Control Science

Control Science

*How Management Made
the Modern World*

Henry Snow

VERSO
London • New York

First published by Verso 2026
© Henry Snow 2026

The manufacturer's authorized representative in the EU for product safety (GPSR) is LOGOS EUROPE, 9 rue Nicolas Poussin, 17000, La Rochelle, France
contact@logoseurope.eu

All rights reserved

The moral rights of the author have been asserted

1 3 5 7 9 10 8 6 4 2

Verso
UK: 6 Meard Street, London W1F 0EG
US: 207 East 32nd Street, New York, NY 10016
versobooks.com

Verso is the imprint of New Left Books

ISBN-13: 978-1-80429-320-1
ISBN-13: 978-1-80429-322-5 (UK EBK)
ISBN-13: 978-1-80429-323-2 (US EBK)

British Library Cataloguing in Publication Data
A catalogue record for this book is available from the British Library

Library of Congress Cataloging-in-Publication Data

Names: Snow, Henry (Labor historian) author
Title: Control science : how management made the modern world / Henry Snow.
Description: London ; New York : Verso, 2026. | Includes bibliographical references and index.
Identifiers: LCCN 2026003789 (print) | LCCN 2026003790 (ebook) | ISBN 9781804293201 hardback | ISBN 9781804293232 ebook
Subjects: LCSH: Labor—History | Management—History | Work environment—History
Classification: LCC HD4841 .S66 2026 (print) | LCC HD4841 (ebook)
LC record available at https://lccn.loc.gov/2026003789
LC ebook record available at https://lccn.loc.gov/2026003790

Typeset in Sabon by Biblichor Ltd, Scotland
Printed and bound by CPI Group (UK) Ltd, Croydon CR0 4YY

To Dad

Contents

Acknowledgments   ix

Introduction: A "Science of Liberty"   1

1. "It Is Our Misery and Ruin Thus to Be Improved":
   Calculated Extraction, 1623–97   4

2. "In Order to Love Mankind, It Is Necessary to Lower Your Expectations":
   Labor Control and Psychological Egoism, 1690–1783   30

3. "Two Sovereign Masters: Pain and Pleasure":
   Mechanized Labor and the Panopticon, 1760–1810   54

4. "They Will Be Compelled of Themselves to Work for You":
   Political Economy in Antebellum America, 1800–65   76

5. "The Whole World Appears Despicable":
   Competitive Evolution and Japanese Industrialization, 1854–1914   103

6. "In the Past the Man Has Been First; in the Future the System Must Be First":
   Scientific Management and "Free Enterprise," 1880–1945   136

CONTENTS

7. "A Fantastic Fairyland":
   *Factory Discipline and
   the Postwar Right, 1946–67* — 170

8. "The Interdependent World We Have Tried to Build":
   *Multinationals, Macroeconomics, and the Road to
   Reagan, 1967–80* — 189

9. "Economics Represents the Actual World":
   Popular Economics, 1981–2009 — 212

10. "No Space to Be Human":
    Dreams of Exit, 2009–24 — 244

    Conclusion: There Is an Alternative — 276

    Notes — 283
    Index — 327

Acknowledgments

The French philosopher Claude-Adrien Helvétius said that to love mankind, you must lower your expectations. This book is a thank-you to everyone I know who has refused to lower their expectations and has loved humanity anyway.

More concretely, though, I owe numerous debts of gratitude to the many people who helped make this book possible. It would be impossible to list all of them. I am grateful to my editors—John Merrick, for taking a chance on a new author with an angry book and very little time to write it, and Leo Hollis, for guiding that book over the finish line. Katie Sinclair's help with the proposal and support thereafter was invaluable. My thanks as well to the many colleagues whose comments and conversation helped make the book what it is, including Milton Achelpohl, Michael Baysa, Akissi Britton, Kim Butler, Sarah Duff, Tim Grieve-Carlson, Philippe Halbert, María Esther Hammack, Alison Hight, Jennie Jiang, Seth Koven, Lynn Lees, K. Sebastian Leon, Ted McCormick, Lauren Michalak, Kim Phillips-Fein, Andrew Popp, Evan Radcliffe, Shantee Rosado, Andrew Shankman, Paul Steege, Margaret Stetz, Anna Todd, and Rob Weisbrot.

Thank you to Arnout van der Meer, my department chair at Colby College, who put me in the ironic position of writing a book billed as "a four-century history of why your boss sucks" while having the best "boss" anyone could ask for. My thanks as well to the staff of the Massachusetts Historical Society, the National Archives in Kew, the American Heritage Center in Wyoming, and the Australian Film and Sound Archive.

ACKNOWLEDGMENTS

Thank you also to my mother, Jennifer Snow, and my father, Peter Warburton, who passed away while I was writing this. Both made it impossible for me to believe in a world of mere self-interest. Finally, let me express my undying gratitude to Rachel Gabrilowitz, my wife, for believing in me and in this book.

Introduction

A "Science of Liberty"

At a conference in Orlando in 2005, the American billionaire Charles Koch gave a speech explaining how he and his audience could protect "freedom and prosperity in the world." While accepting an award named after potato chip magnate Herman Lay, Koch explained that he had conceived a "science of liberty," which he described as "the study and practice of sustainably advancing liberty to create prosperity and social progress." The solution lay, Koch said, in economic analysis—treating every interaction between people as a market exchange. He claimed this "Market Process Analysis" helped him build not only his fortune but also his family life and interpersonal interactions. Out of it he created what he called Market-Based Management (MBM), a theory for managing workers and his business. The science of liberty he outlined in Orlando applied those same principles to government—in America and across the world.[1]

Workers at Charles Koch's web of companies felt differently. One anonymous Koch employee in Wichita wrote that their colleagues were "walking around like they are in the George Orwell book, '1984,'" terrified of the Koch family, the "only major employer in the area," who used their power "to control the employees and their movement within the other Koch entities." Another, in Atlanta, called Koch's extensive training in MBM "brainwashing." The atmosphere, others reported, was "cult-like," and employees were "noticeably unhappy," with fifty-hour work weeks as well as mandatory overtime and weekend work. A software engineer in Bangalore wrote that at

Koch's companies "managers are GOD . . . they can play with anyone's life."²

Some of these disgruntled employees, hoping to convince management to change their ways, insisted they were not "practicing what they preached"—that MBM's *values* were good and simply being misapplied. But Charles Koch had worked on the system for decades. He personally cultivated its materials, and his company forced employees to study them for upwards of five hours a week, according to one review. Some of the values in Koch's system of MBM were simply anodyne—"respect" is its ninth "guiding principle." But the underlying purpose of the philosophy was to extract maximum profit from employees. The science of liberty seemed more like a science of control.

Koch's "science" relied on four connected claims about human behavior that structure economic and political life across the globe today. First, that we should analyze society as merely a collection of individuals, an idea known as methodological individualism. Second, the claim that individuals are motivated only by self-interest, generally though not exclusively in the form of material incentives—or, psychological egoism. Third, an insistence that deliberate planning cannot be trusted: humans are too selfish, and too limited, to make or execute grand plans for society. We should trust the competitive evolution of markets over the cooperative intention of democracy. And fourth, the belief that everything is—and should be—a market. The world consists of competing individuals, and social science exists to figure out how to structure that competition so prosperity arises out of it. This paradigm is known as market fundamentalism.

Proponents of these ideas present them as inescapable truths about the world, like gravity. This scientific posture enables a fifth ideological feature of Koch's philosophy: subordinating the normative "should" statements of ethics to the supposedly objective (positive, in the descriptive sense) "is" statements of economics. If we know how human beings will act, there is no need to speak of how they should act. Thus, "there is no alternative," as the Victorian philosopher Herbert Spencer put it, to these cruel calculations: they are an inescapable truth about human action.

This is a lie. These ideas are not scientific truths that experts have discovered. They are political visions that ideologues have created. This book explores how they were built into law, language, and common sense over the past four hundred years. It makes two arguments. First, labor control efforts in plantations, factories, and warehouses have played a central role in the development of political and economic thought from the earliest days of capitalism. Second, the resulting "science of control"—codeveloped ideas for controlling workers and justifying doing so—is neither scientific truth nor necessarily all that effective as a measure of direct control.

There are other ways we can live and work, and generally most people prefer those alternatives when asked and frequently pursue them when we are not. From Samuel Bentham's program of mechanized and precarious shipbuilding labor to Frederick Winslow Taylor's floundering efforts to optimize pig iron loading, supposedly optimal methods for manipulating workers have generally failed—until their architects relied on political and economic force to impose their ideas anyway. Labor control efforts have often been most impactful as justifications for this coercion. Precisely because there are a multitude of other ways we might organize a society, the insistence that this way alone is possible plays a key role in keeping our world from changing.

Ideas alone don't make history, but I hope that naming and shaming these ideas will contribute in some small way to dismantling the world they have built, and to replacing it with something better. Whoever you are, I believe you deserve that.

1

"It Is Our Misery and Ruin Thus to Be Improved": Calculated Extraction, 1623–1783

In 1623, a child named William Petty was born to a clothier in a town in the south of England. Inarguably talented, young William rose from humble origins: as a teenager, he began his working life hustling neighbors with card tricks and sailors with counterfeit jewelry. While his subsequent remarkable ascent relied on his skill, the contributions of others were invaluable as well, from the nebulous influence of the artisan atmosphere in Romsey to the beeswax sent by his parents, which he transformed, through clever trades, into funding for a Jesuit education.[1] His "greatest delight," according to a seventeenth-century biographer, "was to be looking on the artificers."[2]

Artificers, or artisans, were men who turned natural materials like metal and wood into artificial marvels like clocks and ships. They did their work mostly in little businesses where apprentices and family members and journeymen worked under a master craftsman. Each profession had its attendant differences: potteries were often small family shops, while shipbuilding was conducted by hundreds of men working in concert. They experienced work as toil, certainly, and economic difficulty was common; the vicissitudes of "business" could send a family hurtling into debt or overwork. But they had autonomy most workers today can only dream of. In shipyards, the closest thing to a factory of free laborers you could find in the 1600s, work was organized primarily by what historian Peter Linebaugh has called "heterogeneous cooperation"—not top-down command.[3]

From factories and warehouses to offices, many workers today produce only pieces of a greater edifice, under conditions dictated precisely by someone else, for the profit of owners and shareholders. Artisans in the seventeenth century crafted their own products, on their own schedule, for their own benefit, with their own hands and tools. Their income was their own, not pieces of profit "given" back by a boss. Ancient rights and customs—asserted sometimes through formal guilds, and in other cases through less formal collective action—protected their autonomy and economic power.

Even English peasants, who were much worse off than artisans, had a somewhat similar arrangement. They had the right to graze cattle on common land, glean in forest and fens, and otherwise make a living from the land they lived on. This was far from utopian—it meant relative autonomy and security only within the confines of farming, often as someone else's tenant. Likewise, artisan labor had its own forms of exploitation, particularly of women and apprentices. These shortcomings are not only worthy of critique—they would, in the eighteenth century, become a foundation for new forms of work exploitation. Early modern laborers' autonomy was one good thing in a bad world. This meant that they fought hard to protect it.

Against them were an array of elites who believed the world could be richer and brighter if learned men controlled it. William Petty would become one of them. In 1643, he traveled to the Netherlands to study. Seventeenth-century Europe was an exciting place for a mechanically inclined student. Discoveries and inventions in this period included the microscope, calculus, gravity, the telescope, and blood transfusions. Since natural philosophers—an antecedent to what we call science today—were making new breakthroughs seemingly daily in understanding the physical world, the question of how these insights could be applied to the human world was an obvious one to ask, and an enticing one to answer. Natural, moral, and political philosophy were connected fields with blurry boundaries. Political philosopher Thomas Hobbes studied "motion" as both a principle of matter and a principle of action before he wrote his famous treatise *Leviathan*, which argued for a strong sovereign to control the chaos of human relations.[4]

Hobbes believed he could study humanity just like gravity and geometry because he believed the body was a machine. Society, in turn, was just another slightly more complicated body. At the beginning of *Leviathan*, Hobbes asked, "What is the *Heart* but a *Spring*; and the *Nerves*, but so many *Strings*; and the *Joynts*, but so many *Wheeles*, giving motion to the whole Body, such as was intended by the Artificer," that is, God himself. For Hobbes, society itself was but an artificial body: judges its joints, "Reward and Punishment" its nerves.[5] The question for any ruler or advisor was how to organize and optimize this body—not unlike how a physician might care for a patient. While studying for that profession in continental Europe, Petty befriended and worked with Hobbes.[6] He was a man of diverse interests, and it is not difficult to imagine how the political philosopher's ideas of the body politic might appeal to a physician with ambitions for treating more than bodily problems.

The English body politic was suffering numerous ailments at the time. In 1642, England had gone to war with itself. On one side, the imperious King Charles II; on the other, Parliament and its supporters. The war was driven by an array of interlocking political, religious, and economic motivations, which the king's removal from power in 1646 did not resolve. Religious nonconformists and political radicals in the army found themselves at odds with parliamentary elites over political and religious rights as well as economic inequality. A faction with support in the army, known as the Levellers, argued for expanded voting, legal reforms, and religious freedom.

Even more radical was the vision of the Digger movement. In 1649, the group this became proclaimed to "you, that call your selves lords ... that the earth was not made purposely for you ... but it was made to be a common livelihood to all." "The power of inclosing Land and owning [property]," they argued, "was brought into the Creation by your Ancestors by the Sword; which first did murther their fellow Creatures, Men, and after plunder or steal away their land," and left it to subsequent generations, who in turn claimed that their property was legitimate, whereas the Diggers felt it was, in fact, "bloody and theeving power."[7] Property in their view began with dispossession and was legitimized afterward by inheritors who claimed innocence.

This was a description not only of property in general but also of a specific process of dispossession peasants were experiencing in seventeenth-century England: enclosure. Landowners seeking to increase agricultural profits began kicking peasants off their land through varying combinations of law, purchase and sale of tenancy rights, and intimidation. This frequently led to the walling off of land into separate individual plots, as well as ecological changes, as marshes were drained and common lands cleared for privately owned profit-producing monoculture. As enclosure took off, more and more peasants became landless wage laborers who had to support themselves by seeking work from others. This made them dependent on markets: only by selling their work, buying food, and, if they were lucky, buying land, could they survive.

The Diggers sought neither a redistributive expansion of small ownership within the social order of private property nor even a restoration of the vanishing commons of the past, with its limited rights under aristocratic landholder power. They aimed for an ideal, true commons of the future through collective ownership. The Diggers practiced such common ownership until local lords assembled mobs to violently chase them off.[8] Market dependence was thus not natural or inevitable: it arose through political repression. Subsequently, it had to be maintained by state defenses of private property and by further repression of lower-class political movements.

In this turbulent age, Thomas Hobbes's machine-body-society analogies were comforting for elites. If philosophers could treat the ailing body politic as they could treat ailing human bodies, perhaps there was hope for making order out of chaos. In the same year the Digger movement emerged, William Petty was at work on "new Emploiments or enterprises in which the Poore should bee invited," according to his collaborator Samuel Hartlib.[9] Hartlib was at the center of what we know as the "Hartlib Circle," a coterie of elite intellectuals who dreamed of achieving a "universal reformation" of the world itself through experimental knowledge.[10] Appropriately for such a grand vision, Petty drew on an eclectic range of inspirations, from anatomy, to engineering to natural philosophy, and he concocted schemes in areas from naval engineering to education.[11] He also devised a seed-drill and a perpetual motion device.[12] Petty's most successful and influential creation, though, was "political arithmetic," which brought numbers and quantitative methods to bear on the problems identified by Hobbes and others.

William Petty's career was built on three broad ideas. First, he had a mechanistic and materialist view of the world. Second, he believed the rules of the world could be best understood by experience rather than by rational thought, logic, or pre-existing foundations such as religion. Third, Petty believed the world should be governed like a machine.[13] Where Hobbes had argued that society was a great artificial body, it was Petty who proposed prescriptions for it, with calculated doses. This of course required actually studying the political body as closely as he had studied the physical body. The aftermath of the English Civil War offered a singular opportunity to cut such a body open and to propose radical surgeries.

"Transmuting One People into the Other"

In 1652, Petty traveled to Ireland to serve as "Physician-General" for the Commonwealth army that was then brutally dissecting it. Oliver Cromwell's postrevolutionary state paid for its invasion by promising investors and soldiers millions of acres of confiscated land. For William Petty and the Hartlib Circle, this confiscation was a form of "improvement." As a vision of wealthy men in a country whose elites were primarily landlords, improvement was not a process of maximizing some abstract objective goodness but rather the process of increasing profitability.[14] In the seventeenth century, an "improver" was someone who made land more profitable—particularly by enclosure.[15] The Hartlib Circle, in particular, imagined a capitalist improvement of *all* things as measured by economic value quantified in capitalist terms, culminating in "infinite welfare, benefit and wonderful advantage" and "infinite wealth and happiness."[16] The enclosure and improvement of land could be part of a similar ordering and "improvement" of society itself.

In fact, enclosure in England and confiscation in Ireland were necessary preconditions for improvement: land had to be legally enclosed in order to be physically enclosed. Common rights made certain improvements impossible or undesirable—peasant commoners dependent upon agriculture for food were not about to sanction replacing their economy and ecosystem with potentially more profitable sheep. Only private investors had the authority, and the economic interest, to make investments in improvement—investments that commoners could not afford and in some cases did not want—if they were to reap the benefits. Likewise, the confiscation of Irish land by English elites allowed new political and economic projects on that land.

In 1654, Petty proposed and conducted a massive survey of land, governed by his and the Hartlib Circle's empirical principles. The Down Survey, as it was known, mapped and gauged the profitability of land across Ireland by dividing the work of surveying itself.[17] Rather than hire experienced surveyors to carry out every task, Petty split the work into distinct tasks, so that the paperwork, field work, and geometry were handled by different men. Soldiers could be speedily trained in each individual task more quickly than in all of them. New labor control methods increased workers' efficiency and reduced opportunities for corruption and self-dealing—in other words, by controlling labor, Petty furthered English control of land. The result was a remarkably effective and efficient survey, one that applied the philosophy of "improvement" on an unprecedented scale.

The dissection of Ireland's "political animal" was the genesis of Petty's "political arithmetic," a method for controlling the world by quantifying it. These statistical methods were electrifying: numbers and nature could provide more accurate and more ethical explanations for political and economic problems. Petty calculated that there were enough empty hands and work to be done in England for an additional £2 million annually, an extraordinary sum, if the economy were more efficiently organized.[18] He railed against state monopolies as inefficient and wasteful. Petty even proposed reforming the kingdom's hideously corrupt Parliament around equal representation nearly two centuries before that happened, though he argued for this on the basis of efficiency rather than fairness.[19]

But Petty and others like him, working with states defined by coercion, and economies defined by extraction, did dreadful things when applying numbers to people. William Petty's idea of value was that of a landlord in the era of enclosure and colonial commerce, and he himself became a substantial landowner because of his survey.[20] Petty not only offered his services to optimize land confiscation in Ireland—he proposed extensive solutions for its improvement beyond that. This included forced marriage; to smoothly connect England and Ireland, Petty proposed taking 10,000 "unmarried marriageable" Irish women each year and exporting them to England, while shifting an equivalent number of English women to replace them. By "transmuting one People into the other," he wrote, the need for Irish resistance could be removed by erasing "Irish" as a category.[21]

Improvement required particular kinds of political and economic subjects as well as particular land arrangements. Sheer force was necessary but not sufficient. As historian Ted McCormick explains, Petty's plans for coerced migration were part of a whole constellation of projects meant to "improve" the king's domains. These included new housing in English-style dwellings and some form of religious toleration. Together this was an agenda for remaking the Irish people as political subjects. The resulting "new-model households, linked to towns and ports by improved roads and canals, would produce butter, cheese, linen, and worsted for markets on both sides of the Atlantic, and consume the latest fashions, foods, and manufactures with the money they earned."[22] Petty's plans for "transmuting" Irish subjects were a particular instantiation of the more general effort in "improvement" at changing people themselves.

Petty's political arithmetic offered not only tools for optimizing English rule but also a philosophy for justifying it. In a chapter elaborating recent increases in England's wealth, Petty commented positively on "the accession of Negroes to the American Plantations." They were, he wrote, "Men of great Labour and little Expence."[23] The expansion of colonial settlement was likewise something Petty celebrated. While the kingdom had lost value with the mass death in Ireland, the healthy families of New England were making up for this, producing "an increase of as many People, as were destroyed in the late tumults in *Ireland*."[24] Petty's dehumanizing reduction of African and Irish people to numbers was the product of economic convenience, not personal animus: much like English beggars, Irish subjects and American enslaved people were for Petty merely factors of value.

Numbers allowed theorists like Petty to analyze real experiences while selectively removing unpleasant context—to calculate population loss, say, by stripping the value a million dead Irish had to their grieving families, or estimating plantation productivity without considering the violence involved. It did not have to be this way. Petty was a hands-on experimentalist with roots in alchemy and dreams of universal reformation, not a calculating bureaucrat.[25] He was a "projector," literally a project-doer, in the language of the day, and decidedly empirical. His projects themselves aimed for peace and prosperity.

But political thinkers like Petty, like many of the projectors that will fill this book, consistently and deliberately avoid inquiring into the feelings and judgments of the common people whose world they seek to reform. Their imagined position as disinterested observers is a denial of both the experience of others and the influence of their own political-economic position on their work.

Petty's empiricism without pluralism gave way to a conception of improvement without experiment at all. The emerging capitalist science of control diverged yet further from the reality it meddled in after Petty's death. Where Petty was a projector seeking to transform the world through expertise, his successors were bureaucrats who sought to optimize it through numbers.[26] Many later thinkers who built on the work of their own day's calculating projectors would go further than Petty's successors and reject empiricism and even numbers altogether, insisting that reality itself could not be as objective as abstract reason. William Petty would likely have been baffled at best by their work and methodology. But the rejection of empiricism was premised on a rejection of pluralism that projectors themselves were often guilty of.

In a preface to *Political Arithmetic*, Petty defend his numerical claims as either true or close enough not to matter, offering the Latin phrase *nam id certum est quod certum reddi potest*— "that is certain which may be made certain."[27] This idiom is meant as a practical maxim: if something can be observed, clarity can be achieved. But the methods of seventeenth-century calculators are also described by the inverse of this maxim: that which can be made certain is certain. In his treatise on taxes, Petty noted that for his complex social calculations to work, "the price of labor must be certain." In a market society this was of course impossible without outside intervention—but never fear, Petty wrote, for wages could be made certain "as we [already] see it made by the Statutes which limit the day wages of several workmen." The maximum wage he was referring to was an existing feature of law for several professions; Petty here proposed extending it and adhering closely to it, for "the non-observance of [these] Laws, and the not adapting them to the change of times, is by the way very dangerous."[28] Wages were certain because they could be made so by the power of the state. Coercion and calculation were mutually reinforcing: pretending the world was made of numbers helped shore up coercive hierarchies, while those hierarchies in turn made numerical fictions easier to maintain.

"If You Have One Spark of Human Sensibility"

This kind of accounting of death became central to the economy in the place to which many Irish survivors of Cromwell's brutality were deported: Barbados. While Petty was calculating how to steal Irish land, on the other side of the Atlantic wealthy men in Barbados and their hired agents were calculating the most efficient methods to turn lives into money. The plantation world was in its infancy in this period. Slavery had been a practice in the New World for generations, but mass cash crop agriculture and a slave trade at a similar scale to support it were only just beginning to develop into the transatlantic architecture of death it would become. This system had to be made, piecemeal, by countless individuals seeking greater profit.

The sugar plantations of the New World were precursors to industrial factories. They organized labor with advanced surveillance and control methods and produced a finished product for the market through equally novel engineering methods. Barbados, Antigua, and other sugar colonies were remade from the ground up by European early capitalism; their inhabitants were killed and their ecologies were transformed to make way for industrial production.[29] The Caribbean became a laboratory for capitalism. Its plantations did not produce subsistence goods like grain, or economically useful items like tools or weapons, but wholly unnecessary luxuries, created at an as-yet unseen scale. They were developed using a combination of private funding and state support, similar to Irish and North American plantations.

Initially, state support took the form of penal labor, which turned potential internal enemies of the exploitative state into assets; just as victims of enclosure and England's vicious criminal justice system were made to serve as agents of colonial capital, Irish deportees in Barbados laid foundations for its plantations. On top of deportation and war, many Irish were driven into servitude by poverty owing to their new market dependence. Cut off from land by Cromwell's confiscation and left vulnerable by war, they sought a living by selling their labor as indentured servants. But Barbadian elites quickly developed a greater hunger for lives than Irish deportation or servitude could fulfill. Pursuing infinite profit, and with the backing of a government eager to tax it, wealthy Englishmen expanded the already-existing system of African slavery into a vast architecture of death that maximized profits by draining lives for sugar.

Sugar cultivation is an intense process from start to finish. The harvest is difficult, back-breaking work that occurs on a tight schedule, as is the process of producing sugar from harvested cane, a finicky chemical process conducted in boiling heat.[30] Only massive infusions of manure kept soils profitable for harvest after harvest—in a post-enclosure and early capitalist world where land existed to produce short-term profit rather than long-term subsistence, planters stripped soil of nutrients constantly. Within a generation Barbados lost its trees, which meant that construction and heating for boiling sugar required huge imports of timber.[31] Plantation owners and overseers exacted a brutal toll from workers to make all this happen. A man with 100 slaves, Barbadian planter Edward Littleton wrote, should expect to purchase six new human beings a year—in other words, he estimated a 6 percent annual death rate.[32] Rather than reconsider slavery, or at least reconsider material conditions which might reduce profits, slaveholders worked out how best to replace with new captives those whom they worked to death.

To orchestrate these death factories, planters developed scientific techniques for controlling people, soil, animals, and materials. This began with the planting itself. After initial attempts to plant in rows, slaveholders devised a square hole method, in which enslaved people were forced to dig rows of holes for planting cane. These captured the limited rain that fell on Caribbean islands while maximizing surface area for agriculture and limiting soil erosion. Highly labor-intensive, the cane hole method exacerbated labor problems by adding an extensive digging phase, at the cost of further exhaustion and injury to enslaved people. Cane hole planting also required further fine-tuning. Writing in instructions to overseer Richard Harwood in 1679, enslaver Henry Drax of Barbados outlined a specialized system of periodic raised beds, facilitating gutters and trenches, to increase irrigation. This method, however, risked further erosion.[33]

Early planters presented themselves as embattled entrepreneurs struggling against hostile nature; in reality, they were the aggressors. Plantations were hostile to nature. Refusing to abide by any constraints—nitrogen in the soil, water needs, the limits of the human body, and the limits of free labor—enslavers made war on the soil under their feet and the people who worked it. They treated each front of this war similarly: optimizing human life and death was for them a task like any other. Drax coldly wrote that Harwood should expect "a yearly Recrute of 10 or 15" to "supply the places of those that shall be deseased or Dy."[34]

The greatest threat to plantation owners, however, was the very basis of their profits: enslaved people themselves. Slave revolt haunted planters. An odd glance in the morning from the cook might mean breakfast was poisoned, while whispers in the evening or unfamiliar songs could be harbingers of rebellion. On larger islands, and across the Americas, fugitives from slavery created large maroon communities through armed revolt and mass flight. On islands like Barbados and Antigua, however, this was impossible. Those islands had rapidly lost their wilderness, as slaveholders devoured the land itself. Enslaved people knew how tenuous life was in these hellscapes planters had constructed. Stripped of soil nutrients and dependent on imports, their islands could neither sustain life on their own nor hold out against an imperial onslaught that would inevitably follow a revolutionary capture of the islands. Absent large-scale regional upheaval, this strategy was not available to them.[35]

Accordingly, organized resistance in the sugar islands often took the form of subversion rather than rebellion. Henry Drax claimed that enslaved people were "addicted to thieving" and drunkenness. His linking of the two exemplifies a simultaneous pathologization and criminalization that became central to Atlantic racism. For the slaveholders who seeded and cultivated this rhetoric, tropes of addiction and ill demeanor were convenient, portraying enslaved people as crazed criminals rather than rational resisters and starving victims. Drax hints as much himself, writing that if thieving "be for there body," that is, to avoid starving, "its the more excusable."[36] Enslaved people did indeed steal to survive, supplementing meager diets of imported fish and whatever they could grow on poor-quality land not dedicated to sugar. But such theft was just the tip of an iceberg of resistance and subversion. Enslaved people constantly undermined slavery, materially and socially. Plantations were houses built on sand, always threatening to crumble under the weight of their own oppression and exploitation.

Planters were therefore forced to devise new methods of surveillance and punishment to control enslaved people. Each was based on brutal violence and the threat of death, but this violence was deployed and structured in ways to maximize profit—starting on the far end of the Middle Passage, at the African coast. In coastal forts and then on slave ships, slave traders calculated precisely how much they could starve enslaved people without killing them and losing profits, creating what historian Stephanie Smallwood has termed a "rationalized science of human deprivation."[37] The ships carrying captives across the Atlantic packed men and women in like cargo in greater and greater numbers, as slave traders built increasingly large and specialized vessels, with correspondingly increasing issues of ventilation and health, all of which also needed to be managed—not for the sake or health of enslaved people, whose deaths were considered acceptable, but to optimize profit per voyage. To support the burgeoning slave trade, European elites built complex legal and financial infrastructures: "slave codes" stripped enslaved people of any rights, insurance protected their murderers from the costs of their deaths, and new investment structures split the profits extracted from their lives.

Once captives arrived in places like Barbados and Antigua, slaveholders worked to maximize profit by controlling their labor. Constant surveillance was central to this: enslavers were always on the lookout for the slightest disobedience. Plantation owners hired overseers to surveil and manage plantations, and these overseers in turn commanded enslaved workers, known as drivers, to manage other enslaved people.[38] This entire hierarchy was kept running with violence, most notably, but by no means exclusively, via the whip.

Anyone seeking to escape or evade slaveholders' control infrastructure was punished harshly. Without written permission, enslaved people were expected to remain confined on the plantation. Being found without a pass was grounds for severe punishment; those permitted to sell at markets on Sundays were required to wear metal collars.[39] In cities, slaveholding authorities' violent punishments and executions, carried out on gallows and in public cages, were used to discipline and terrorize enslaved people.[40]

Slaveholders' new modes of exploitation did rely on foundations built under older hierarchies. Slavery was a foundation for the development of modern capitalism, but it was grown in part from the fertile soil of feudal authority and class repression. The state-funded Royal African Company accelerated and expanded English slavery beginning in the 1660s. Feudal law backed up new legislation and court decisions that enabled English slavery.[41] The passes that restricted enslaved people's movement were similar to the paperwork by the same name which kept England's poor from begging outside the parish in which they were born. In Barbados, the cage used to discipline enslaved people was originally created to punish sailors.⁴² Drax repeatedly insisted that his plantation was a family.

As slaveholders constructed their vast apparatus of death, they simultaneously built new justifications for it, creating a bridge from early modern class repression to increasingly modern racist and capitalist exploitation. The Diggers had it right when they pointed out that landholders "justifie the wicked deeds of your Fathers," in maintaining their oppressive system; to rule is to justify rule. Like enclosure and settler colonialism, the process of making and operating the plantation was inextricably linked to the process of legitimizing it. To whip and cage and starve and hang human beings systematically, by the millions, was to create new philosophical justifications for whipping and caging and starving and hanging.

Slaveholders were defending themselves against the objections of abolitionists before any such movement existed. Enslaved people crossed linguistic and cultural barriers to fulminate against slavery from its inception. In the mid-eighteenth century, a man named Syneyo, for example, railed against his enslavers:

> Are you a Christian people? Then do unto us as we have done unto you; strip us of these chains, and conduct us back to our own shores. If Christianity will not move you to perform so just an act, look at those little fatherless children, whom you kidnapped from their parents; hear their cries, behold their sufferings, think of the bewailing of their bereft parents ... if you have one spark of human sensibility, or even the least shade of humanity, if you are what you profess to be, a christian; repent and let us, whom you call heathens, return to our once happy shores, thereby, if you cannot obliterate, heal as much as possible the wounds you have made.⁴³

The captain of the ship carrying Syneyo across the Middle Passage responded to his eloquent oration with a few curses and threats, which he then carried out, of whipping and starvation, both precisely calculated—"fifty stripes," lashes, and "twelve kernels of corn per day" alone, the latter of which was in fact a mass punishment for all the Africans on the ship.

Europeans could not ignore enslaved people's objections and resistance, for they constructed societies in which they were vastly outnumbered by those they kept in bondage. Elaborate ideas about power, necessity, psychology, prosperity, and society were necessary for enslavers to make their violent project function at all in the face of enslaved people's resistance.

In the words of Barbadian slaveholders such as Richard Ligon, Edward Littleton, and Henry Drax we can see three attempted justifications for plantocracy and subsequently white supremacy. The first was a claim that enslaved Africans needed less of everything: less food, less rest, less freedom. Richard Ligon, writing in his 1657 *True and Exact History of the Iland of Barbadoes*, reported that enslaved people received only "one bunch a week" of plantains for food, and for lodging "at night a board, with nothing under, nor any thing a top of them."[44] He reassured his readers, however, that they were "happy people, whom so little contents, if they be not spoyled by the English." Ligon's warning about "spoyled" slaves dehumanized Africans by arguing even their basic human needs were contingent on their treatment by slaveholders.

English ideas of improvement promised infinity for English elites, but the price of this unbounded prosperity above was a reduction of human life below. The same kind of calculations that promised ever-larger estates in England produced ever-smaller diets and ever-shorter lives in the Caribbean; the metropolitan infinite was guaranteed by the colonial finite. While the English economy was quantified for maximization, enslaved people's lives were quantified for minimization. When planters spoke of themselves, "need" and "contentment" and "desire" meant the need for a return on investment and to pay creditors, contentment with a comfortable life, and desire for growing wealth. When planters spoke of the men and women they enslaved, need meant whatever was necessary to avoid immediate death or revolt. This division of human need into tranches was part of the broader construction of Atlantic racism; the quantification behind it reflects a sinister new atomization of humans into quantifiable units.

Barbadian planters also claimed that, independent of needs, enslaved people *deserved* less. Ligon argued there was a "marke set upon these people . . . of their cruelties when they have advantages, and of their fearfulnesse and falsnesse," and that ethical individuals among them were rare exceptions.[45] Henry Drax's claim that enslaved people were "addicted to thieving" likewise reflects a theme that became prominent in slaveholder rhetoric: the supposed immorality of enslaved Africans. Such claims were complemented by the related claim that Africans were "irrational." Witnessing a revolt plot, Ligon claimed it was the work of the "high spirited and turbulent," in other words that it was motivated by irrational emotion rather than a rational response to sleeping on boards, being worked to death, and the starvation even Drax privately admitted was a problem. Between claims of immorality and claims of irrationality, slaveholders portrayed Black subjects as unworthy of basic rights and decency and even unable to receive their benefits—there was in this view no reason to allow them better living and working conditions, let alone freedom, if they would "irrationally" rebel anyway. Both tropes became and remain important pillars of racist discourse.

Their third justification was that slavery's brutality was, simply, necessary. Edward Littleton illustrated this amply in a pamphlet defending planters and arguing for reduced tax burdens. Because the "poor planter" could not spare even a penny for new taxes, he wrote, they certainly could not afford to pay for free and willing labor. But economic necessity as a justification for economic exploitation went deeper than individual slaveholders' claims about costs. Costs and prices were subject to human influence: taxes were a significant cost, transportation costs were the product of another area of the economy altogether, and sugar prices were determined in part by just how much sugar slaveholders were producing. Economic "necessity" occurs within particular economic regimes—in this case, a regime of extraction. This extraction was called "improvement." The insistence that slavery was economically "necessary" was not an objective description of inevitable reality—it was an admission of culpability by the architects and beneficiaries of the institution.

Ironically, Littleton himself complained that improvement came at his own expense. He wrote that "Projectors," those behind new taxes meant to turn colonial profit into government revenue, "talk of Improving the Plantations to the advantage of *England*," rather than Barbados, "just as a Landlord would improve his Mannor, by racking his Lands to the utmost Rent, or as the Masters of Slaves, improve and contrive their Labour to their own best advantage."[46] The effect was supposedly disastrous, with the "poor planter" starving just like an oppressed renter—"it is our misery and ruin thus to be improved," he complained. Littleton and other plantation owners who used whips and chains and nooses to take everything they could from enslaved people were outraged that the creditors they borrowed from, the slave traders they purchased captives from, and the empire that protected this activity all took as much as *they* could from slaveholders.

"A Little Burning Felt"

Two features of English political thought helped elites justify this fractal of extraction: pessimism and calculation. Influenced by the ideas of Swiss reformer John Calvin, English Puritans believed all of humanity was invariably defined by sin and that nothing could be done about this. Salvation was something no one could deserve. Only a small elect were elevated above this state, and then only by the will of God. Critically, this elect was saved without cause: contrary to what the name might make one think, "predestination" did not mean God determined one's fate prior to living based on a pre-judgment but rather an arbitrary lottery. Because no reason could suffice for saving man, the elect were saved for no reason.

Puritans believed both in a utopia and in its absolute futility. Humanity had been cast out of Eden—a place where land was held in common and inhabited rather than dominated. There was no sense in trying to re-create it now. Not with the damned masses. If all were sinners and the vast majority in a permanent fallen state, then society had to be structured to control and mitigate their sins.

This was the purpose of the state that William Petty originally worked for. Cromwell and his supporters' Puritan ideology perfectly justified wage ceilings, the coercion of Irish plantation, and the repression of radicals. Petty himself was not a true believer in Puritan ideas, but he did not need to be. Cromwell was as much a bourgeois oligarch as a theocrat, and Petty's primary political commitment was to optimization of the state, not to radical ideas or reactionary royalism. The fact that Cromwell was brutally reducing Ireland was an opportunity, not a crime, and if his Puritan government wished to close some theaters—well, that was hardly a physician's problem. Would-be technocrats looking to shape state policy found it necessary to work with whatever state was at hand.

After the Puritan state fell, it took its elect as a state logic with it—and a projectors' logic built on similar theological foundations soon moved in to replace it. The man who would design them, John Locke, came from less humble origins than William Petty. His father, like generations before him, was a successful cloth merchant. Locke is best known today for his political theory, including arguments for (limited) religious toleration and consent in political systems, which helped influence the American Revolution. But until the later eighteenth century, his most widely read work was on the philosophy of minds rather than politics.

In 1689, Locke wrote that "good and evil . . . are nothing but pleasure or pain."[47] These words come from Locke's influential *Essay Concerning Human Understanding*. The work built on empiricist insights about senses and calculation seen in Petty and Hobbes but now applied more narrowly to the individual mind instead of collective society. If humans were machines, the impulses that moved them could not be mysterious religious concepts: they had to be something we could discern and understand.

The answer to this lay in pleasure and pain. For Locke, these were the core of all motivation, the means by which we decide between one thing and another. Locke broke complex emotions up into pieces of pain and pleasure for analysis. "The being and welfare of a man's children" may be described as love, but love and hate are merely "dispositions of the mind, in respect of pain and pleasure."[48] Envy and anger are mixed pleasure and pain applied to others. Using this psychological arithmetic of pain and pleasure in conjunction with formal logic, Locke believed moral rules could be made "as certain as any demonstration in Euclid," the ancient Greek father of geometry—morality could be like a geometric proof.[49] He rejected arguments about goodness based in anything but sense and logic—including existing religious morality. Locke was still a Christian, and he insisted the moral rules one derived through his methods coincided with Christian ethics, but his framework was entirely different. It exploded any idea of good or evil.

Rejecting any higher abstract good (which would be impossible to calculate), Locke claimed that "good and evil, as hath been shown . . . are nothing but pleasure or pain, or that which occasions or procures pleasure or pain to us." Thus "men judge of the most considerable moral good or evil of their actions" by "by comparing them to [God's] law," which, like human law, assigns consequences of pain or pleasure to actions. Given this, "moral good and evil . . . is only the conformity or disagreement of our voluntary actions to some law"—morality is only "that we call reward and punishment."[50] Good and evil are just consequences, and morality is only a legalistic system that attaches them to actions.

Elite ideas about God's authority were also ideas about man's. Consider the meaning of Locke's understanding of good and evil in practice—say, in parenting. Locke never had children, and perhaps if he had he might have raised them with ethics beyond what his epistemological treatise suggested, but to a child asking their parent how they know right from wrong, the Locke of the *Essay* would respond: what I told you to do is right, because I can and will bring you pain if you don't listen. Locke attempted to soften the blow and save some room for more traditional morality by arguing that all ethics are ultimately comparisons to the laws of the final arbiter, the final parent, the final lawmaker: God, who apparently has "goodness . . . to direct our actions to that which is best."[51] But it is unclear why one would need *goodness* to justify imposing law if the imposition of law is all that good actually is; it is likewise unclear what *best* means other than that authority said so.

Critically, Locke argued human selfishness was inevitable but also morally acceptable, even necessary. If all humanity could do was pursue pleasure and avoid pain, then we could not condemn ourselves for doing so. In a lengthy series of passages on the "greater good," he passionately argued that humans cannot motivate ourselves to do good only by thought and intention. Locke claimed that a poor man could not be convinced by himself or others to want money, nor a "drunkard" to give up alcohol—only "uneasiness" could make them change. His choice of examples here is a giveaway: he imagines a poor man "content" with poverty, and in comparing this to alcoholism he implies both are individual rather than systemic failures.[52] This cynical theory of psychology was a bridge from traditional Christian ethics and its pessimism about sin to a new proto-utilitarian ethics, one that was pessimistic about the mind.

The solution to poverty was not philosophy and discourse but psychology and mathematics. *Uneasiness* had to be generated. Since all emotions are ultimately pain or pleasure, this meant the pauper and the drunkard must be offered one or the other to directly motivate action. Locke firmly believed that pain was a stronger motivator. Quoting the Apostle Paul—"it is better to marry than to burn"—Locke wrote that "a little burning felt, pushes us more powerfully, than greater pleasures in prospect draw or allure."[53] To improve a man's action, one should not preach to him—one should instead approach him as an automaton, find the "uneasiness" dial, and turn it up. In other words, men had to be coerced for their own good.

Locke's arguments about pain, pleasure, and ethics provided new cover for domination and new methods for exploitation. In 1697, Locke drafted a memo on welfare as part of his work with the powerful Board of Trade. It was a proposal for reform of the Elizabethan Poor Law, which offered limited but significant support for the poor.[54] A recent "multiplying of the poor," which required an increase in taxes, prompted calls for reform across the long eighteenth century. The real causes of this increase were complex but ultimately linked to dispossession and exploitation. Enclosure had robbed a great many people of their ability to support themselves. The slow rise of wage labor was increasingly creating a class of people—not in-demand artisans but less-skilled urban workers—whose finances depended on the whims of the wealthy. A proper reform to the poor law might have involved asking the poor what would help them find work and considering what had *changed* to produce their increase. It might have invested in their welfare, promoted an increase of wages, weakened the power of the renter class, helped stabilize prices, considered why certain sectors of the economy were not working, or aided particularly ailing regions.

John Locke's proposal did none of this. His assessment of the "cause of this evil" (an increase in the numbers of the poor) ruled out shortages in both food and employment with the brisk insistence that "God has blessed these times with plenty, no less than the former." Instead he offered the dubious claim that there had been a "relaxation of discipline and corruption of manners; virtue and industry being as constant companions on the one side as vice and idleness are on the other." It is worth keeping in mind here that discipline and virtue were synonymous for Locke, who was skeptical of the very idea of virtue in any other sense. England's poverty problem was thus a control problem. Locke's theory of the mind, and the nascent field of political economy, offered solutions.

Locke proposed the same approach he believed to be God's: control through reward and punishment. Existing law recognized people's ability to rely on the support of the parish they were born in—but in the age of enclosure, most rural communities had limited work available, and limited wealth to share. Accordingly, the poor often ventured to more distant cities and towns in search of work and—especially the disabled, elderly, and mothers—charity. Poor Law reformers targeted such "vagrants" specifically. Locke's first remedy was consigning any man found begging in maritime areas to "hard labor" in the nearest seaport until a ship came in, "where they shall serve three years under strict discipline, at soldier's pay." If you forged a pass, you would have your ears cut off.[55] If you were a woman found begging without a pass, you would be dragged home and fined; if you did this again, you would be sentenced to three months in a "house of correction." Anyone who insisted that they required charity because they could not find work was to be immediately offered as an employee at a "lower rate" to anyone who would take them. Children found begging would be sent to a specialized facility, whipped, and forced to work for a day; if they were far from home, they would be forced to work for six weeks.

The specialized facility in question, a "working school," consolidated Lockean psychology and ethics into an instrument of profit. Children under the Poor Laws were not forced to work, which for Locke was a problem: it meant that the government could only begin profiting from the labor of the poor once they turned fourteen. To make poor children properly useful, Locke therefore proposed schools that would ensure children would "from infancy be inured," or used to, "work." Locke approvingly noted the children would then come to school and work hard "because otherwise they will have no victuals" and would starve. He helpfully computed the costs and benefits of working children, beginning from the age of three.

Had it been implemented, this proposal would have been ruinous, because the plan included nothing to increase the demand for labor. An influx of forced maritime workers would drive wages down, and since the "working schools" were to train children and force them to work in the acceptably profitable wool trade, textile wages would naturally fall as well. With working schools and maritime beggars taking a share of existing labor at a far lower price, the proposal would have rapidly worsened poverty among populations that were doing disproportionately well, since these had previously been good jobs. Wool prices would fall, too, further exacerbating the problem there; this in turn would harm sheep farmers. Even granting Locke his premise that the poor were all refusing to work rather than unable to find work at living wages—a premise that was undoubtedly wrong, particularly given how low poor rates were—and even putting aside the ethical issues with forcing three-year-olds to work, this was a profoundly bad idea for economic reform.

It was, however, an effective blueprint for controlling the poor. John Locke's Poor Law reform plan is not significant as an example of policy, as it was not actually implemented, although it does grimly foreshadow policies that were put into practice later by his intellectual descendants. Rather, it is an example of what his philosophy meant in practice. Lockean psychology justified state coercion, violent punishment, and dismissive political rhetoric, along with cheap labor for capitalists and an expansion of early modern carceral institutions. If human beings were fundamentally automata designed to avoid pain and pursue pleasure, then a violent system of powerful laws was necessary for their own good.

Locke's *Essay on Human Understanding* was immensely influential, spreading these ideas far and wide. His Poor Law proposal tells us exactly what these beliefs about the mind could lead to. The ear-chopping child labor advocate might seem like a person entirely different from the freedom-advocating philosopher beloved by American revolutionaries, but it is a mistake to divide these two sides of John Locke. Locke worked for much of his life within institutions—Oxford University, the Board of Trade—and it was these and the elites whose favor he often required who ultimately determined what ideas had influence. Those with political and economic power could sift Locke's pro-authority ideas from his more revolutionary ones, keeping only the former. Locke's limited opposition to slavery was so effectively overriden by the state and by subsequent events that historian Holly Brewer had to piece that opposition back together centuries after the fact.[56] And his *Essay on Human Understanding* was more immediately influential than his semi-democratic political theory, which published anonymously while he was in exile in the Netherlands.

Locke's ideas, including his political theory, were a product of the society they were incubated in. Private property was central to John Locke's politics. In the second of his *Two Treatises on Government* he argued that revolt is legitimate "whenever the Legislators endeavor to take away, and destroy the Property of the People."[57] He listed a second reason for revolution, when legislators "reduce [the people] to slavery under arbitrary power," after rather than before threats to property.

More broadly, he imagined property to be a basic right on par with life, even a logical necessity of human relations. Ironically, he used American Indians as an example of this. Imagining an Indigenous hunter who had killed a deer, Locke wrote that "his *labour* hath taken it out of the hands of nature, where it was common . . . and *hath* thereby *appropriated* it to himself. Thus, this law of reason makes the deer that Indian's who hath killed it."[58] Real rather than hypothetical Indigenous hunters would have disagreed—had he asked them. What Locke imagined as a "law of reason," even an "original law of nature"—private property—was only a human invention. Even some of his countrymen knew this: the same essay included a detailed rebuttal of claims that Adam's receipt of Earth from God created common, rather than private, property.

This property-centric worldview was part of Locke's property-centric world as a successful bourgeois Englishmen in the mid-1600s. Neither a noble with a firm inherent belief in hierarchy nor a worker with experience in what that meant, Locke generated moving and influential critiques of governments but could not imagine a world without property. Law was central to his ethics, property to his politics, and both to his universe. Locke the man was defined by the institutions he lived and worked in even as the best of his writing on liberty expanded powerfully beyond them. The machine John Locke wanted to improve and optimize was a brutal empire, and his idea of improvement was that of a profit-minded English landholder.

Political arithmetic, "universal reformation," morality as geometry—English elites dreamed of philosopher-physician-mathematicians organizing the world through a universal science of ethics, minds, and politics. Yet Locke, Petty, and other seventeenth-century theorists' unwillingness to engage with the masses—their attempts to decide rather than ask what was good for the poor, the Irish, Indigenous people, and enslaved Africans—ensured their technocratic dream of how the world should be was defined by how the world already was. Calculation gave English elites new ways to optimize and justify this business. William Petty wanted to concoct a new world of prosperity. John Locke wanted to free human beings from tyranny. What they instead helped produce was a science of control.

2

"In Order to Love Mankind, It Is Necessary to Lower Your Expectations": Labor Control and Psychological Egoism, 1690–1783

In the early 1690s, two Dutch strangers came to Bradwell in the county of Staffordshire. During the late seventeenth century, this region was home to around a thousand potters, who lived in small villages of thatched dwellings connected by poorly maintained highways.[1] The newcomers, brothers by the name of David and John Philip Elers, came with secrets: they knew how to make a dark red stoneware, imitating much-valued Chinese red pottery that Europeans called "Boccaro."[2] All told, it was a simple enough business plan: mixing German/Dutch engineering, English clay, and Chinese style. But they had a problem: English workers. Staffordshire potters bitterly rejected attempts to hoard knowledge and individually profit from it. The Elers brothers knew that the local potters would readily adopt the methods they brought with them—not only imitation Boccaro, but also a white "salt-glaze" technique—and took appropriate countermeasures.[3]

According to local oral history, they concealed their trade secrets with a novel labor surveillance system. First, they divided their works into different parts, so that no laborer knew the entire process. The brothers hired workers with what we would now call intellectual disabilities, figuring they would have greater difficulty learning and communicating the brothers' process. These workers were locked inside by day, and when they left were searched and interrogated. Some labor had to be conducted outside, which put it dangerously in view of other potters' interested eyes—so the Elers brothers made sure it was done "beneath the shadow of the trees" to keep their gaze away. A speaking tube connected their warehouse to their workshops, from which the former could warn the latter if anyone suspicious was coming. They even shipped out their wares at night. Through these efforts, the brothers aimed to profit from Staffordshire's clay and labor without contributing to its community, and to preserve the competitive advantage that allowed them to sell a single teapot for two to four times what a journeyman potter might make.[4]

The Elers brothers' system was antithetical to the artisan tradition local to the region. Potters worked in "pot-works" consisting of roughly eight men. They did not divide their labor: all of them engaged as needed in the many tasks involved in pottery. Children also participated, while women labored outside of the pot-work itself by selling the product.[5] Artisan labor like this was far from equitable, but it afforded many potters a great deal of autonomy—autonomy they were keen to defend from the Dutch strangers.

According to local tradition, a young man by the surname of Astbury feigned disability to gain employment with the Elers brothers. Once in, he carefully observed, and finally stole, their methods. There are inconsistencies in the Astbury legend, but whatever actually occurred, the story's celebration of what we would now call intellectual property theft is indicative of early modern Staffordshire potters' values.[6] Potters acted as a social collective, bound by a combination of tradition and material interest.

In the early eighteenth century, a man named Ralph Shaw attempted to claim ownership of multiple advances and variations in pottery work, asserting a patent in 1733. He ended up in a lawsuit with John Mitchell, who was backed up by "almost all the master potters." Mitchell and the community succeeded in having Shaw's patent invalidated, to the "manifest joy of a vast crowd" assembled at the court in July 1736.[7] The community firmly rejected the monopolization of their trade, which was built by far too many to belong to any one person. Against the mobility of capital, the potters believed in the value of home; rejecting the Elers brothers' consolidation of knowledge and profit from it, they insisted that potters should share in the spoils of new ideas. This was a very different ethos from the rising amorality of imperial commerce.

"Vice Is Beneficial Found..."

In 1713, Bernard Mandeville's *Fable of the Bees* made a different argument about profit and ethics: selfishness is good. In the *Fable*, Mandeville used a fictional beehive as an allegory for Britain. He painted a bleak moral picture of the Brit-hive: "All Trades and Places knew some Cheat / No Calling was without Deceit."[8] His bee-lawyers search laws for loopholes the way "burglars" search "shops and houses... to find out where they'd best break through," while physicians are selfish men who value "Fame and Wealth / Above the drooping Patient's Health."[9] He was equally critical of the justice system, writing of Justice that "Her Left Hand, which the Scales should Hold, Had often dropt' em, brib'd with Gold."[10] Britain's eighteenth-century justice system was brutal. Mandeville wrote of the injustice of executing "the Desp'rate and the Poor" for crimes of hunger, merely to protect the wealthy. The hive's residents are all cheaters and hypocrites, bemoaning dishonesty while engaging in it themselves.

When Jove, the Roman god Jupiter, answers their prayers for a virtuous world, "Honesty fills all their Hearts," and they transform their society.[11] In the new hive, bureaucracy is cut to a third of its size, as one honest official on salary can do the work of three paid via graft. The hive gives up foreign wars fought for "empty Glory," and doctors tend to their patients with honesty and diligence.[12]

But the result is a tragedy. Priests, bureaucrats, merchants, and construction workers all lose their superfluous jobs, and workers rush into the few remaining necessary trades, which already have too many workers. Countless bees leave, and the hive is attacked by its enemies, whom it defeats only at great cost before retiring from the hive structure into a hollow tree, which is presented as less of a luxury. Without dishonesty, the entire hive collapses.

Mandeville depicted this moral transformation with profound cynicism. Pages earlier, Mandeville told his readers that the allegorical British justice system unfairly executes poor people to protect "the Rich and Great." Yet later, he argued that such a justice system should remain—because otherwise locksmiths would lose their jobs.[13] "The Indies have been ransack'd," he wrote, and he knew this meant slavery, for wealthy landowners' fancy furniture, but Mandeville insisted that this was how things must be.[14] Only "fools," Mandeville claimed, pursue societal honesty: clear-eyed observers must understand that virtuous ruin was the only alternative to vice-ridden luxury.

Mandeville's defense of self-interest was part of a broader argument for elite control of labor. This is particularly clear in an essay on charity schools that accompanied the *Fable* beginning in its 1723 edition. The idea behind them was that economic opportunity through education might help at least the children of the poor. Charity schools did not necessarily threaten existing hierarchies. They were not a call for redistribution.

Yet charity schools were still too radical for Mandeville, who believed they were a threat to Britain's political and economic structure. Mandeville believed that there was little or no difference between being an ordinary worker and being a king. Both positions, he claimed, had benefits—kings might envy a peasant's lack of responsibilities and their "Peace of Mind," and anyway peasants were used to "Dirt and Squalor."[15] The "Hardships" of poverty, Mandeville claims, "neither seem nor are such to those who have been brought up to 'em, and know no better. There is not a more contented people among us [than the uneducated poor.]"[16] Since class hierarchy did not make a person better or worse off, there was no reason to care about inequality. Being poor was, all things considered, fine. Educating the poor was an injustice, since then they *would* know better—an echo of Richard Ligon's argument about enslaved Africans—and suffer accordingly.

Fears of underclass envy naturally led to Mandeville's broader political and economic concern that, motivated and aided by education, the poor might seek to change their position. Europe's political and economic system was, he knew well, based from the ground up on coercion, though he did not necessarily know or believe there were other ways to arrange a society. "No Body will do the dirty slavish Work that can help it," he warned.

Education would "encourage" common people, "Country Wenches," and conniving servants to demand "more than Masters and Mistresses can afford."[17] Schools would not only make this class of people dissatisfied, it would give them the tools to conspire against the elite. "No Creatures submit contentendly to their Equals," he warned—making them feel they were intellectual equals, or even just a few steps closer to, their superiors was a recipe for disaster.[18] In contrast, poverty was convenient and useful—Mandeville provided precise arguments for actively maintaining it. There was plenty of "hard and dirty Labour" around, he believed. "Where shall we find a better Nursery for these Necessities than the Children of the Poor?"[19]

All of this amounted to both justification and instructions for economic hierarchy. To the extent he was making policy recommendations, he argued for limiting education, cracking down on organizing activities, and keeping a large force of poor and semi-employed people—what Engels later called a "reserve army of labour"—to drive down wages.[20]

Beyond justifying inequality, Mandeville's bleak worldview developed existing political ideas into a quietist argument for political apathy. The *Fable of the Bees* built on Lockean pessimism in new ways: where Locke had merely argued that individuals inevitably pursue their own self-interest, Mandeville insisted that their doing so was also good. Even if we could rid ourselves of selfishness, we should not do so. Likewise, the cold calculations of political arithmetic were a necessary part of Mandeville's fable. Conservative morality treated vice as a sin worth combating, but only a system that turned morality into math could justify maintaining a corrupt and thieving bureaucracy for the public economic good, let alone maintaining prisons as (functionally) a jobs program.

This was a far cry from William Petty's project, which had been transformative—an effort to remake the world itself. For Mandeville, no universal reformation was necessary; society would engineer itself according to the principles of commerce anyway. Mandeville doubted that any normative project was sustainable in the face of human vice, and he insisted that the pursuit of vice produces an optimal outcome. In the *Fable of the Bees*, then, we can see an early form of what would later become the libertarian tendency known as *laissez-faire*, or "let it be," *economics*. The term is misleading; after all, markets and market dependence are political creations that rely on the enforcement of rules like property rights. Even Mandeville believed that "Vice is beneficial found / When it's by Justice lopt and bound." While control science's architects disagreed about how the law should be used to optimize human action, they all agreed that it was necessary.

"When It's by Justice Lopt and Bound"

Claude Adrien Helvétius was both a very likely and a very unlikely proponent of capitalist self-interest. Born in 1715 to the French queen's personal physician, Helvétius used a generous state stipend as a tax farmer to fund a wealthy lifestyle and intellectual exploration.[21] But Helvétius identified with the oppressed as well. He was an ardent and early opponent of slavery and a genuine philanthropist. While his 1758 magnum opus, *De l'esprit*, or *On the Mind*, forwarded Lockean and Hobbesian arguments, it also contained a thoughtful takedown of racist arguments that climate produced biological differences that made Europeans superior to others. An anecdote published shortly after his death offers a more personal example of his egalitarianism. One day a peasant's cart blocked the way of Helvétius's coach. He disembarked and prepared to argue with the man, who scolded him for doing so, exclaiming, "You think that just because you ride around in a coach that I'm a bastard and you're not." Helvétius thanked him.[22]

But like Locke, Helvétius was deeply pessimistic about humanity. He believed that all action was motivated by the pursuit of pain and pleasure, a view he justified with an elaborate account of sensation and memory. Helvétius did not shy away from the extreme implications of psychological egoism. In response to an imagined mother stating that she loves her son for his own sake, Helvétius dismantled parental love, insisting that there are parents "who see their children only as playthings and pastimes."[23] He compared the death of a child to the killing of a Bastille prisoner's pet spider, claiming the resulting tears come

> frequently . . . for nothing but for the lassitude and want of employment into which they fall. If mothers appear in general more afflicted by the death of a child than fathers employed in business, or given up to the pursuit of ambition, it is not because the mother loves her child more tenderly, but because she suffers a loss more difficult to replace.[24]

Our lack of self-awareness only compounds the problem: we are selfish *and* unaware of our selfishness. "In order to love mankind," he insisted, "little must be expected from them."[25] This meant coercing people into being better, rather than convincing them.

For Helvétius, human self-interest could produce great suffering on a societal level, and in contrast to Mandeville he viewed inequality as a problem, offering an insightful description of its compounding growth and arguing that economic inequality could become "as cruel as it is incurable": as rent-seeking increases and small farms are annexed to large ones, the number of wage laborers increases, which lowers the price of labor, further worsening inequality.[26] In such a society, propertyless artisans were displaced from their villages into workshops, and then from those workshops into yet other workshops, losing their attachment to place itself, making them unable to defend the nation.[27] While modern policing had not yet been invented, he also warned of state surveillance and punishment in remarkably modern terms. "In policed countries," he wrote, "the art of the law has often consisted only of making an infinite number of men contribute to the happiness of a few; of keeping, for this purpose, the multitude under oppression, and violating all their rights of humanity."[28]

Where Mandeville claimed market avarice strengthened the hive and virtue weakened it, Helvétius suggested the opposite might be true: inequality could weaken a nation's military strength. He was not systematically anticapitalist and shied away from embracing such antiluxury claims fully, but he was attuned to the ethical problems of capitalism. Helvétius even argued that wage increases for laborers were necessary and proposed redistributing land to that end. For Helvétius, human self-interest, and self-deceit about it, needed to be kept in check.[29] At stake was what would come to be known in later Benthamite thought as the duty-interest junction. If everyone is selfish, how do we make people's self-interest match and thus encourage their ethical duty? Mandeville suggested they were already aligned; Locke implied that God had ensured that alignment.

The solution Helvétius proposed was coercive law. "We cannot flatter ourselves into thinking that we can make any change in the ideas of the people," he wrote, "without having changed the law."[30] In conjunction with his views on inequality, this could have been an argument for democratic regulation of markets, even socialism—but Helvétius did not advocate for democracy. His treatise focused on changing individual behavior rather than inequitable systems, and it proposed doing so by way of silent technocracy, "insensibly" remaking humans from their "imbecility." Legal changes needed to come from enlightened men above.[31]

This entirely top-down view of human action made the lawmaker and legal philosopher a kind of factory manager. To guide these laws, Helvétius sought a "science of morality" which would "furnish us with the means of rendering people more happy, and empires more durable."[32] Using his understanding of self-interest, "moralists" could take the existing "vain science" of morality, which had so far "contributed little to the happiness of mankind," and "make of it a science useful to the universe." A later English translation rendered this "a science of universal utility."[33] Human society was a mechanism to Helvétius, one that could be described with the same methods as the natural world and operated as a system via laws. And in Helvétius's day, perhaps no group of elites had more experience coercing masses of people via law than slaveholders.

While Helvétius was working on *De l'esprit*, Antiguan slaveholder Samuel Martin published an influential how-to guide for Caribbean slavery known as the *Essay upon Plantership*.[34] Like Helvétius, Martin believed rational elites could use law to align incentives. In this case, the relevant elites were planter-legislators like himself—Martin was also a prominent figure in Antigua's colonial government. The *Essay*'s introduction claimed that important planters should naturally be leaders in government and that these men should "understand the whole science of good policy."[35] This included dividing land into smaller plots and giving them to settlers so as to increase the colony's white population and produce "a body of white men interested in the soil," enabling better defense against both foreign invasions and slave revolts.[36] This was a classic example of Helvétian cooperation: law transforming individual interest into cooperation for the general interest.

For Martin, controlling enslaved people was part of a broader set of scientific control methods encompassing land, animals, and plants. He described the plantation as a "well-constructed machine, compounded of various wheels, turning different ways, and yet all contributing to the great end" of profit—"but if any one part runs too fast or too slow in proportion to the rest, the main purpose is defeated."[37] Careful optimization was necessary. Proper plantership, for example, required good animal care, since soil depletion made dung critical to sugar cultivation. Martin offered experience-backed suggestions for feeding animals calculated for maximum financial efficiency, including heavy reliance on sorghum. Calculated proposals for its cultivation and conversion into fodder are included in the *Essay*: sorghum should be planted in May and cut in July, then stored in oval-shaped "ricks" measuring sixteen feet wide, thirty feet long, and seven feet high.[38]

Martin was similarly calculating about enslaved laborers—indeed, he began his treatise with suggestions for their management. For their diet, he proposed nutritional diversity, including plantains, yams, and potatoes. He advised keeping their houses separated by short distances to avoid fire and offering space for planting provisions. Health preservation in the harsh environment in which he and other enslavers forced enslaved people to work entailed attention to the burdens of labor. Martin noted that hoeing was "heavy labor," which should be split up with "easier work" and assigned based on age and health.[39] His management strategies pertaining to people were connected with his proposals regarding land and animals. The diverse diets he proposed also improved soil health, while he advocated animal management partly because animals could undertake labor that would be hard on human workers.

Analyzing "what is the right or rational method of treating" enslaved people, he insisted, "Rational beings they are, and ought to be treated accordingly."[40] But "rationality" for Martin, on a plantation run by his rules, meant obedience. Martin's insistence that enslaved people's resistance was calculable and manageable was a product of the political context of mid-eighteenth-century Antigua as well as the philosophical context of Enlightenment Europe. The island's slaveholding elite was shocked and terrified by a well-planned 1736 revolt attempt, which was only narrowly stopped at the last minute.[41]

In the aftermath, Antiguan planters passed new laws to crack down on plantation conspiracies. Moreover, Martin's own father had been killed by the people he enslaved. If any reduction in violence did come from his ideas, we might actually understand it as the fruit of these resisters' labor, via Martin's own fear. Samuel Martin's calculus was an attempt to claim control in the face of resistance that could not be controlled, to justify the violent institution his wealth was based on, and to set the conditions under which resistance occurred and was interpreted.

Samuel Martin justified slavery using the same logic he suggested should guide the system's operation: economic calculations of self-interest. Martin argued that it was in the interest of slaveholders to act with "kindness and good nature" toward enslaved people and that "good discipline is by no means inconsistent with humanity."[42] By providing enslaved people with sufficient and healthy food—beyond the "scanty" cornmeal that sustained life but did only that—he argued that slaveholders, who had a literal financial interest in the people they enslaved, would "reap a much larger product . . . than the most cruel Egyptian task-master."[43]

His solution to the duty-interest problem, where slavery was concerned, was not a solution at all—he simply claimed that slaveholders' duties and interests were inherently aligned. This was inaccurate, of course. Slavery requires terror and violence by its very nature: capturing and enslaving people in the first place requires force, and keeping them from running or simply refusing work does as well. Martin wanted to optimize this unfathomably vast array of daily violence for maximum profit.

John Locke had invoked God's benevolent will to render his selfish system compatible with Christian ethics. Samuel Martin now argued that God had structured the world in a manner that made slaveholders' economic interest congruent with their ethical obligations. After claiming that slaveholders' financial interest and ethical duty were in agreement, he thanked God for making them that way, writing: "So bountiful is the Creator, to make that most for our interest, which is most our duty."[44]

In Samuel Martin's plantership guide, European political economy, philosophy, science, and work management coalesced into Helvétius's "science of universal utility" and Locke's Euclidean ethics. Though neither would have approved, given their views on slavery, Martin's control science arose naturally from their principles. The *Essay upon Plantership* went through multiple editions after its initial publication and represents the widely shared views of an influential figure in colonial society. Turning to South Carolina, we can find similar calculating principles in the activities of another slaveholding elite, Henry Laurens.

"Gentlemen of Fortune"

Henry Laurens's business was calculating the value of human lives. The letters he sent to his correspondents traversed the globe, and while they do not directly invoke philosophers and were not written for public consumption, he was as good an indicator of enslavers' worldview as any other and an influential figure among the eighteenth-century colonial elite. The firm he founded, Austin and Laurens, was the largest slave trading business in North America, and Laurens was a regular fixture in the port city of Charles Town (now Charleston), where Laurens sold beings for, in his own words, "a monstrous price."[45]

The yard he sometimes used for allowing buyers to inspect his human "merchandise" could contain and display for sale more than 100 human beings at any one time.[46] His letters recommended tailors in London, advised on transatlantic slave markets, and contained dispatches to magnates and officials throughout Britain's Atlantic empire.[47] This empire ran on dehumanizing calculation, transforming human beings into numbers. Laurens made his fortune by ruthlessly maximizing them. His friend and business partner Richard Oswald calculated that a "life . . . employed on indigo in the back parts of the province, would be worth ten years purchase more than one employed on rice in the maritime part."[48] Enslaved men with artisan skills, such as carpenters, appeared in his example spreadsheets as "valuable negroes."[49]

Enslavers' quantification created a parallel world in which brutality was rational, sanitized, and inevitable. Turning human beings—infinitely complex, diverse, freely acting entities—into single numbers was no easy feat and only ever an approximation achieved with violence. South Carolina planters preferred purchasing captives from particular regions, having come to believe that men from "Calabar" (a slave-trading center in present-day Nigeria) were rebellious and that those from east of the Gold Coast were more likely to escape slavery by ending their own lives.[50]

Of course, slave traders like Henry Laurens were not about to interview enslaved people on the cultural influences of resistance in order to better predict it. But they did not have to. It did not matter to Laurens whether the oversimplified and ill-informed stereotypes of purchasers were true. The market transformed the subjective preferences of slaveholders into "objective" financial reality: Calabar captives sold for less.

Actual people captured in Calabar may or may not have engaged in differing forms of resistance, but Henry Laurens was selling and buying the sanitized and violently controlled idea of a person, a fiction maintained only with whips and nooses. When captives arrived half-dead on American shores, some slave traders tried to sell them as healthy potential workers by oiling their skin. Others used the rough maritime sealing material known as oakum to seal captives' orifices, silencing their protests and hiding their dysentery.[51] But they did not see people, or goods, or ships. They saw numbers. Laurens lived in a world of account books, handshakes, and receipts.

When reality broke through, Laurens's disinterest dropped, revealing the unspeakable violence that lay beneath. In 1757, he wrote to an acquaintance on behalf of a shoemaker named Patrick Hind, who had purchased one captive from a recent voyage. Artisans like Hind regularly purchased and trained enslaved workers in lieu of apprentices—their services were cheaper, their legal rights weaker, and their labors eternal. The £150 Hind spent must have been a sizable sum to him, and he seems to have purchased a sicker captive, "very Mauger & full of sores," at a discount.[52] Laurens claimed Hind planned to get the unnamed person, probably a child or adolescent based on the language used, medical care, and then profit as usual. But the £150 price did not match the reality of what Hind could get out of him: after his purchase, Hind discovered the captive was, he wrote, "an Idiot"; Laurens referred to him as a "Creature" rather than a person.

We cannot know whether this apparent disability was psychological, physiological, or perhaps even feigned. Whatever the case, Hind and Laurens defaulted to the reality they knew—the "boy" was "not worth a Groat," and Hind was bleeding money to pay for his food and shelter. Laurens's sympathy was for Hind only, of course—this "poor man" was burdened with a "Loathsome Carcass." Slaveholders' paper-and-profit world flattened enslaved people into numbers, and this young person's number was less than zero. Hind went on to live a long and prosperous life, perhaps with Laurens's help in this instance. It is unclear what fate the unnamed man he purchased came to.[53]

In the world enslavers had created, what happened to this unnamed man was not a horrible act of violence but an ordinary act of accounting. When Martin spoke of treating enslaved people with "rational methods," this too was included: maximizing the productive output of a plantation naturally included minimizing costs, which meant minimizing standards of living within reason and calculating the value of enslaved laborers. Laurens's friend Oswald proclaimed Carolina a profitable colony precisely because in its environment enslaved people could, and therefore could be forced to, hunt and fish for their own subsistence.[54] A kind of capitalist rationalism was coalescing as both the epistemology and the morality of commerce on both sides of the Atlantic.

"Make Such Machines of the Men as Cannot Err"

As slavery and colonialism created new methods for extracting profit, their proceeds created new markets for luxury goods. One such good was pottery. And while Staffordshire pot-works produced impressive output, they could not produce nearly enough to meet its newly rising demand. The latest advances in chemistry were an opportunity to develop new wares that might appeal to elites—but artisans were largely happy with the pottery economy as it was. It would take a capitalist to transform it into an industry. That man was Josiah Wedgwood, and while he was hardly the only person behind this transformation, he was a central figure in it.

Born in Staffordshire in 1730, Wedgwood came from a well-off family on the boundary between artisans and petit bourgeois, born to a father in "easy, if not affluent circumstances."[55] In fact, he was a nephew of Samuel Astbury, the hero who had stolen the Elers brothers' secrets. Every sign in his life pointed to a successful future as a master potter, likely one who would become slightly wealthier than his father before him, as his father had compared to *his* father, and so on. But in childhood, a battle with smallpox left him with a "disorder in his knee."[56] This was potentially devastating, as making pottery involved using a pedal-powered wheel.

Since he could no longer work a pottery wheel, Josiah instead moved to learn the rest of the trade, becoming a designer, an inventor, a chemist, and a marketer. Wedgwood's innovations were impressive indeed. Working on a class of decorative ware that attracted eyeballs and coins by imitating fancy materials like agate and marble—a specialty of one of his relatives—Josiah set himself to experimenting with different chemical mixtures and soon developed what was apparently the first effective imitation of the mineral porphyry.[57]

Just as his painful knee drove him to a new understanding of his art, Josiah's uncooperative older brother Thomas unintentionally drove him to a new understanding of business. Josiah learned as an apprentice under Thomas, but when his apprenticeship period ended, the elder Wedgwood refused to become Josiah's business partner—perhaps because of jealousy, or a difference of opinion. Whatever the reason, Wedgwood was forced to find other investors if he wanted to fulfill his growing technical and financial ambitions. He went into partnership instead with the potter Thomas Wieldon and slowly amassed wealth. When inflammation following a bone bruise, perhaps exacerbated by the previous damage to his leg from smallpox, confined him to his room for months in the early 1750s, Josiah set himself to reading. His focus was on chemistry, but this was the era of natural philosophy, not science, so his reading undoubtedly brought him into contact with works of political and moral philosophy as well. By the early 1760s, he made an important friend engaged in all of these intellectual pursuits: the chemist and philosopher Joseph Priestley.[58] Motivated first and foremost by religion, Priestley was not quite a devotee of the emerging field of political economy, though he was influenced by Locke and was later an influence on Jeremy Bentham—but he was also captivated by the ideas of "improvement." Priestley believed in an ever-improving world that could be guided through reason to moral perfection. He became a fond, almost Mandevillian, believer in commerce and business, which made him an obvious ally of Wedgwood.

Priestley's ideas about economic inequality have been fairly summarized as "paternalistic liberalism."[59] While he rejected ecclesiastical and aristocratic hierarchies, he remained comfortable with economic inequality—believing it rational and even ordained by God himself. Like Locke, he proposed abandoning the Poor Law, arguing that it encouraged laziness. In its place he proposed a combination of private charity, mandatory insurance, and interest manipulation. Society, he believed, had to render it in "the visible interest of every man to be industrious."⁶⁰ On top of this, Priestley's ideas could be outright authoritarian. When he heard of a Bavarian welfare program that forced the poor into workhouses, he praised it warmly. It was, he said, "good government." Historian Isaac Kramnick described his work and that of his pupil Thomas Cooper as a "science of domination."⁶¹

Josiah Wedgwood put Priestley's chemistry and philosophy into action as he grew his business in the 1760s, specifically in his megafactory Etruria, built in the late 1760s with the proceeds from his growing business. Even before it opened in 1769, it was a site of brutal labor discipline. In June 1768, Wedgwood found out that his architect, Joseph Pickford, was treating the workers constructing Etruria too harshly. In an unknown incident involving a mortar-maker, Wedgwood observed that "mr. P. has much of the Bashaw in his treatment of workmen," that is, he treated them like a supposed Ottoman despot would, "& does not seem to consider their having any feelings at all." Wedgwood sympathized with the workers and considered speaking with Pickford about the "proper treatment of our inferiors."⁶²

His thinking centered on a Lockean/Helvetian vision of ethics. "*Our humble friends*," Wedgwood wrote, "are capable of feeling pain, or pleasure." However, they only felt this "*nearly* [emphasis mine] in the same manner as their Masters."⁶³ Similar to Samuel Martin, Wedgwood reduced workers not merely to the pleasure-seeking automata of Lockean psychology but to a slightly lower suborder of a humanity already characterized by that psychological egoism. This patriarchal liberalism was of a piece with Martin's "rational" slaveholding ethos. Both identified those at the bottom of the hierarchy as actors worthy of moral consideration but also insisted that the hierarchy itself was fundamentally just, while differentiating and othering workers from the enlightened elite.

When Etruria opened in 1769, Wedgwood applied this same body of ideas to control its workers. Every aspect of manufacture was under his direct control, and the infrastructure of his facilities was built to limit as much as possible the agency of individual workers. The mass production and, critically, marketing of pottery demanded uniformity, which required a complete reorganization of labor. A single master potter and fewer than a dozen men and apprentices working at a traditional potbank could not produce in the quantity Wedgwood wanted, nor could their mode of production make hundreds or thousands of nearly uniform pieces. In order to reorganize production, Wedgwood attempted to "make such *Machines* of the *Men* as cannot err" out of artisans who prized their autonomy.[64]

To do so, Wedgwood used surveillance, incentive appeals, behavior manipulation, and simple tyranny. He hired what he called a "Clerk of the Manufactory" to oversee production; the clerk was charged with enforcing the cleanliness of the facility and keeping a close eye on workers to ensure exact adherence to Wedgwood's regulations on things like clay dampness and mixing.[65] Taking control of production meant taking control of workers, not because they had low standards but because they had different preferences, goals, and interests—something unacceptable to Wedgwood. He wished to *use* artisans like machines rather than negotiate with them as people. Talented artists who might once have designed a product and seen what began in their mind transformed into physical reality were reduced to reproducing Wedgwood's designs.[66] The loss of autonomy was agonizing.

In addition to alienating workers from their work, central managerial control also took more concrete things from them. It was normal for a potter to take time off for "a wake [a community festival] or a fair," and artisans were used to flexible workdays under their control.[67] Wedgwood demanded regular scheduling, and while he was not in the short term successful at breaking local festivals, he did institute what the historian E. P. Thompson described as "time discipline," now a normal feature of the modern workplace. Wedgwood even developed a rudimentary time-clock system.[68] Wedgwood also instructed the clerk to "distinguish" the best workers "from the less orderly part of the work people by *presents or other marks suitable to their age*," while punishing those who were late and counting the hours they missed.[69]

In doing so, he alienated workers from each other. Wedgwood had each worker's productivity calculated so they could be pitted against each other. Then as now, groups of workers might include a team member who kept everyone's spirits up, or an older employee who worked more slowly but knew the process better than anyone else and kept everything running, or a grieving parent, or disabled worker, or ill colleague. All of these people could be reduced to a number, a purely economic value. For Wedgwood's workers, this modern capitalist labor system was a departure from a bygone world in which they could control their lives, recognize their work in their hands at the end of the process, and—especially in larger workplaces like dockyards—share a sense of camaraderie with those around them. All this was now a bitter memory made more painful by how recent and clear it was, and how fast it seemed to have vanished.

Tyranny and coercion were necessary for this vast transformation of work. Wedgwood personally smashed pieces he found unsatisfactory with the announcement that "this won't do for Josiah Wedgwood." His workers, he wrote, "are frighten'd out of their wits when they hear of Mr W. coming to town, & I perceive upon our first meeting they look as if they saw the D[evi]l."[70] This direct coercion functioned in a background of broader economic coercion. With factories churning out pottery en masse, each with powerful marketing arms and financial connections, traditional potbanks could not compete. Changes in skills and training made workers more vulnerable to economic coercion as well. Wedgwood trained workers not as general potters who might be able to autonomously navigate the whole of production, as they once had, but as specialists, which put them at the whims of the market: when gilding fell out of fashion, his gilders lost their livelihoods.[71]

A knowledgeable and lucky worker might still take advantage of market demand himself by seeking out Wedgwood's competitors (particularly in America or France) to bargain for a higher wage.[72] To keep this from happening, Wedgwood resorted to coercive measures of knowledge control. He argued that the postmaster should have the legal power to open letters of those suspected of recruiting or being recruited for foreign enterprise. He printed and distributed pamphlets insisting that work outside of Britain was a nightmare. In 1783 he personally warned and threatened his workers with a speech that included stories of shipwreck, destitution, and penury. His speech also appealed to their patriotism—but toward its end fell back on persuasion by force. It concluded with Wedgwood reading from laws threatening manufacturing workers who sought employment in other countries.[73]

Josiah Wedgwood was not satisfied with reducing labor from a practice to a market in which workers sold their time—he wished to skew that market itself. The laws he wielded against them were what the "science of legislation" looked like in practice: coercive rules meant to forcibly align workers' incentives with those of the elites who controlled the British state. The purpose of Wedgwood's discipline, surveillance, training, and even facilities was simple: he sought to excise human will from human work. In the words of historian Neil McKendrick, who was sympathetic to Wedgwood, wages were "very adequate compensation for [workers'] loss of freedom," from a man who demanded "complete obedience, and complete submission."[74]

John Locke's philosophy, which Wedgwood was undoubtedly in contact with, if not directly then via Priestley, was an invaluable part of this. Psychological egoism was perfect for a man who wished to reduce men to "machines that cannot err" because it in effect claimed they already *were* machines. Workers' desires, like participating in community festivals, could be reduced to pleasure-seeking or pain avoidance, thrown into the same category as alcoholism and overridden.

"Degrading, Slavish Chains"

Control science on both sides of the Atlantic was an intellectual, social, and technical project for meeting capitalism's profit imperative. Caribbean slaveholders' methods of control aligned with those of British manufacturers through a process of convergent evolution: they were both fundamentally about excising human will from profit-making. This included even their own will. Josiah Wedgwood was not a heartless man. In 1768, just before Etruria opened and put into action his plans to make workers into machines, Wedgwood feared he was doing the same thing to himself. He expressed his worries in a letter to his beloved friend and business partner, Thomas Bentley. In it, he wrote that he wished to be "released from these degrading slavish chains, these mean selfish fears of other people copying my works."[75] He proposed two paths forward.

One future he imagined was what we would now call an open-source dream, sharing designs and processes throughout Europe for the good of all. "So far from being afraid of other People getting our patterns," Wedgwood wrote, "we should Glory in it, throw out all the hints we can, & if possible have all the Artists in Europe working after our models." Instead of the "narrow mercenary selfish trammels" of running a cutthroat business, he could embrace his role as a designer and share his work with the world. Notably, this also would have inevitably granted greater power to workers, since the employer's monopoly on manufacturing knowledge and design was a key asset against workers. He had talked about this vision with Bentley on the road from Liverpool one day, and had not forgotten "how *our hearts burned within us*" as they did. Wedgwood believed that his own creativity would flourish if he were free of the profit motive, that he had "always wish'd to be released from it & was I now free I am persuaded it would do me much good in body, more in mind."

The alternative was the "narrow, mercenary, selfish trammels" of business, prioritizing profit over all else. Wedgwood despaired at what this business plan would cost them: at "the coats of mail we are forgeing for our reluctant hearts, to case & hamper them in their journey through life, & prevent all benevolent overflowings for the good of their fellow Citizens." Market self-interest meant turning themselves into hollow metal men operating only according to the dictates of the market—only according to material self-interest. To become the boss, Wedgwood feared he would have to repress his own virtues. Bentley suggested combining Wedgwood's two plans, and Josiah took him up on that—but his subsequent business activities suggest the "mercenary" vision was more powerful.[76]

On the other side of the Atlantic a year after Wedgwood's letter, Henry Laurens wrote to his son with similar ethical concerns. "You know, my dear son, I abhor slavery," Laurens claimed. He argued that as a slave trader he was "not the man who enslaved them" and that while he hoped to free the people he enslaved "great powers oppose me—the laws and customs of my country, my own and the avarice," that is, the greed, "of my countrymen."[77]

We should not, of course, take ethical doubts from one of the inventors of the factory and one of the largest slave traders in the world seriously. In the same letter to his son, Laurens claimed that the people he enslaved had never attempted to run, when in fact he had taken out advertisements seeking bounties for exactly this reason—for example, a September 3, 1753, advertisement for a man he referred to as Footbea.[78] He was not quite lying in the same way about the power of the slaveholding establishment—it really did consist of "great powers." But part of the reason that those powers existed, and that they were so "great," was Laurens's earlier decision to invest time and effort in the slave trade. Slavery's eventual end was a result of political efforts, including by people far less powerful than Laurens himself.

Capitalism's market dependence was self-reinforcing: it empowered those who exploited workers, and it disempowered those who did not. Having directly contributed to the extension of market dependence into pottery, Wedgwood found that the market tied his own hands as well; the "degrading slavish chains" he complained of were partly of his own forging. Wedgwood did not create a morally neutral system of commerce and then discover that it involved ethical compromises—his system was itself an ethical breach from the beginning. Any of these men could at any point have abandoned their malevolent work and set their energy to making a different world possible. For elites, the market was resistible in a way it was not for workers. If Wedgwood stopped exploiting workers, he would be less rich and perhaps have to take up a different living; for the men laboring in his factories, stopping work meant death. Control science was not only an economic practice for optimizing profit but also a political discourse for legitimizing it. As capitalists were devising new methods to exploit workers, they were also coming up with new excuses for doing so. And the best justification for the unjustifiable was, simply, saying that nothing better was possible.

Wedgwood knew the world could change, and in other areas he believed in trying to change it. His friend Thomas Bentley was an antislavery activist, and when Bentley died, Wedgwood honored his memory by supporting the movement to abolish the slave trade. But while he tried to create, and helped the movement to eventually achieve, a world without slavery, he could only imagine a world without the profit motive. "Political arithmetic" provided a new language for control of the masses, while "improvement" promised infinite dividends for doing so—a promise that justified any action. "Self-interest" and the development of natural philosophy offered an air of inevitability, presenting elite control as natural and elite victory as foreordained. These ideas were codeveloped with practices of control that produced early capitalism's vast profits. While developing influential production and marketing practices, Wedgwood was absorbing influences from people like Priestley and hobnobbing with the developers of the steam engine, Matthew Boulton and James Watt.[79] It was in the 1770s through the 1790s, as capitalism and empire were threatened by revolution, that practice and theory properly converged. Samuel Bentham, a young shipwright working for two empires, devised a new way to control workers: the Panopticon.

3

"Two Sovereign Masters: Pain and Pleasure": Mechanized Labor and the Panopticon, 1760–1810

Samuel and Jeremy Bentham came from a well-off London family. Their father, Jeremiah, was a successful lawyer. Samuel, the younger brother, was born in 1757, and was mechanically inclined from a young age. He built a carriage for a childhood friend, Cornelia Knight (later a notable novelist and artist), and managed to convince his reluctant and disapproving father to allow him to go into shipbuilding.[1] Of course, no Bentham was going to be a common shipwright: Jeremiah secured Samuel a top-tier apprenticeship, training for a supervisory position. In this position, he learned not only the craft of shipbuilding but the latest in geometry and mathematics, while pursuing studies in French and chemistry as well.[2] Like Josiah Wedgwood, he became equipped with both a tradesman's knowledge and bourgeois European science.

The Royal Dockyards Samuel entered as an apprentice were a patchwork of modern labor protections and ancient rights. They had a form of pension and a form of tenure (workers could generally count on lifetime employment). Workers had significant power, collectively, over the timing and intensity of their work. They lived in longstanding craft communities composed of friends and family, with centuries-old traditions. When managers threatened their pay or working conditions, shipbuilders reacted with well-coordinated strikes as well as quieter forms of subversion, like fudging paperwork to increase pay. They took care of each other and for the most part, within trades, made the same wage—an egalitarian tendency they defended proudly. The yards were far from perfect, of course. Apprentices often suffered grievously, and egalitarianism often existed only *within* trades—shipwrights did not stand up for ropemakers, for instance. The work was hard, and the hours long. But it was one of the best places in England to be a worker.

Samuel probably did not fit in as a dockyard man. His apprenticeship set him apart from the others. While they were toiling away in the early morning cold, he was studying geometry. After a long day at work, he was practicing French while they were going home to their families, or nearby pubs. The dockyard was a tight-knit and well-organized proletarian community brave enough to repeatedly and illegally strike and win.[3] Samuel, however, was a lawyer's son and the stepbrother of a future parliamentarian. The common men of the yards probably resented him, all stiff-backed in his fine clothes, a lawyer's son who had parachuted in from the bourgeoisie because he liked ships but was more comfortable with a protractor than an adze. And he resented them in turn—slouched in their tradition, designing the most complicated weapons in the world by eye-balling it, working with rules of thumb instead of rules of math.[4] His work ethic and attitude set him apart from the other elite apprentices as well. He refused to skip or slow work, as they often did, and was dedicated to his craft.

In the dockyard, Samuel developed the twin convictions that most anything could be done better than it was currently being done, and that he could figure out how this was possible. Scientific methods—examining, testing, comparing, and developing theories—were the means he relied upon in every area of work. While he learned shipbuilding from artisans and from hands-on experience, he also sought to advance knowledge of it in new ways. A private shipyard operator, in conversation with Jeremy, described Samuel's work as a "second branch" of shipbuilding, better called "'computing' or 'comparing' or some such word."[5]

Like Samuel, Jeremy did not fit quite right in his own profession—law. Although he met his father's expectations by pursuing legal study, he soon dashed those expectations by failing to actually practice law. Skeptical of fuzzy concepts like "natural rights," as well as the blurry institutions that supposedly guarded them, Jeremy came to detest the legal system he had trained for. Instead of England's common law, which relied heavily on judicial precedent, Jeremy preferred a system of civil law—a central body of codes, a scientific rule set for a scientific age. Jeremy's worldview mirrored Samuel's, and they developed their work and their philosophies together. The brothers were close and wrote to each other often, inspiring and encouraging each other. Jeremy called his younger brother "my only friend, my second self."[6]

In 1775, Royal Dockyards shipwrights went on strike against a new work program developed along "self-interest" lines. John Montagu, fourth Earl of Sandwich, had a simple plan to replace workers: pay was to be tied to productivity. The fastest workers would be paid more to get more work out of them, and based on the resulting improvements, the rest of the workforce could be fired to cut costs. In this way, Montagu hoped to fire half the shipwrights of the Royal Dockyards. Workers denounced this task work as "progressive suicide on our Bodies" and proudly rejected individual self-interest in favor of a semi-egalitarian, communal ethic. Dockyard artisans demanded an across-the-board pay raise, not mass firings and harder work for the rest. They pursued these demands with petitions and strikes, coordinated across England.[7] It took several months, but their strike halted Montagu's plans. But workers did not have the last word.

It is unclear exactly how Samuel felt about the strike, but it is not hard to guess. Samuel spent some of the strike period on a family trip to France, but he was certainly aware of it and was present in the dockyards when the strikes began in June. His brother had assigned him "the divine Helvetius" as reading and forwarded him correspondence from Joseph Priestley. Perhaps Samuel read the strike, cynically, as an expression of workers' self-interest, or as another eruption of rebellion that needed to be quelled.[8] Certainly, this was Jeremy's attitude in the same period toward America's rebellion. Both American rights rhetoric (if not practice) and British shipbuilding tradition insisted that certain things were unconditionally, and thus unquantifiably, valuable: liberty, say, for subjects or workers, was important in and of itself, and not subject to compromise. In contrast, the calculating worldview the brothers were developing held that nothing was important in and of itself.

Jeremy Bentham's 1776 *Fragment on Government* articulated the scientific morality he believed in. The *Fragment* is an exhaustive and amusing takedown of legal theorist William Blackstone, whom Bentham accused of mincing words and hiding circular arguments behind tedious semantics. Blackstone, for instance, stated, "As the power of making laws constitutes the supreme authority, so wherever the supreme authority in any state resides, it is the right of that authority to make laws."[9] Bentham spends several pages explaining precisely why this statement is circular and reduces to (my words, not his) "the people who can make laws can make laws."

For Jeremy, this kind of sophistry got in the way of truth and justice. Unclear language was prone to misuse, and impossible to argue about—rights, for example, were incoherent, as were "duties." Jeremy believed, building on Locke, that duty meant an obligation guaranteed by punishment. The state, therefore, could not have any duties to the people, because duties were what the state imposed upon the people through the law. Instead of duties or rights, Jeremy believed that all legal and political concerns should be determined by rational calculus of costs and benefits, one example of the broader mathematical approach to ethics that defined his moral philosophy.

Jeremy claimed that Wedgwood's associate Joseph Priestley gave him the phrase and the idea "the greatest happiness for the greatest number." A good world was not one that met particular obligations, or provided minimum standards to all, but one in which the sum total of happiness was maximized, whoever was happy and whatever the reason for their happiness. Jeremy was clearly influenced by Priestley, had read his work, and moved in adjacent social-intellectual circles.[10]

God, in Priestley's view, wanted us to be happy and shaped both human nature and the universe itself to that end. Since he did not want us to seek our happiness "at the expense of that of others," God had devised an "admirable constitution" that aligned our happiness with that of others.[11] In contrast, Jeremy wanted to improve the existing world, but he was motivated by a belief in rational science rather than theology or class justice.

The fact that the brothers were enemies of the existing "system of management" in courts and dockyards did not make them friends of shipwrights or prisoners.[12] Jeremy opposed the vicious executions Britain conducted under what was known as the "Bloody Code," but he proposed prisons for the poor instead of death. Samuel wanted the dockyards to be better managed, but for the purposes of the state rather than workers. Both wished to optimize rather than replace existing hierarchies. Jeremy's editor John Bowring quotes him as saying that in this era, he "never suspected that the people in power were against reform." They only needed "to know what was good in order to embrace it."[13] In a slavery-funded empire that maintained power by the hangman's noose, his naivete was stunning . . . and convenient. If all those in power needed to do good was a little knowledge, men like Jeremy were the solution.

Reformers rather than revolutionaries, they hoped to wield rather than challenge imperial power. As America rose up, the brothers fled Britain and headed for imperial Russia—Samuel first, in 1780, followed by Jeremy in 1786. There, Empress Catherine the Great wielded nominally absolute power, although in practice she was constrained by court politics and other forces in the state. In Russia, Samuel believed that he could practice his new science of shipbuilding unhindered by organized workers and entrenched bureaucracy. Jeremy, meanwhile, hoped that Catherine was the answer to his dreams of sweeping aside convoluted legal traditions: he believed that she could in a single stroke make the sweeping changes he wished to see. Russian autocracy, the Benthams imagined, could be a shortcut.

They could bypass institutions and authorities, customs and rights, and make labor and law as they should be with a wave of the empress's hand.[14]

The "Central Inspection Principle"

Imagine for a moment that you are a Russian worker in St. Petersburg in late 1782. Your job is to drive piles into the ground using a towering contraption of weights and pulleys. By pulling on connected ropes, you and a squad of others lift a heavy weight and then release it to ram a pile into the ground for construction work, building piers and foundations. The work is immensely taxing, and it produces a natural rhythm: heavy pulling, brief rest.

One day a British man in his twenties marches into your workplace with a design for a machine supposedly meant to solve all of the problems with your work. Perhaps his proposals will protect your aching back. But no, Samuel Bentham's problems are your employer's problems, not your problems. Samuel has been traveling the country consulting for wealthy elites on how to optimize their estates; the previous year he worked on salt mines. He would like you to work faster and believes you are engaged in "habitual skulking." But one man's skulking is another man's rest. The natural rhythm of pile-driving provides plenty of reasons for breaks, and your role in that rhythm makes it easier to create time for them.

Samuel has proposed a machine that would "put an end" to this rest by using you and your coworkers' weight as well as your strength. His contraption is easier to move from point to point, which makes construction faster. Samuel's first problem was not the efficiency of the machine, it was the efficiency of the workers—its entire purpose was to address skulking, according to his wife Mary's later summary. While we do not have a diagram of Samuel's pile-driving machine, Mary described it as "a kind of ladder which yielded downwards on every step that the men took," presumably not unlike a

StairMaster or a treadmill.[15] This invention was one of the first in a series of contraptions he designed to control workers.

Samuel's pile-driving machine was only the beginning. Between 1780 and 1791, his career took him far and wide across Russia, where he consulted on everything from salt mines to glassworks. Imperial Russia in this period was dominated by powerful nobles like Grigory Potemkin, a prince, lover, and favorite of the empress who directed Russian expansion onto the steppes near the Caspian Sea. This meant conquering Indigenous people in the kind of colonial expansion more commonly associated with Atlantic empires. Russia was not a commercial capitalist empire like Britain, but Potemkin and nobles like him promoted the latest in technology and hoped to profit off it. This, of course, was made easier by the widespread use of convict labor.

Samuel's unwillingness to consider what workers wanted, and his willingness to wield power over them, reflect a broader personal tendency of his: in both his work and his personal life, Samuel could be a poor listener. In early 1783 he informed Jeremy he had fallen "deeply in love" with Countess Sophia Dmitrievna Matiushkina.[16] The relationship was troubled by opposition from her family, and Samuel made matters worse by failing to listen to Sophia's advice on how to navigate that opposition. At one point she was so distraught by a plan of his involving a letter that she broke social protocol at a party, publicly grabbed him by the arm, and begged him not to deliver it. He did anyway. If Samuel was unwilling to listen to the advice of someone he loved, he was certainly not going to seek the perspective of the pump workers affected by his pile-driving machine. Whether they might be comfortable with "skulking," or what *they* might feel was fair to do about it, did not influence his decision-making.

Throughout his career, Samuel treated labor as an engineering challenge. If he could determine an objectively superior method for joining planks or firing cannons, then why not do the same for workers? Skulking was as objectively undesirable as timber waste. He did not seriously consider any perspectives that might have challenged his own. Like Wedgwood, he entrusted only himself with the responsibility of changing the world. Samuel combined this scientific elitism with penal labor exploitation, serving imperialism and aristocratic profit, to develop the Panopticon. After Samuel gained the favor of Potemkin, he went to work at his facilities in Krichev, where Potemkin manufactured tools for Russia's imperial conquests.

Samuel's job, first and foremost, was to build ships. The younger Bentham was a talented shipwright, but his knowledge of shipbuilding and other enterprises was useless without other men to actually do and manage the work. He therefore invited British artisans to Russia. When they arrived, Samuel soon found out that these workers brought with them their own assumptions about what work was and how it should be governed. They treated orders and schedules as suggestions more than commands.

These men were not acting unruly. Rather, they were operating according to a different set of rules: the semi-egalitarian artisan moral economy of tradition rather than the Benthams' nascent science of management. Samuel and Jeremy had come to Russia because of its authoritarianism, and they were not about to create an egalitarian workplace within it.[17] Accordingly, Samuel devised a system to control English workers, train Russian serfs, and surveil foremen.

It began with the central inspection principle: workers should be watched at all times, working within "a building so contrived as that the whole of the operations carried on in it should be under observation from its centre."[18] Every aspect of production could then be overseen with the minimum number of managers, which was both more efficient and in line with Samuel's belief in "individual responsibility"—the consolidation of final administrative authority in one person.[19] The all-seeing manager could identify workers who needed further training, problems in the production process, or skulking, with ease. Functionally, this system was meant to minimize the will of anyone not at its center while magnifying and extending the central manager's agency across the entire workplace.

Central inspection began as a particular solution to labor problems in Russian manufacturing, but Samuel always had broader goals. In the next few years, Bentham's activities ranged from helping Potemkin win a war against the Ottomans with experimental ships to building a strange worm-like vessel for Catherine's 1787 trip through new territories. It was on that trip that Potemkin, according to legend, built fake villages full of happy peasants for the empress to look at with pride. These infamous "Potemkin villages" did not in fact exist, but if they had, it would have been Samuel Bentham who built them.

Between 1786 and 1787, Jeremy visited his brother in Russia. Like Samuel, he hoped to use the empire as a laboratory. He planned to win Catherine over to his designs for a comprehensive and entirely new legal code based on his mathematical morality. John Locke, Joseph Priestley, and Adam Smith had all tempered their views of calculable happiness with an inconsistent but real belief in rights and ethics.[20] Jeremy avoided internal contradictions by abandoning these incalculable things altogether. Rights, in his formulation, were "nonsense upon stilts," inefficient barriers that got in the way of social optimization through law.[21] Even emotions could be reduced to math. "Passion calculates," he insisted. Bentham expanded on Smith's economic arguments while abandoning his ethics, just as he adopted Locke's vision of self-interest without his vision of political rights.

Underlying this was an extreme adoption of Lockean psychological egoism. "Nature," Jeremy wrote in 1789, "has placed mankind under the governance of two sovereign masters, *pain* and *pleasure*. It is for them alone to point out what we ought to do, as well as to determine what we shall do." "Right and wrong," he wrote, "[and] causes and effects, are fastened to their throne." Behavior had to be predictable and controllable if it was going to be manipulated by calculation—and Jeremy Bentham's utilitarian philosophy, as it came to be known, was defined by cold calculation above all else. The right thing to do was whatever produced the most pleasure and the least pain for the largest number of individuals.[22]

On the surface, this may not sound like a bad thing, and to someone in the Benthams' position, a mathematical ethics had undeniable appeal. Philosophy seemed to create problems, while science and mathematics solved them. English intellectuals had already been calling for a calculated remaking of the world along empiricist principles, and rapid advances in science could only make a believer in this vision more confident in the possibility of achieving it. Bentham read the writings of, corresponded with, and met men stumbling through new discoveries: oxygen! Electricity! Steam power! Day by day, more and more of the world could be described by equations and manipulated by engineers. Jeremy hoped to do the same with law.

This was the motivation behind his plans for legal reform, which he meant to advance during his visit with Samuel in Krichev. Jeremy was not content to stew in these ideas or write a few pamphlets, but he was spectacularly unsuccessful in winning Catherine over to his schemes. For a practical philosopher, the introverted Jeremy was poor at advocating his ideas within the halls of power. He failed to finish his legal code before the opportunity to meet the empress arrived, and when it did, he made sure *not* to meet the woman on whom his plans hinged.[23]

With his own plan foundering, he latched instead onto his brother's promised labor control schemes. Working together, they developed the central inspection principle into the circular concept known as the Panopticon. In the hands of the philosopher and erstwhile jurist, Samuel's idea became the foundation for an improvement, a project that channeled a century of political economists' obsessions through the person of Jeremy Bentham into a building made to change the world. When Jeremy and Samuel returned to England, they brought this project home with them.

"Dexterity and Good Will Rendered Unnecessary"

The classic Panopticon design is a circular building with a central tower from which an inspector can watch all prisoners without them being certain they are being watched. But the Panopticon was a workplace before it was a prison. Jeremy's 1791 *Panopticon, Or the Inspection-House*, began with the kind of sweeping claims improvers had been making since the seventeenth century: *"Morals reformed—health preserved—industry invigorated—instruction diffused—public burthens lightened—Economy seated, as it were, upon a rock—the gordian knot of the Poor-Laws not cut, but untied—all by a simple idea in Architecture!"* He promised to finally reform the Poor Laws, improve manufacturing, innovate in schools and hospitals, and save the state money—or even make money—in the process. Profit was central to the Panopticon's operation: it was a private prison (or school, or asylum). "I would farm out the profits," Jeremy wrote, "to him who, being in other respects unexceptionable, offered the best terms."[24]

Why? Finances were one reason. Taxation is always unpopular with the wealthy, and Jeremy's primary constituency *was* the wealthy. When he spent years trying to get his prisons built, he was meeting earls and cabinet ministers. But Jeremy's idea to run the world through profit was a matter of far more than convenience. By generating and structuring profits, Jeremy could structure the self-interest of every actor involved in the prison. Selfish wardens would choose to engage their prisoners in the most profitable and thus economically useful trades.

Where profit alone would not properly structure self-interest, law would: Jeremy proposed fining his contractors for dead prisoners to discourage overwork and encourage taking care of their health. This was a close parallel to the financial incentives that slaveholders argued encouraged "humane" treatment but which, as we have seen, led in fact to an entire infrastructure made to quantify and exploit human life. Despite this, Jeremy trusted in a combination of transparency and market operations to produce happiness through profit.

Profits meant labor control. Accordingly, the Panopticon did not just *happen* to evolve from workplace discipline, it was part of its core functions and goals. The language I use in this book, "extracting" labor value, is the same as Jeremy Bentham's—the thirteenth item in the *Panopticon Letters* he published is "means of extracting labour."[25] To make profits possible, Jeremy took up the call to manage the masses' interests, chiefly through coercion. He wrote, "[I] would give my contractor all the *powers* that his interest could prompt him to wish for," with "only some slight reservations."[26] This despite acknowledging that contractors were "a good-for-nothing set of people . . . ranked with sinners."[27] Jeremy proposed denying them the power to physically *beat* prisoners, because it was unnecessary. Instead, wardens of the Panopticon could envelop prisoners in darkness by controlling the amount of light their cells received. The warden would address them via speaking tubes, so they could not know when he was or was not busy with another. This also, of course, meant they were always potentially being listened to as well as watched. Prisoners would receive bread, water, and possibly darkness if they refused to work, while those who did work could count on meat, beer, and "whatever else" they could purchase with earnings, which Jeremy acknowledged would be meager thanks to the warden's monopoly.

But the most insidious mechanism for forcing work out of workers was psychological deprivation. These men were kept completely cut off from one another, "without a soul to speak to."[28] Jeremy might have underestimated the psychological toll of solitude—he reportedly enjoyed having plenty of it himself—but we shouldn't. Today, solitary confinement is considered torture for good reason. In the Panopticon, the only distraction from the existential crises, unfathomable depression, and hallucinations produced by solitary confinement would be work.

For the twentieth-century French philosopher Michel Foucault, the Panopticon was emblematic of "a certain technology of power" under which the "soul is the prison of the body."[29] I would venture instead that the Panopticon was meant to work by threatening to destroy workers utterly—that Bentham's planned prison was designed to kill the soul so it did not have to kill the body. Bosses did not want workers to think or feel. In the Panopticon, workers themselves wouldn't want to.

Surveillance, time discipline, and the calculation of human value—core goals of control science—came together to form an emerging mindset and tool kit for *the boss* in this period. Labor exploitation was not new, of course, but the boss was. He watched you constantly with one eye on your hands and another on his account books. He mercilessly fired you the moment you were no longer needed. He paid you as little as he possibly could and used force and law to crush guild-like activity that in the past might have resisted him. Self-interest embodied in a person: a manager threatening you with destitution for going a minute over on a break.

The Panopticon was not the first example of this mindset, but it was a pivotal moment in its development, combining Wedgwoodian time discipline, Lockean and Helvetian psychology, and capitalist ideas of management and accounting in an attempt to produce the quantified perfect worker. Samuel and Jeremy's Panopticon was a project of its day, conceived in absolutist Russia and expanded in counterrevolutionary Britain. The 1790s were a terrifying time to be rich and British. Revolutions and strikes had only spread. Samuel made his way home from Russia in the twilight of the *ancien régime*—according to Mary, the engineer was in the Duke of Richelieu's box at the opera on the last night King Louis ever attended.[30] Increasingly radical ideas pulsed on both sides of the Channel, as some oppressed English workers found little in their French counterparts' revolution to oppose. The Bentham brothers returned from Russia into a rapidly changing world full of both opportunity and peril. They answered the moment with a forward-looking vision of control based on scientific principles.

New technology was central to this vision. When Samuel returned to England in 1791, he went on a tour to see the latest in manufacturing facilities. A few years later he collaborated with steam engine manufacturers Boulton and Watt, who were acquaintances of Wedgwood.[31] He also began prototyping the Panopticon in the backyard of their recently deceased father's house, which Jeremy had moved into. The Benthams had speaking tubes installed in the house and constructed a miniature prison behind it as a demonstration of their Panopticon plan.[32]

In 1796, Samuel became Inspector General of Naval Works, a position with a complicated relationship to authority but a broad mandate for rooting out inefficiency and advancing British government shipbuilding. As part of his vision of labor in both the Panopticon and the dockyards, Samuel undertook and oversaw the development of new machines. Their purpose was the excision of human will from human work. As Jeremy wrote in a letter in 1793, "Dexterity and Good Will" on the part of workers could be "rendered equally unnecessary by my brother's mechanical contrivances."[33] The contrivances in question were machines for manufacturing, and they were critical to the Panopticon. Since its confined and suffering workers would lack both the skills and the desire to work, simplified machine labor was a necessity. As he had with pile-driving, Samuel broke the human rhythms of woodworking into abstract movements, specifically a "reciprocate Motion" (sawing) and a Rotary Motion."[34] In his position as inspector general he pursued numerous mechanical innovations, from milling machinery to steam-driven pumps.

This mechanical engineering was also social engineering: from his early days as an apprentice, Samuel had imagined different work and ethics as well as tools; disruption to workers' social ties and power was a feature, not a bug. Samuel wished to optimize labor the way he optimized cost accounting—by top-down quantification. The rebellious shipwrights he grew up around would never allow this. They resisted him, as they had long resisted administrators, not merely because he wished to make them work harder as individuals but because they had an entirely different vision of what work *was*. Dockyard shipwrights believed that disabled, older, and simply slower workers deserved equal and livable pay. They insisted that they should have a say in their working hours and conditions.

For Samuel this was inefficient and wasteful. He wanted to replace equal pay with pay by productivity, bottom-up control with top-down supervision, and flexible hours with twenty-four-hour shift work.[35] The inspector general did not so much wish to replace shipwrights with machines as he wished to make them work like machines. Their beliefs and resistance were irritations to be engineered away, like waste in ship construction or weaknesses in hull design.

The resulting clash between control science and community culture was explosive. Rebellious workers sabotaged Samuel's inventions and continued massive fraud efforts that inflated and equalized their wages.[36] Samuel also met resistance from above as well as below by corrupt contractors and conservative administrators. He began to prevail in remaking dockyard labor only by forming an alliance with the tyrannical John Jervis, Earl of St. Vincent, who became First Lord of the Admiralty in February 1801. Jervis was a brutal and rigid man. In 1798, when the crew of the *Marlborough* mutinied to protect one of their crewmates from execution, Jervis had the *Blenheim* draw in close and load its guns, and ordered the mutinying crew to hang their friend themselves or die together.[37] They complied. When dockyard shipwrights organized to demand higher wages, Jervis took a similarly hardline approach by simply firing hundreds of them for daring to resist.[38]

Samuel had big plans, ranging from day and night shifts to working gangs of different ability—and with Jervis in charge he began to implement them. He took advantage of the strike-breaking moment to abolish waste wood privileges and reorganize work itself, stripping artisans of privileges and taking full control of the social organization of work. The dream of task work, pay by productivity, became a reality.[39]

Dockyard shipwrights saw their workplace was somewhere they contributed to society, a place where they (uneasily) shared power and thus deserved certain rights and protections. They would fight to protect them. Samuel's view was much simpler: in his view, workers were another component of a system to be engineered. Critically, Samuel developed this view not in profit-oriented private institutions but on behalf of the state. Private economic actors obeyed a profit imperative. Forces ranging from market competition and debt to individual avarice and elite status competition pushed these early capitalists to extract more and more from their laborers. The British state in the 1790s did not face these same pressures. Public dockyards sought savings, certainly, but not profit.

Ideas about how to manage workers ricocheted between elites in the state and in private industry, developing new justifications and methods all the while. The Bentham brothers' 1790s proselytization properly fused ideas on how to manage people with practices for doing so, while iterating further on both. The result of Samuel Bentham's engineering of people was the beginning of a new world of work.

The result for dockyard artisans was devastating. Jervis's mass firings were only the beginning of a long and painful decline. In 1833, Royal Dockyard shipwrights lost their autonomy, independence, and security when administrators created a new category of temporary workers—one that would in time encompass most shipwrights.[40] Though the Panopticon existed in the real world only as a backyard miniature, its ideas were already being implemented to remake the largest production facilities in the world.

"A Multitude, Though Not a Crowd"

While Samuel was off stomping on dockyard workers, Jeremy was busy pitching the Panopticon to London elites. Among them was William Wilberforce, a man known today for his role in the abolition of slavery. Jeremy and Wilberforce soon became unlikely friends. The former was practically an atheist, and disdainful of conservative morality; Wilberforce, meanwhile, was devoutly religious. But the two were alike in one key respect: each man had a particular vision of social order that he believed in with unwavering zeal.

Neither supported revolutionary change from below. The Panopticon offered both subtler and more profound control of the populace, which made it attractive to Wilberforce and served as a catalyst for his friendship with Bentham: a visit to the backyard miniature version in April 1795 was how they met. Afterward, Wilberforce began promoting the project to friends in government. Over the next few years, the project encountered many obstacles—it was slow-walked, killed, revived, killed again. Through it all Wilberforce was a staunch supporter. In 1796, after one disappointment, he wrote to Bentham, "[I] need not repeat that it will ever give me pleasure to cooperate with you, or desire you always to call on me for aid."[41] Wilberforce was a true believer in the plan, insisting that the public deserved its "Practical Benefits" and that its opponents would yield if they had but "a little, ever so little [more] Religion."

For Wilberforce, the Panopticon promised order in a disordered age. He was a staunch advocate of that long-lasting theme in British elite politics, the "reformation of manners," which argued for religiously inspired changes to commoner behavior. Such behavior control was the Panopticon's specialty. It split individuals from their communities, inhibiting what Wilberforce saw as sinful influences, and focused the observational and punitive power of the warden on them like ants beneath a magnifying glass. As Jeremy put it, the Panopticon's prisoners were "to the keeper, a *multitude*, though not a *crowd*; to themselves, they are *solitary* and *sequestered* individuals."[42] It de-individualized but still individuated, making manageable individuals—uniform but alone. Cut off this way, they could be reprogrammed by Jeremy—"Mr. B the Reformer of the Vitious," as Wilberforce jokingly but tellingly referred to him on one occasion—into ideal, obedient subjects.[43]

Bentham's and Wilberforce's visions of exactly what kinds of subjects the Panopticon should make were not identical. For Wilberforce, obedience was a primary political and religious virtue. In his view, Christianity taught that the poor's "more lowly path has been allotted to them by the hand of God . . . [and] it is their part faithfully to discharge its duties, and contentedly to bear its inconveniences."[44] Indeed, the poor should be grateful, for they had less to tempt them to sin than did the wealthy. Moreover, even the poor's "situation in life, with all its evils, is better than they have deserved at the hand of God," thanks to humanity's inherent sinfulness. And such earthly concerns were temporary in the face of eternal life. Accordingly, the poor—who in this period were often rioting over their inability to feed their children—should shut up and wait for salvation. The task of government policymakers in this chaotic era was to make them do so.

Bentham, in contrast, did not believe obedience was inherently a virtue. But he did believe human beings were pleasure-maximizing, selfish individuals and thus that these disordered masses had to be kept in line. In a June 1799 letter to his stepbrother, member of Parliament Charles Abbot, Jeremy argued for loosening the harsh provisions of Abbot's proposed Treason Forfeiture Bill, which prevented children of those convicted of treason from inheriting from *any* ancestor—part of the broader British "Terror" against radicals. Arguing that it punished the innocent and had unintended consequences, Jeremy encouraged him to "pick out the innocent," citing the Gospel of Luke: "*Father forgive them, for they know not what they do.*"[45] Yet before any of this, he concurred on the fundamental righteousness of the cause. He had "not the smallest objection to" placing "the Jacob*ins* . . . upon the footing of the Jacob*ites*," rebels who wished to restore the Stuart dynasty and whom the state had repeatedly crushed.

Which treasonous men exactly did the bill target? Who deserved such treatment? Men like the radical Thomas Spence, who dared to argue for a universal vote across gender and property, social support for disabled people, and an end to child poverty and abuse. In a September 1800 letter to Samuel, Jeremy mentioned a mob action over corn prices and a subsequent right-wing mob counterattack.[46] He claimed to have known "nothing about" the source of corn prices but noted that his "preposessions [were] certainly in favour of liberty and Adam Smith"—in other words, he did not sympathize with those who wanted the government to step to lower corn prices.

Jeremy did not have Wilberforce's faith in God or his agents on Earth to preserve order, but he arrived at a similar argument for deference to elites through his belief in markets and the power of capitalism to allocate resources. Likewise, his skepticism of human goodness mirrored his conservative friend's. Jeremy's liberal pessimism—the idea that we must optimize the selfish for their own good—and Wilberforce's conservative moralism—his belief that we must control the sinful for their own good—were ultimately manifestations of the same underlying British Protestant misanthropy.

"Objects of Useful Industry"

Wilberforce, Bentham, their audience, and ultimately their intellectual descendants, shared a commitment to whatever could "render men useful members of civil society."[47] These are Wilberforce's words, but they could just as easily have been Bentham's. Usefulness, *utility*, is the center of the philosophy he is best known for today, utilitarianism. This was the "science of universal utility" Helvetius had called for, and the Euclidean ethics Locke had aspired to. Its maxim, to create "the greatest happiness for the greatest number," might sound positive, but it demanded the quantification of feeling and allowed elites to manage it. It promised certainty, and scientific clarity, in morality and politics.

Such certainty and clarity were dangerous fictions that justified oppression. Amid debates over Poor Law reform, Jeremy's friend Joseph Townsend argued characteristically that the poor *must* exist so "that there may always be some to fulfill the most servile, the most sordid, and the most ignoble offices in the community." This included the military. Poverty in the turbulent eighteenth century was exacerbated by the labor disruptions, burned crops, agricultural deaths, and resource waste of frequent warfare; grotesquely, and entirely obviously to contemporary observers, poverty also created useful conditions for the enlistment of large armies. Townsend felt that the effects of poverty on this and other undesirable forms of labor were not just necessary but *salutary*—when the poor fill the worst positions in society, "the sum of human happiness is thereby increased." Townsend's positions were characteristic of "natural law" critiques of the Poor Laws, which held that poverty was a necessary evil built into nature itself.[48]

The humanitarian opponents of these natural law critics also used the quantifying methods of control science. One such opponent was Thomas Gilbert, who gathered large quantities of data to support his reform proposals. Wilberforce did much the same during the mid-1790s debates over the Poor Laws. Yet no matter how well-meaning and detailed their investigations were, their answers came up short. Gilbert's 1782 law provided only a mechanism for voluntary cooperation of rural elites to administer the existing Poor Law. Later, when the revolutionary upheavals and subsequent war of the 1790s made the problems of poor relief more acute, the government's response to devastating food shortage and related riots was to call for the voluntary reduction of wheat consumption by the wealthy and the encouragement of nonwheat breads.[49]

Wage regulations fared no better. Whig MP Samuel Whitbread proposed in 1795 to use magistrate authority previously relegated to setting a *maximum* wage to instead set a *minimum* one, indexed to wheat prices. William Pitt opposed this, citing Adam Smith's warnings against interfering in the market. His own bill instead ordered the parish to supplement wages that were beneath the ill-defined "full rate" locally. In other words, Pitt found it more logical to force cash-strapped parishes to supplement wages than demand employers pay a living wage.⁵⁰ Pitt's own Poor Law reform bill failed to pass—it was brought low by the reflexive opposition of those attached to natural law theory. Others, like the doomsaying prophet of overpopulation Thomas Malthus, proposed revoking the Poor Laws entirely, to avoid funding the creation of poor families, and advocated "moral restraint" (backed by the threat of starvation) as a remedy.

Jeremy Bentham disagreed with Townsend's and Malthus's "let them suffer and die" proposals. Instead, he argued for making the poor useful. Like the man armed with a hammer who sees everything as a nail, Jeremy's solution to poverty was the Panopticon. His "Pauper Plan" proposed the creation of a private joint-stock company called the National Charity Company—a kind of East India Company for poverty instead of empire.⁵¹ This authority was to run a system of 250 workhouses. The contracted overseer would receive the profits of the labor of the people they controlled, with abuses theoretically checked and humanity encouraged by putting a price on each inmate's life. Each year of a child's life would reward an official with "head-money," while the death of a womaen in childbirth would bring a penalty.

This system of profit echoed slavery's violent calculations. Ostensibly, Bentham opposed slavery, and he moved in abolitionist circles, but he wrote little on the matter, and what he did write was marred by calculation and hesitance.⁵² During his years of friendship with Wilberforce, one of the most significant elite abolitionists in Britain, Jeremy appears to have done nothing for the cause beyond this initial argument. Likewise, the existence of enslaved people figures little in his correspondence. The fact that Jeremy did not consciously think much about these matters does not mean they did not influence him. In fact, his apathy tells us a good deal about how they likely did influence him.

Jeremy Bentham and William Wilberforce both supported an end to the international slave trade, but only a gradual end to slavery itself. They were far from the only proponents of gradual abolition: slow death, and even continued life, for slavery, both managed by control science, were the dominant elite abolitionist opinions in this era. In the early 1800s, Wilberforce increasingly relied on arguments that the slave trade and later slavery should end because they were economically inefficient and against the national interest.[53] This quantifying, calculating view, fundamentally concerned with imperial economics and market mathematics rather than justice helped slavery last longer and made its eventual end worse: everything had to bow to the market. To argue that the slave trade and slavery should be abolished for economic reasons was a clever strategic move. But it also implied that an alternate system of racial domination and economic exploitation would be fine as long as it produced more profits, more stably.

In his classic work *Capitalism and Slavery*, the historian and future first prime minister of Trinidad and Tobago, Eric Williams, famously argued that Britain abolished slavery only when it was no longer profitable. More recent historians have countered that slavery remained profitable to the end. The economic reality is less important for our purposes than the fact that economic perceptions became central to abolitionist discourse. Whatever the trajectory of slavery's profits, the fact that elite abolitionists made those profits part of their argument, the fact that they made their moral conundrums moral *calculations* using the same arithmetic as enslavers, ensured that slavery's accounting of death and the commercial world-as-market would outlive slavery itself. By preserving existing hierarchies even as they brought a legal end to slavery, and viciously putting down revolution and its possibilities wherever they could, British elites aimed to ensure that labor control would survive and thrive after slavery.[54]

4

"They Will Be Compelled of Themselves to Work for You": Political Economy in Antebellum America, 1800–65

"Human labor," Nathan Appleton wrote in 1844, "is the only source of wealth."[1] Appleton was one of the architects of American industry, and his fortune was built on the hard work of thousands of mill workers—and hard work controlling them. He was one of the "Boston Associates," a group of investors that also included Francis Cabot Lowell. They built a vast manufacturing enterprise from scratch, including an entire city that bears the latter's name. From the machinery and architecture of their facilities to control of the workers within them, the mills required precise methods for aligning workers' incentives with management's interests. Once this system was built, managers also had to defend it against market competition and political conflict. An observant Unitarian and avid reader of philosophy, Appleton had to justify his money and power to himself. As a state and federal politician, he had to justify it to his country as well. This he did through the nascent science of political economy.

Political economy was the macro-scale arm of control science, and Appleton took to it eagerly. He read the work of John Locke, Adam Smith, Joseph Priestley, and John Stuart Mill, who as a child was tutored by Samuel and Mary Bentham and went on to become a disciple of Jeremy Bentham's. Appleton and his associates also employed control science on the level of the workplace: their power looms were taken from English industry, and their labor control methods were devised in response to it. Their cotton came from plantations in the

American South ruled with an iron fist through evolving legal and social frameworks of domination—frameworks justified by Priestley devotee and Benthamite utilitarian Thomas Cooper. Like the Benthams, Wedgwood, Laurens, and Petty before him, Nathan Appleton was part of a broader transatlantic conversation about how the few could control the many. Both political economy and workplace management were attempts to answer this question.

In the early nineteenth century, the corporation, the boss, and the government took recognizably modern form. The two centuries of ideology we have been following served as a blueprint for all of them. If the Benthams outlined the *what* of impersonal market domination, the *how* of implementing that domination became the focus of their later counterparts. Mill tycoons built empires on colonial extraction and international trade while redefining the relationship between capital and the state, in particular through iterations on the corporate form. In their quest to extract ever more capital from labor, these elites produced technologies and tactics that shape our work today as well as discourse and ideology that shape our politics.

"The Selfish System"

In a memoir written a few years before his death, Nathan Appleton recalled with pride his "first appearance in public" as a young child at the town school. He had recited from Alexander Pope's translation of *The Illiad*:[2]

> I fix the chain to great Olympus' height
> And the vast world hangs trembling in my sight

Nearly seventy years after the event he could still recall the attendees who praised him for delivering those lines, part of a speech from Zeus, or Jove, king of the gods. Delivered in wrath, the lines are a kind of boast of power. The next two lines go:

> For such I reign, unbounded and above;
> And such are men, and gods, compared to Jove

For a man who became so powerful and wealthy, this is almost too perfect a childhood memory. But he also chafed against authority in his youth. He grew up in what he described as the "strictest form of Calvinistic Congregationalism"; classes at the school he attended ended early one year when the older students tore down its chimney in protest of their evidently violent teacher, Mr. Hedge.[3] This was not the kind of Jove he wanted to be.

Appleton and his future business partner, Francis Lowell, built careers in commerce on the back of longstanding American exploitation. Both came from long-established New England families, and the foundation of their early wealth was land stolen from Indigenous communities. Colonial rule in India and slavery in the West Indies contributed to their fortunes as well. Both Lowell and Appleton got their starts as merchants in the mid-1790s, with Lowell importing textiles from Asia and later expanding into rum.[4]

During a trip to England between 1810 and 1812, Lowell began scheming to set up a mill of his own. He covertly memorized the highly coveted secrets of the power loom. It was also on this trip that he first met Nathan Appleton and solicited his investment in what would become the Boston Manufacturing Company (BMC). While the usual method of founding a mill relied on starting small and working as a partnership, Lowell and Appleton began the new venture by selling stock in the firm, a process that had the useful side effect of uniting influential Massachusetts elites, who became known as the Boston Associates, behind the project.[5]

The BMC's first mill was built in Waltham in 1814 with a mountain of capital—their 1813 act of incorporation permitted them to raise the huge sum of $400,000, in an era when many laborers made less than a dollar a day. They were thus able to start on a grand scale and plan on a long time horizon.[6] The Waltham mill improved upon existing competition in New England both in scale and process thanks to the power loom. Previous American mills produced yarn and then relied on domestic producers to weave it. The weavers therefore controlled the quality, quantity, and frequency of their work. For the new manufacturers, this was a problem: when household income was healthy and thus domestic weavers did not need the extra income, production fell, and mill managers could do nothing about it. Using the power loom, the "Waltham-Lowell" system brought this step of the production process in-house, improving control, productivity, and profit with it. The consolidated mill was a success, and the BMC expanded with a second mill in 1816.

Lowell and Appleton's business was meant to be both more profitable than America's limited existing manufacturing and more ethical than Britain's. In 1802, while visiting Manchester, Nathan Appleton remarked, "[It] has the worst name of any town I know . . . universally considered as having no hospitality and very little honesty," a problem that he identified with its industrial character.[7] But his concerns were hardly pro-worker: the problem was not that their wages were too low but that they were too *high*. High demand for workers had produced the "serious evil" of high wages: in the past, "every penny [workers] could earn by constant labor barely sufficed for their subsistence," Appleton wrote. "Now, 4 days labour supports them a week."

These concerns about labor closely mirrored an earlier pamphlet by Joseph Priestley, who had a similar characterization of "the poor": "whatever they do get by their labour more than is sufficient for their immediate occasions [i.e., subsistence], they too often waste in the most extravagant manner."[8] Priestley and Appleton both saw working people as sinful drinkers, "degraded," "debased," and lacking motivation thanks to the plenty of supposedly high wages and strong poor relief. They wished instead for workers to save, educate, and improve themselves. Thus the Waltham-Lowell system "included the then new idea, that corporations should have souls," as mill worker Harriet Robinson later described, which meant they should "exercise a paternal influence over the lives of their operatives."⁹

Paternal authority in the mills was very literal: to better serve money and morals alike, the BMC's managers decided to employ women. This had the advantage of being cheaper than employing men. The autonomy and security that artisans like Wedgwood's potters stood to lose from factory labor was something many women already lacked. Women in early-nineteenth-century America could expect to live their lives under the authority of men—first fathers, then husbands. The domestic labor of keeping a household and raising children did not bring them a cent, and whenever they did do work that brought in cash in one of the few professions open to them—weaving, working as a domestic servant, teaching—their husbands controlled that money. Before marriage, their families might expect or demand it. In Harriet Robinson's words, "the law took no cognizance of woman as a money-spender. She was a ward, an appendage, a relict."¹⁰ Women resisted this as best they could, but the legal and social system was stacked against them.¹¹ Patriarchy effectively subsidized capital accumulation in early industrial America—factories could attract women merely by offering something better than the coercion they faced at home.

Even with the limited alternatives available to women, convincing them to embark on employment in an industry with long hours and a poor reputation required mill owners to make the job attractive. Comparatively high wages were a significant part of this: in the mills, even children made two dollars a week, which was quadruple the fifty cents weekly that a woman would make as a domestic servant, and more than double the seventy-five cents a week she could make as a "tailoress."¹² Overseers who ruled by mutual interest rather than terror inspired "conscientious" women to take "pride in spinning a smooth thread, drawing in a perfect web, or in making good cloth"—a phenomenon Harriet Robinson characterized as the practice of "that principle of true political economy—the just relation, the mutual interest, that ought to exist between employers and employed."[13] This principle of mutual benefit was often deployed to defend cruel and unjust orders. But this did not mean it was a sham or a mirage in all circumstances. Presenting mutual benefits to workers, within limits, could secure control and loyalty in a way nothing else could.

Robinson's account of mill life includes memories of both pride and horror, good managers and bad, fair pay and exploitation. She and other workers seized the opportunity the mills provided. Robinson took pride in the "self-cultivation" of mill girls, who took advantage of their urban surroundings, the fellowship of other workingwomen, and their wages to make new lives for themselves.[14] This, in fact, was the origin of Robinson's career as a writer. Workers like Robinson managed to limit labor discipline in certain cases as well. Women who quit mill jobs, for example, were supposed to provide advance notice and receive an "honorable discharge" if they wanted to remain employable at any of the Boston Associates' mills in the future.[15] In reality, this rule appears to have been routinely broken or ignored outside of moments of heightened labor-management tension, and women who broke it were still rehired.[16]

The mutually beneficial aspects of the mill existed alongside coercion, and both worked in tandem to secure capitalist profits. Mill towns provided educational opportunities for women and children alike as well. One unnamed woman came to the city specifically in order to have access to books she could not find in her rural home. As a child, Robinson got to read them herself in exchange for picking them up and returning them from the library while the woman was at work, an opportunity she recalled with joy: "What a scurrying there used to be home from school, to get the first new book!"[17] Robinson praised the education she got in school and at work—but she also recounted her own experience as a ten-year-old of being hit repeatedly by her teacher.

When she was wrongly accused of destroying a "one cent multiplication table," her teacher Mr. Hills beat her "till she could not see, for pain and terror" until she finally "gave in" and confessed, "whipped into a lie," an incident she recalled with great pain more than sixty years later.[18]

The sum effect of the pleasures, pains, and performance regulations of the mill was to inculcate discipline—in Robinson's words,

> We were obliged to be in the mill at just such a minute, in every hour . . . We went to our meals and returned at the same hour every day. We worked and played at regular intervals . . . and we were taught daily habits of regularity and of industry; it was, in fact, a sort of manual training or industrial school.[19]

Managers worked to form workers into the kind of subjects they needed them to be.

Mill architecture itself was designed to control workers. Lowell and Appleton's company constructed housing for its workers, becoming both employers and landlords. The work itself happened in an enclosed complex of mills and other production facilities.[20] This spatial arrangement both reflected and enabled business centralization. The Boston Associates optimized their workers' lives around profit. Their mill complexes performed every aspect of production, receiving cotton and outputting finished cloth, while the mill town contained every necessary component for worker maintenance. As historian Thomas Dublin put it, "the overriding concern of management . . . was control" of both process and people.[21]

What did this look like in operation? Divisions of gender, age, and skill placed workers in different tasks. Young children worked as doffers, who ran up and down lines of equipment replacing the bobbins that gathered yarn once they reached capacity. This work was not constant—doffers worked for "about fifteen minutes in every hour"—but it was taxing.[22]

They worked "nearly fourteen hours a day," which according to Harriet Robinson was "the greatest hardship in the lives of these children."[23] The children found solace in the idea that they were at least better off than those working in England; when she was young, Robinson and the other children sang a lament called "The Factory Girl's Last Day," about an English child who dies at work.[24]

Adult workers faced more constant supervision. On average, they worked twelve-hour days in six-day weeks.[25] The integrated mill complex made it easy to police workers' time: the main gate was open only for opening and breaks, while late workers had to make their way through another entrance past supervisors. Different rooms of the mill complex held different parts of the production process, and the base operatives worked as machine tenders, optimizing their assigned parts of the process.[26] Such a heavy division of labor tended "to convert man into a machine," as political economist Thomas Cooper admitted in 1826.[27] Managers wanted long hours and machine-like consistency from workers.

The nature of their labor had changed in a profound way from that of their artisan predecessors. Whereas weavers had been the primary agents of production—starting, continuing, and stopping work—Lowell workers were machine attendants: replacing spools and bobbins, connecting broken threads, identifying problems. Mill workers had little power over the pace of work, which managers could and did increase unilaterally, leading to fewer workers tending more and faster machines. They could not take breaks, choose their own pace, or easily conceal information from managers. The shift from tools that aided workers to *machines that workers aided* simultaneously created greater need for "order and regularity" in the workplace to keep machines running and aided managers in pursuing such regularity as a goal.[28] As with Samuel Bentham's earlier machines, this was by design: machines were created to replace rather than assist workers.

Social architecture worked in concert with the mills' physical architecture to achieve control. Robinson described company agents as "autocrat[s]" who ruled over Lowell workers.²⁹ Agents functioned as the company's representatives in the facility, keeping an eye on workers and process alike. They "usually lived in large houses," Robinson wrote, separated from workers' housing and "surrounded by beautiful gardens which seemed like Paradise to some of the home-sick girls."³⁰ Agents were the local incarnation of company directors, meant to make their will reality at individual sites of production.

Beneath them were overseers, who generally lived next to the boardinghouses and more directly ordered workers around. Both layers of management exerted power over the lives, not just the work, of their employees. Regulations required workers in company boardinghouses to attend church and abstain from drinking.³¹ Boardinghouse keepers controlled visitors. Corporate paternalism turned sexual morality and gender norms from a potential liability—if the mills developed a reputation as dens of iniquity, they would have trouble recruiting workers—into an asset. By policing sexuality and gendered behavior norms, the Boston Associates' firms protected the gender divisions that made women cheaper to hire.

The mills relied on exploitation along racial lines as well as gender and age. Critically, they depended on a supply of cotton from Southern plantations, and Southern elites cooperated in building out this economy. In 1816, Francis Lowell convinced influential South Carolina Congressman and slaveholder John C. Calhoun to support a tariff protecting American manufacturing from British competition.³² Two years later, Calhoun personally visited the Waltham mill and, according to Appleton, did so "with the apparent satisfaction of having himself contributed to its success."³³ Calhoun was a leading man among a malignant Southern elite that Appleton expressed disgust and horror for only a few years earlier. On a visit to Charleston, South Carolina, in 1804, he recorded recoiling at the sight of the "sale of human flesh," which he remarked must have been motivated by "cotton mad avarice."[34]

How did Nathan Appleton justify treating this avarice as an opportunity instead of a sin? It would be easy to say the money did it for him—that he was simply pursuing his own self-interest. But it would also be wrong. Even if Appleton had been a coldly profit-optimizing robot, he would still have needed a narrative to present to the people around him, and because he wasn't, he also needed a coherent narrative for himself. He found it in moral philosophy.

Around 1828, as his factories were taking off, Appleton wrote notes responding to Scottish philosopher Thomas Brown on the topic of "selfishness." Brown had denounced the "selfish system" of other philosophers, a system with which we are familiar: the idea that people are motivated purely by self-interest. While he did not specifically reference Bentham or Priestley, his use of both happiness and utility indicates that this was part of the same broader philosophical conversation about motivation and morals they had contributed to. Against their psychological egoism, Brown offered a vigorous and amusing defense of human virtue. He had particular scorn for the idea that when we do good for others, we derive pleasure, and we are thus selfish because we act out of a desire for that pleasure. Brown claimed that this was both absurd and irrelevant, insisting that any happiness we might feel from doing good is not the reason we do it, and the fact that we do feel it proves we are virtuous, rather than selfish.[35]

Appleton appears to have disagreed. In his notes, he mounted a defense of the "selfish system" clearly derived from Adam Smith's *Theory of Moral Sentiments*, a book he owned.[36] Despite "every possible denunciation" offered by Brown, the Boston merchant insisted that a "certain modification" of the selfish system offered "the only scheme of all human action" and the "only rules To guide us in morals."[37] After all, there was "but one intelligible motive to action: the doing of good to the agent." While

Appleton mused that this "may be stated" in various ways—"the desire of happiness—of enjoyment—of well-being"—he believed that this self-interest was "not only consistent with the highest efforts of benevolence, but that it is the parent of any virtue."

For Nathan Appleton, virtue began with looking out for number one. "The only benevolent System is the selfish one." "What a situation would the human race be in if each individual instead of having the care of his own happiness was only occupied in providing for his neighbours? . . . what disappointment." Selfishness was, however, insufficient to provide for everyone's happiness. To connect the happiness of *each* with the happiness of *all*, he drew on the notion of sympathy in Adam Smith's work. "Powerful physical feelings of sympathy," Appleton wrote, "make the suffering of each principal to all." Following these sympathies meant Benthamesque calculations of what actions, and what rules for action, would produce the greatest happiness for all.

Within this framework, Nathan Appleton could imagine himself as at once a self-interested individual and a manager connected by bonds of sympathy to the thousands of people whose lives he touched. But nothing in Appleton's framework suggested a need to listen to, let alone empower, workers themselves. Through sympathy, the interests of others could supposedly be calculated without necessarily asking or empowering them. These calculations were the subject of the new discipline of political economy.

"They Will Be Compelled of Themselves to Work for You"

"Political economy," Thomas Cooper wrote in 1826, "is that science which develops the sources, the distribution, the accumulation, and the consumption of national wealth."[38] It extended "the maxims of domestic economy" to the nation. Like the traditional patriarchal household, political economy relied on the extraction of labor. Its foundational insight was that "human labor employed in conferring utility or value on some material object, is the sole foundation of all wealth."[39]

Like Jeremy Bentham, Thomas Cooper was born in the London area to a lawyer father. In the 1780s he became a lawyer as well as a textile manufacturer. In 1785, he moved to the manufacturing hub of Manchester, where he befriended steam engine manufacturers Matthew Boulton and James Watt, as well as Joseph Priestley, who became his mentor. Priestley's Lockean views and proto-utilitarianism inspired him as they had Jeremy Bentham, and Cooper collaborated with Priestley and various other Manchester luminaries on interests both scientific and political. He supported causes like expanded voting rights and increased religious tolerance for non-Anglican Christians.[40]

In 1787 Cooper published a series of letters against the slave trade. These amply demonstrate both the promise and the shortcomings of the elite British abolitionists' worldview.[41] Cooper depicted slavery's hideous violence and condemned all those who participated in the trade in human beings. He countered Samuel Martin's earlier argument that cruelty and violence were "against the planters' interest."[42] Cooper insisted that Black people were not subhuman and thus worthy of slavery, but part of the same universal species as their enslavers, with the same intellectual capacities.[43] To defenders of slavery who argued that the institution was necessary to grow crops in the West Indies, Cooper responded flatly, "It is better that the islands remain uncultivated to eternity, than that their cultivation should be encouraged at the price of such extensive villainy."[44]

But his abolitionism was flawed from the beginning. "French slaves are all well treated," he claimed, because French planters lived on and oversaw their own estates—implicitly if not explicitly reflecting a commonly held elite abolitionist belief that slavery *caused* problems, when in fact slavery *was* the problem. His arguments also pointed toward a bleak post-slavery future. As an alternative to slavery, Cooper advocated for the colonization of Africa for the purpose of exploiting labor, and his pamphlet referenced the work of James Ramsay, an important figure in abolitionist efforts to control enslaved people's lives and bodies.[45] While he did gesture at support for an end to slavery as well as the slave trade, he reassured slaveholders that after slavery, free Black people "must do something for their living: you need not feed them unless they will earn it, and then they will be compelled of themselves to work for you."[46] Like Wilberforce, Cooper recoiled at the physical violence of slavery but was perfectly comfortable with indirect economic coercion. For Cooper, the alternative to slavery was not freedom but mute economic compulsion; instead of overseers threatening with whips, markets would threaten with empty stomachs.

On certain questions of political rights, Thomas Cooper was ahead of his time, advocating not just for an expanded franchise and broader religious freedom but also women's rights. Like many of his peers, he was uncomfortable with certain forms of violence and rigid political hierarchy. Yet this did not extend to the realm of economic hierarchy—even when it was built upon open violence and rigid political authority. Thus, like many of those in his circle, he managed to alienate both conservative elites above him—who bristled at rights for Catholics and insults to the king—and commoners below them. Who were these chemists and philosophers to propose emancipation for Catholics while exploiting hard-working, God-fearing Anglicans? In 1791, Joseph Priestley's house was attacked from above and below (in class terms) by a mixed mob motivated by this combination of grievances.[47] Cooper, though, was undeterred. The following year, he excitedly headed off with James Watt's son (James Watt Jr.) to revolutionary Paris, where he fell in with moderate revolutionaries.[48]

France during his visit was experiencing similar economic and political tensions within liberal ideology. Cooper reportedly made an enemy of the Jacobin leader Maximilien Robespierre relatively quickly. In his later telling, he supposedly fell in with factions more moderate than Robespierre's after an interpersonal squabble with him and later plotted to assassinate him by challenging him to a duel.[49] Whether the details of this account are true or not, Cooper's broad trajectory is clear: he arrived, grew to oppose the revolution as it became more radical, and then left.

Cooper's vision of liberation was one led by enlightened elites. Where he felt common people supported his goals, he promoted democracy and freedom. But when he had to choose between the people and his own ideas of progress, he preferred the latter. When he returned to England, he risked being caught up in England's *anti*-Jacobin terror. Since neither British conservatism nor French radicalism seemed to fit him, Cooper tried his luck in America. In 1794, he set out for the new nation with two members of Priestley's family.[50]

America fit Thomas Cooper perfectly. It lacked a king and established church, but its nascent democracy was also relatively elite-dominated. In *Some Information Respecting America*, a published work organized as an introduction to America for Joseph Priestley, Cooper praised it as a "rising country" characterized by a "freedom from artificial poverty, and the universal diffusion of the common comforts and conveniences of life."[51] Certainly the economic situation of America, particularly its low population density and relatedly high price of labor, helped.[52] But Cooper also believed that the precise character of the state did as well. America protected many of the rights he believed in without the government taking a more active role in the economy—he was particularly scathing about what he viewed as wasteful manufacturing subsidies in Europe.[53]

Unsurprisingly, he and Priestley fell in with Jefferson and his southern anti-Federalist faction, whom he characterized as the "outs" to the "ins" of the Federalists, albeit while praising what he viewed as the more moderate nature of political conflict in America.[54] After convincing Priestley to come over in 1794, Cooper embarked on a life as a Southern gentleman. In his subsequent scandal-ridden career as a jurist, academic, university administrator, and government advisor, he worked to align the world with his political vision. By 1826 he was a slaveholder himself.[55]

Cooper's views on manufacturing similarly shifted over time. In *Some Information* he wrote that he "detested the manufacturing system" for converting people into "mere machines, ignorant, debauched, and brutal," so that "the surplus value of their labour of 12 or 14 hours a day, may go into the pockets and supply the luxuries of rich, commercial, and manufacturing capitalists."[56] Decades later, in *Lectures*, he still conceded that manufacturing "tends to convert man into a machine," but "if he can read and write, he has the means of profitably improving his leisure . . . his lot cannot be considered as a hard one."[57] Cooper conceded that "the introduction and improvement of machinery, then, appears to me always productive of more or less misery among the poor," at least briefly, but insisted that they add to the mass of capital.[58] As a result, machines "are therefore beneficial to the nation because the ultimate effect is a balance of good."

A "Science of Modern Date"

The process of taking value from workers undermines itself. By Cooper's day, capitalism had already produced mass poverty, sparked mass strikes and revolutions, and exhausted critical natural resources. Factories drove down the prices of their own output to the point of potential ruin. Capitalists therefore needed a powerful ideology to push the laws they wanted, legitimize assaults on workers, advance global exploitation, and blame the resulting misery on anyone but themselves.

Enter the political economists. Their scientific analysis of political economy bordered at times on the facile—it's hard to imagine anyone being blown away by economist and philosopher Francis Wayland's breakdown of industry in his 1837 *Elements of Political Economy* into changing the "elementary form," "aggregate form," and "place" of matter, or more prosaically, changing stuff, shaping stuff, and moving stuff.[59] Nor was political economy entirely consistent—Wayland criticized slavery on many of the same grounds that Thomas Cooper defended it.

But first and foremost, political economy served an ideological role. Its internal contradictions, like those of the moral philosophy to which it was connected, were useful in defending the always-contradictory system of capitalism. Men like Appleton could believe themselves sympathetic enough to take the poor's needs into account, while simultaneously believing the poor were too selfish to have power or a voice of their own. Slavery could be too expensive to accept for men of conscience like William Wilberforce, and too cheap to abandon for men of avarice like John C. Calhoun—both figures who phrased important public arguments in the language of political economy. Yet Britain's "father of abolition" and the grandfather of the Confederacy could agree on vicious crackdowns on lower-class political movements, pervasive surveillance of Black people's very bodies, and rule by a wealthy, paternalist elite.

Thus political economy flexed around regional and political differences while creating a broad elite consensus on the necessity of capital accumulation and a government that facilitated rather than impeded it. Political economy also justified this elite consensus to the increasingly politically important masses. By early in the mid-nineteenth century, political economists' defenses of free trade and capital accumulation echoed from Nathan Appleton's study to the church his workers gathered in for classes: Wayland's *Elements of Moral Science*, a work of moral philosophy shaped by the same scientific and quantifying mindset as *Elements of Political Economy*, served as a textbook for an ethics course at Lowell.[60]

Political economists argued that the world they believed in was inevitable. The "evil" that machines did to workers, in Cooper's telling, was something they are "unable completely to provide against."[61] Scientific framing and methods were helpful here. By claiming they were engaged in the latest science, a "science of modern date," political economists claimed that the social world was as predictable and controllable as the natural world. Just as Archimedes could tell you not to build a ship that was too heavy or it would sink, Thomas Cooper could tell you not to give charity to the poor. The "only way" to improve their situation was "the addition of riches to riches." Writing of the "future subsistence" of children, he insisted, "nothing but capital can give it."[62]

Inevitability and its twin, necessity—we must do this or else ruin will come, there is no other way—justified the most brutal forms of exploitation. For Cooper, this included slavery: since Cooper had not seen "black teachers, black preachers, black physicians," in a few decades of limited freedom, "improving their condition," they were clearly incapable of improvement. He claimed that "the first object of every negro" was "a life of idleness, freedom from all kinds of labour and exertion." Thus they *had* to be forced to work. This was on one hand how Benthamite self-interest characterized all humanity, and on the other hand a racialized manifestation of it that speaks to *Homo economicus*'s origins in a world defined by slavery.

The actual propositions these strategies supported were remarkably defensive. Cooper's *Lectures* consists largely of negative advice: do not redistribute wealth, leave economic planning to private individuals, shun tariffs, keep taxes low, let "liberty be truly the parent of equality, and be cautious of governing over much."[63] This, and the libertarian right program today, grew out of Smith's argument that private self-interested actors were best able to optimize economic decisions.

Political economy became what elites needed it to be in order to justify new regimes of exploitation: a dominant language for discussing basic economic features, and a dominant ideology for understanding them. Men like Appleton invoked it in forums ranging from newspapers—where Appleton occasionally wrote on political issues—to congressional chambers—where Appleton acted as a key spokesman for merchants in 1812 before later becoming a congressman himself.[64] At the beginning of the century, Dugald Stewart offered the first undergraduate lectures on political economy, building on the earlier work of eighteenth-century figures like Adam Smith.[65] By 1898, even former mill worker Harriet Robinson was referencing political economy in her autobiography.

Thirty-nine years after he had written that no price calculation could justify the "extensive villainy" of the slave trade, Thomas Cooper used price calculations to justify slavery. Insisting that it was economically necessary for places like South Carolina, he calculated in his *Lectures* that a twenty-one-year-old white laborer cost a thousand dollars to "produce," while an enslaved Black laborer would only cost five hundred.[66] Based on the prices of cotton, he calculated that slavery produced several hundred pounds of profit, while free labor cost as much. Cooper of course ignored the fact that the price of cotton would rise without forced labor producing it, but political economy did not have to be rational or even internally consistent: it simply had to justify exploitation.

"The Remedy Is Not with Us"

Working conditions in Lowell started deteriorating in the 1830s. As prices fell, mill directors came together and decided on a significant pay cut for workers. Later in the decade, mill agents sought to increase output to make up for declining prices. They began to increase the speed and number of machines an individual worker supervised, and they gave significant bonuses to *managers* based on the productivity of the workers underneath them.[67] Some women sought to work more machines for higher wages (though notably their productivity increase was far greater than their wage increase). The rest could be forced into greater productivity by managers: seeking bonuses, overseers pushed their workers harder and punished less productive workers. Incentive alignment produced cruelty: in the words of one overseer, the "necessity which [the overseer] is under of producing work, of the quality, and in the quantity his employers desire of him, compels him (even when he has dispositions to do otherwise) frequently to be harsh and unmindful of those employed under him."[68]

These developments leveraged every tool in control science's toolbox. Machines gave central managers the ability to set and monitor the pace of work. Economic power drove some workers to push themselves harder and managers to pressure the rest to do the same. Social and physical architecture provided them the ability to do so. Ideology, as we will see, restricted the state's response. Capitalists had secured a previously unknown level of control over work itself.

Workers could not possibly respond to this assault in every area. Women could not vote, laboring men were ill served by early American democracy, investment capital was firmly in the hands of elites, and although many mill workers were prolific writers, there was no competing with centuries of ideology ensconced in popular wisdom, university systems, and law itself. American workers instead chose a more winnable battle: fighting over the length of the workday rather than control of work.[69] They launched a campaign that became known as the Ten-Hour Movement. Building on earlier efforts for a ten-hour day, they organized rallies, formed associations, wrote in newspapers, and lobbied state legislatures—here it helped that men, who could vote, were a part of the movement as well.[70]

In political economy, state officials found a justification to say no. Deciding not to regulate the workday, the Massachusetts legislative committee investigating the ten-hour movement's grievances cited the political economists' laissez-faire maxims. They wrote that the "question of wages" was something "much better regulated by the parties themselves than by the legislature."[71] The committee further claimed that in America, "labor is on an equality with capital." Whether or not the committee had read Cooper or conspired with Appleton is immaterial. They undoubtedly had read or spoken with others who read his work or who had read the same treatises he had. Political economy was becoming a dominant paradigm in public discourse.

Government legally created the corporation, defined and protected property rights, set legal boundaries on the pursuit of profit, and issued the very currency capitalists competed for. It had power, and its legislators had a choice. Yet even though the Massachusetts committee believed that "there are abuses" and "that it would be better if the hours for labor were less,—if more time was allowed for meals, if more attention was paid to ventilation and pure air in our manufactories, and work shops, and many other matters," they insisted, "The remedy is not with us."[72] This was the power of political economy as ideology: it allowed men to tell themselves that a system entirely of their own making was beyond their control.

Unable to actually make workers into machines, capitalists contented themselves with forcing them to act like machines. Nonetheless, pesky human will always asserted itself, even under the threat of death. Capitalists thus resorted to wielding the full might of economic power to compel workers and managers alike to act in the firms' interest rather than of their own will, ideologically attacked any challenge to capital's dominance, and violently cracked down on any resistance that remained. They managed to hold onto power despite the internal contradictions of nineteenth-century capitalism. But in the same period, capitalists were increasingly facing threats from another set of contradictions—and specifically threats from each other.

"A Covenant with Death"

Capitalists could do more together than they could alone. It was mass capital accumulation that enabled the Lowell system's triumph over its Rhode Island competitors through larger factories, more capable (adult) workers, and more advanced machinery. The Boston Associates achieved this by coming together as a corporation and issuing shares. The Merrimack Manufacturing Company drew on the fortunes of Nathan Appleton, Patrick Jackson (Lowell's brother-in-law), Paul Moody, John W. Boott, and Kirk Boott—who had between 60 and 180 shares each—but also pulled capital from a number of smaller shareholders, like future Secretary of State Daniel Webster (4 shares).[73] Their founding agreement offered the possibility for future expansion by selling more shares, and in it the founders agreed to seek a corporate charter from the state.

What's so useful about a corporation? The typical answer consists of three parts: corporations do not die, they allow for capital accumulation beyond what an individual or partnership (like Bentley and Wedgwood) could accomplish, and they limit the liability of individual shareholders. All of these are real advantages in business. But we should add a fourth: corporations do what control science says humans are supposed to. Individual human beings do not always act in their material self-interest. Corporations, on the other hand, have to do so. Literally an artificial legal person, corporations are automata of paper and flesh that rigidly conform to the profit imperative. Unsatisfied with how real people act, capitalists created their own. Nineteenth-century elites began to transform the special-purpose instrument of the seventeenth- and eighteenth-century chartered corporation into the modern corporate form.

Capitalists also needed to be protected from their own self-interest and from competition. Well before the famed robber baron trusts of the late nineteenth and early twentieth centuries, the Boston Associates functioned as one in New England thanks to close personal and financial ties. Their firms "shared waterpower rights, technological developments, labor policies, and market strategies," as well as "mill architecture, labor policies, and marketing strategies."[74] The 1830s strikes were a response to inter-company collusion to reduce wages, something that happened on other occasions as well. Major shareholders were similar across companies—Appleton and Jackson, for example, were directors of twelve and ten of the firms, respectively.[75] The Merrimack Manufacturing Company sold a piece of itself to the Boston Manufacturing Company early in its history.[76] Boston Associates firms engaged in a kind of friendly competition, pursuing their own individual optimizations while sharing every technique and result.

This kind of collusion worked well for the Boston Associates, but keeping capitalists aligned more broadly required broader strategies. Ideologically, the axioms of political economy served this purpose. The argument that the government should not intervene in the economy was a call not to attack competitors through state action, for example, recognizing that such assaults ultimately disadvantaged capitalists as a class. Classical political economy was simply bourgeois class consciousness. Its axioms in turn contributed to the creation of laws and constitutions that further created a collective interest among capitalists.

But ideas and laws could not completely bind economic interests together. Where they directly conflicted, the best that capitalists' new rule set could do was restrict that conflict. As entangled as Northern manufacturing was with Southern slavery, planters and factory owners had divergent economic interests. These different interests began to make tariffs controversial early in the century. The 1816 tariff Appleton had argued for and Calhoun had supported was meant to be temporary, but soon Northern manufacturers managed to pass successive tariffs and increasingly make protectionism a part of the national economic fabric. Southerners, facing increased import prices and with the War of 1812 further behind them, were anything but pleased and fought back out of a combination of motivations both economic (real and imagined) and political (Jeffersonian antigovernment rhetoric and regional particularism).

In 1828, Southerners including John C. Calhoun created a tariff bill meant to fail. This onerous "Tariff of Abominations" was not intended to pass—the intent was for it to fail, sinking tariff increases and damaging support for President John Quincy Adams in the process. But the Southerners' plan backfired. A number of Northern legislators, blocked by the South from amending the bill into a better form, voted with middle and western states to pass the bill.

The result was a tariff that threatened to split America in two. Calhoun erupted, arguing the states should be able to "nullify" laws they viewed as unconstitutional, this one included—despite the fact that he was partially responsible for it. He had powerful allies and ideological frameworks supporting him. Calhoun invoked the "most refined principles of political economy" in an 1831 address to the people of South Carolina railing against the tariff.[77] Thomas Cooper also advocated for nullification, apparently quite effectively—a federal agent in South Carolina during the crisis claimed that Thomas Cooper specifically had "poisoned" the "public mind" in the cities of Columbia and Charleston.[78] When an 1832 compromise tariff failed to convince Southerners, South Carolina's legislature passed an "ordinance of nullification" in November, declaring that the tariffs were unconstitutional and could not be enforced after February 1, 1833.

With just over a week remaining before this possible deadline for civil war, a recently elected Nathan Appleton delivered a speech before Congress. Speaking "as a representative of a great amount of capital" as much as a representative from Massachusetts, he too drew on "universally admitted theory in political economy"—but to defend the tariff.[79] Specifically, he cited the claim that all wealth comes from labor, then argued that the destruction of capital resulting from tariff reduction would harm laborers by reducing wages. Moreover, he doubted Southern calculations, appealing to the "science of political economy" to argue that Northerners paid a fair burden in tariffs as well. Appleton even accused his enemies of engaging in "French Jacobinism, in the worst periods of the revolution, when the cry of Rich aristocrat! met the response of '*à la lanterne!*' and consigned the unhappy victim to the nearest lamp post."[80]

Southerners were threatening to break the country over this—and Appleton's response was to insist that if their "war upon property be carried out," "preserving the Union . . . will not be worth the pains." Their war upon property struck at "the root of the principle of accumulation—the very foundation of all civilization." Finally, he warned slaveholders that if *Northern* property was not secure, theirs wasn't either: "Will it strengthen their confidence in the security of their peculiar property to see ours sacrificed without remorse? Will the name of rich slaveholder be a better security, in this warfare, than that of grasping monopolist?" He had bitterly rejected that label for manufacturers earlier in the speech.[81]

Calhoun and Appleton both won, and both lost. Nathan Appleton rightly accused "certain leading politicians" of having "formed bright visions of a Southern confederacy."[82] But these visions would not come to pass just yet. Senator William Wilkins of Pennsylvania had already (on January 21) proposed a bill authorizing military action to ensure revenue collection, and a month later Congress passed the Force Act, which did exactly that. Nullification, whether or not South Carolina believed in it, would be treated as insurrection. Shortly thereafter, Calhoun and Henry Clay rushed through a compromise tariff, one that temporarily preserved many of the high rates but scheduled them to slowly fall. For now, Southern and Northern capital would remain tense allies.

Both faced a rising threat though: abolitionism. Calhoun, of course, was a vicious defender of slavery. But Appleton also vigorously opposed abolition. In an 1860 letter to Virginian William Rives, he outlined his theory of the escalating conflict between North and South. He found fault on both sides but blamed Northern abolitionists for initiating conflict. In his view, the "first aggression was made by the North, or rather by a few individuals residing in the North," namely William Lloyd Garrison, Edmund Quincy, and Wendell Phillips, who "about the year 1830" formed what was in his view an inflammatory abolition society.[83] This was personal for Appleton: Wendell Phillips in particular was a childhood friend of his son, and each of these men was a part of the same elite Boston circles.[84] Appleton then traced subsequent developments in what he viewed as a back-and-forth escalation between regions.

Nathan Appleton regretted polarization more than injustice. In his view, each time peace was possible, overreaching Southerners or moralizing Northern abolitionists lit another fuse—thus there was "fault on both sides."[85] He conceded, "We of the North consider Slavery a social evil," but he felt "regret . . . that the subject has been so mingled with religion."[86] His account sympathized with Southern actions, characterizing them as unnecessary or miscalculating, but understandable, reactions to perceived threats, while uniformly condemning Northern abolitionism as a zealously anti-American betrayal of the Constitution and the Union. An earlier draft of his letter to Rives, as well as public statements made previously over the leadup to the Mexican War, suggest that abolitionist characterization of the Constitution as a "covenant with death and an agreement with hell" (for recognizing slavery) particularly incensed him.[87] Still, at least according to his public statements, Appleton was willing to risk the Union to protect Northern property. He was not willing to risk it to deprive Southerners of theirs. This was a perfectly consistent position: he believed first in property, second in the Union, and not very much at all in freedom. Even though he thought the 1832 crisis was explicitly an early secession plot, he believed in compromise with the South.

The increasingly distant role in management that enabled Nathan Appleton to have vast political influence perhaps made it easier for him to dismiss and deny the problem, and he ultimately proposed only tariff policy as a solution.[88] Of course the real problem was much more fundamental than mid-century market conditions. Extracting greater profits from workers meant forcing them to work longer, harder, and in worse conditions. No amount of sympathy could moderate a program of exploitation and control. Only a few months after the first shots at Fort Sumter, the man who made a fortune from blood-stained cotton heard the news in 1861 that his daughter Fanny—ironically, an abolitionist herself—died when her clothes spontaneously caught fire. He died the day after her funeral.[89]

The plantation world Nathan Appleton and Thomas Cooper defended was brought down by a national movement that extended across race and class, one rife with contradictions, flaws, and factional conflict. Though Appleton's account of the political conflict over slavery completely ignored Black Americans, they had in fact been abolitionists before the movement or word existed and were significant participants in the movement throughout the period Appleton covered. After his death, Black Southerners secured an end to slavery with what W. E. B. Du Bois characterized as a "general strike" in the South, pushing the pragmatic President Lincoln to issue the Emancipation Proclamation. The plantation was thus undone in no small part by the kernel of truth at the heart of classical political economy: all wealth does come from labor.

The victory of abolition was, however, only the beginning of a new struggle for justice in America. As Wendell Phillips put it with the passage of the Thirteenth Amendment, "We have abolished the slave, but the master remains."[90] For while slavery was dead, the science of control persisted. Abolition was a very real victory, but the coercion slaveholders had justified for two centuries was still a part of America's economic fabric. Capitalists in America came to rely on exactly the economic coercion that young abolitionist Cooper argued would protect Caribbean planters. Formerly enslaved people "must do something for their living: you need not feed them unless they will earn it, and then they will be compelled of themselves to work for you." Economic *compulsion*—the same language mill workers described overseers' actions regarding bonuses with as well—became the order of the day. This impersonal but powerful market coercion relied on the labor control advancements that nineteenth-century American elites made in three areas. First, they expanded techniques for the exploitation of individual workers. Second, they continued to exploit vulnerable populations, using racial hierarchy, patriarchy, and the desperation of immigrants (themselves victims of extraction and exploitation elsewhere) to minimize wages and maximize control. Third, they turned increasingly popular economic ideas into dominant ideology.

And in this same period, they began expanding those ideas, along with the economic forms they were meant to justify, to new parts of the world. In 1851, Secretary of State Daniel Webster, an attorney for and investor in the Boston Associates, signed a letter to the Emperor of Japan, asking him to open his nation to American commerce.[91] He was not asking, he was demanding.

5

"The Whole World Appears Despicable": Competitive Evolution and Japanese Industrialization, 1854–1914

Secretary of State Daniel Webster's planned expedition to force open Japan arrived there in 1852, Commodore Perry demanded open trade and refused to take no for an answer. The resulting political and economic turmoil—the transition from the early modern closed Tokugawa period to the modernizing Meiji era—turned the nation upside down. Tokugawa Japan had an equivalent to "political economy," according to intellectual historian Tetsuo Najita: *keisei saimin*, which can "be rendered more precisely as 'ordering the social world'—*keisei*—and 'saving the people'—*saimin*."[1] The phrase was a call to consider means as well as ends: how to save the people, yes, but "in ways that were ethical both in purpose and consequence," as Najita put it. When Japan was forcibly integrated into nineteenth-century global capitalism, Japanese intellectuals imported and studied books reflecting the latest and most widely read European thought. They encountered a different Western vision of political economy that increasingly argued against morality altogether: the worldview of Herbert Spencer.

The industrialists and intellectuals we have encountered so far endeavored to remove will from work. In the middle of the nineteenth century, their ideological descendants began to go further, both to address the existing failures of labor control and political economy and to meet the new challenges of global expansion. They aimed to nullify human intention not just at work but in political and economic life altogether. This was nothing so obviously tyrannical as controlling individual choices. Rather, they imagined a world where individual choices did not matter—one where they could be predicted and directed along a clear path of progress. As science's power and prestige grew, political economists aimed to calculate human action the same way they now could predict the movement of gases. But to truly make control science a science, to make self-interest as inevitable as gravity, they needed humanity to obey their findings. These men claimed they were seeking to discover the rules that govern all human action.

In reality, they were writing and imposing those rules themselves. Herbert Spencer was the most influential nineteenth-century proponent of the science of control. A philosopher who wrote on subjects ranging from biology to religion, his work became a global success, read from Britain to America to Egypt to Japan.[2] Like other proponents of control science both before and after him, Spencer presented himself as a man offering hard truths about how the world really works, in contrast to the naïve idealism of his opponents. Anyone who did not agree with him needed only to wait: control science was an objective account of human action, and those who rejected it were doomed to fail.

By examining Japanese industrialization, this chapter paints a different picture. Isolated from foreign trade for centuries and then forcibly opened by American gunboats, Japan offers a useful example of a nation adjusting all at once to industrial capitalism, and to how control science could work and could fail, outside the context it was originally conceived in. As Japanese elites worked to assess which European ideas to adopt and which to discard, they experimented with Herbert Spencer's theories. Like European technology, European ideas proved useful in expanding labor exploitation. But Spencer's cutting-edge European political economy failed: Japanese elites kept Europe at bay by ignoring the dogma of control science and adapting to the situation on the ground. Spencer's doctrine, like the later economic thought built on it, was a fallible ideology, not scientific fact.

Up to now, we have been dealing with technocrats. Each of them dealt with a growing tension between elite rule and psychological egoism. If all human beings were selfish, how could we trust even enlightened experts to rule? Herbert Spencer finally answered this question: embracing psychological egoism more profoundly than any of his forebears, he argued against ethics and intention altogether. A proper world for Spencer consisted of individuals competing in a "survival of the fittest," a phrase he, not Charles Darwin, coined. Spencer and his libertarian inheritors call this freedom.

Spencer's work and the rising current of right-wing economic thought he helped form were defined by amorality rather than liberty. The most significant contribution of this ostensibly liberal ideology was not its "small government" rhetoric and "laissez-faire" economics, neither of which actually produced the results they were supposed to. Rather, Spencer's contribution to world history was an assault on ethics itself: the abandonment of the earlier technocrats' ideas of ethical rule altogether. Control science would no longer try to balance or justify itself in ethical terms. A man who believed in nothing, Spencer proposed a world without *should*.

"The Great Scheme of Perfect Happiness"

"There is no life of which I have a really intimate knowledge which seems to me so inexpressibly sad as the inarticulate life of Herbert Spencer," wrote Beatrice Webb, his friend and protégée, in 1883. "Poor man ... there is something pathetic in the isolation of his mind, a sort of spider-like existence; sitting alone in the center of his theoretical web, catching facts, and weaving them again into theory ... I see what it is in him which is repulsive to some persons."[3] The only lover he ever had, the novelist Marian Evans, better known as George Eliot, claimed he had a "tremendous glacier" inside him.[4] He declared his love to her first, but when she reciprocated, he rejected her and claimed she was not attractive enough for him. The real reasons he drove her away were, perhaps, harder for him to face: he feared he was incapable of love and that his abusive father's mental state would be inherited by any children he had. When he argued that the weak and the unfit should be wiped off of the face of the Earth by the force of evolution, he did not believe he should number among the survivors.[5] The only thing Herbert Spencer had a dimmer view of than humanity was himself.

In some respects this miserable philosopher might seem an unlikely villain for a story of control science's global conquest. He wrote against colonialism and war, and he denounced Jeremy Bentham. But people contain multitudes. Spencer imagined the mind as an assembly in which different emotions and impulses might sometimes take the "presidential chair."[6] In both his own writings and their real world influence, the impulses that most frequently occupied this seat were cruelty and indifference rather than compassion.

Spencer is a founding figure in what adherents call "libertarian" thought. It argues for minimal government and low taxes—today's libertarians can be found arguing in the name of freedom against everything from pollution regulations to government-funded fire departments. Critics of Spencer have long tied him to "social Darwinism," the eugenicist belief that humanity evolves through struggle. Spencer biographer Mark Francis has claimed that Spencer was neither a laissez-faire libertarian nor a brutal Darwinist but rather a thoughtful liberal who wanted a utopian, cooperative future.[7]

He was all three: Spencer did argue for libertarian political and economic positions, but those positions are in fact a core part of the social Darwinist vision. He was also a liberal in the nineteenth-century sense, and he did want a peaceful and cooperative future, but he opposed every effort to achieve it. The defining characteristic of his philosophy was a hostility to human intention: to the willful decision by an individual or by a group to change themselves or the world. He believed only nature should do that. His ideology, and his main contribution to world history, was a theory of control rather than freedom.

As Francis himself puts it, Spencer wanted to "rescue freedom from democracy."[8]

Spencer was born in 1820 into a world where the ideas we have been following had become firmly established and popular. Between his personal and political environments, Spencer developed three core features of what would become his ideology: a hostility to command, an interest in science, and a belief in progress. Their sum was a doctrine of scientifically described progressive evolution without command, which he outlined first in his 1851 work *Social Statics*. Intended to finally meet the Helvetian, Lockean, and Benthamite demand for a mathematical ethics, Spencer's focus in the book was a system of "pure ethics" devised from first principles and applied reason. Just as the human "geometric sense," produced "geometric axioms, from which reason may deduce a scientific geometry," it fell to the "moral sense to originate a moral axiom, from which reason may develop a systematic morality."[9]

Social Statics relied on a rationalist rather than empiricist methodology to achieve this. Spencer acknowledged that "it seems at first sight a very rational way of testing any proposed rule of conduct to ask, How will it work?" But Spencer felt this empiricism was an "absurd" standard clouded by changing human nature (something he felt was adaptable, not constant) and the political notions of the questioner. "Humanity," he wrote, "cannot be used as a gauge for testing moral truth."[10] Human experience was likewise a "subordinate means of acquiring knowledge," as biographer Mark Francis summarizes.[11] In later work, like his *Principles of Biology*, Spencer did rely on scientific thought, and all of his work includes (often crude and erroneous) historical examples. But his intellectual methodology and political practice across his career were hands-off, an attempt to rise above messy reality and experiment. Herbert Spencer did not exactly have a consistent epistemological position, but "pure" reason was at the heart of *Social Statics*.

What made Spencerian "pure" ethics useful was the *necessity* its purity implied. The phrase "there is no alternative," famously associated with Margaret Thatcher, was perhaps first written in the same sense by Herbert Spencer—it occurs twice in *Social Statics* verbatim and is more generally one of the core arguments of the book. Summarizing his arguments at the end of the treatise, Spencer wrote that "moral truth, as now interpreted, proves to be a development of physiological truth," and meanwhile, that "the injunctions of the moral law, as now interpreted, coincide with and anticipate those of political economy."[12]

Morality, physiology, and political economy converged into a "law of the perfect man" of laissez-faire in most human activity—politically, this was what there was no alternative *to*.[13] Spencer's central rule was that individuals' "sphere of activity" must be limited as little as possible.[14] He justified this with a Locke- and Bentham-influenced line of reasoning on pleasure and action. Happiness in his view came only from "the exercise of [man's] faculties."[15] Because God wants us to be happy, "it is man's *duty* to exercise his faculties," and this duty should be respected as much as possible.[16] He conceded that some limits on human action were necessary—murder was not to be allowed, for instance—but insisted these must be kept few in number. Important rights included property as well as the "right of exchange" and the "freedom of contract."[17] Perhaps the best element of Spencer's program, an argument for common land use, was one he later backed away from.[18] Another emblematic right was the "right to ignore the state," which undergirded a broader anticollective stance and vision.[19]

The very title of Spencer's well-known later work *Man versus the State* is instructive. Like his intellectual predecessors, he divided the world into individuals, in his case literally atomizing it—he compared individuals to the atoms that chemist John Dalton had recently theorized.[20] Freedom was something for these individuals, not collectives. If a majority of people decided, contrary to Spencer's proclamations, that they wanted to provide poor relief, redistribute property, regulate commerce, or even fund public education, they were in violation of the fundamental rules of the world itself, and with them the "Divine Will."[21] Spencer was not exactly a political individualist—he hoped his competitive principles would lead to the evolution of a more cooperative society—but he was decidedly a methodological individualist.

Labor control was an area where Spencer's moral law and political economy coincided especially well—when explaining how they align in his closing summary, all of his examples are class warfare. The state cannot regulate wages or prices. It cannot restrict speculation in food markets—a common working-class demand down to the present—or interfere with trade. "Legislative interference with manufacturing processes" was likewise forbidden, and naturally, moral law and political economy had both proven that it was wrong to restrict mechanization. Usury should be legal as well, of course.[22] In Spencer's world, poor workers could choose from any factory job on offer, but they could not organize state action to make those jobs better or make their economy fairer. The "Moral Sense" was valid if it pointed toward factory labor and invalid if it pointed toward socialism, as it did for an increasing and increasingly repressed number of Europeans.[23]

Spencer's worldview thus left a vast array of evils and injustices in place. This was intentional. As he put it, "a system of pure ethics cannot recognize evil," by which he meant it could not concern itself with particular cases or harms toward anyone. Anyone who did so lost the certainty Spencer prized: "his decision is no longer scientific and authoritative, but is now merely an *opinion*."[24] This was a shot at Bentham, who proposed calculating what *was* an evil and using the state to minimize it.[25] Spencer argued that humanity was too discordant and degraded to agree on utility, and that the state Bentham hoped would act as the "umpire" of happiness was thus doomed to fail.

Herbert Spencer had scorn not only for the Helvetian ideal legislator but for the idea of well-intentioned good altogether. Government and classical ethics based in the real world necessarily concerned the "crooked man," rather than the perfect "straight man" that a "pure" moralist should rightly be concerned with.[26] Spencer did not believe that the state, or anyone else, could make a crooked man into a straight one. He believed human nature could and must change, but he did not believe we could choose how to change it—any human attempt to do so was prone to failure and, anyway, necessarily tyrannical.

Since virtue was suspect and intentional collective change impossible, Spencer put his faith for progress in competitive evolution. Like John Locke and Samuel Martin, Spencer claimed that God directed human behavior by arranging the natural consequences of our actions—"punishment attaches to the neglect" of the exercise of faculties.[27] It followed from this that people should not be protected from those consequences, even and indeed especially when they were painful. We must instead allow all individuals the maximum possible freedom to act so that the inherent rules of the universe, the social equivalents of gravity, will suppress bad behavior and promote right action.[28] "All nature" is characterized by a "stern discipline" that he believed "weed[ed] out the sickly, the malformed, and the least fleet or powerful."[29] This "purifying process" forces adaptation and, with it, happiness. Spencer conceded that

> it seems hard that an unskilfulness which with all his efforts he cannot overcome, should entail hunger upon the artisan. It seems hard that a labourer incapacitated by sickness from competing with his stronger fellows, should have to bear the resulting privations. It seems hard that widows and orphans should be left to struggle for life or death. Nevertheless, when regarded not separately, but in connection with the interests of universal humanity, these harsh fatalities are seen to be full of the highest beneficence—the same beneficence which brings to early graves the children of diseased parents, and singles out the low-spirited, the intemperate, and the debilitated as the victims of an epidemic.[30]

Those who could not adapt were better off dead. If the state did not let them die, it would inhibit the winnowing force of evolution. The proper role of government was to protect individual rights, especially property rights, and never to pursue any kind of collective public good—especially not poor relief.

Spencer's competitive process was biological as well as social, thanks to his (incorrect) Lamarckian vision of heredity, in which attributes acquired during life were passed down to offspring. The evolution at the heart of Spencerian ideology was in fact more closely related to political economy than biology. From political economists' progressive accounts of history and stadial theory he drew a faith in "universal progress."[31] The division of labor into increasingly specialized and distinct tasks, like spinner and gilder and manager, became in Spencer's hands a process of civilization analogous to the "physiological division of labour" seen in the natural world.[32]

He advanced his predecessors' portrayal of a base and hedonistic humanity—the selfishness of *Homo economicus* was one of the few constants he insisted on, in a human nature he otherwise claimed was flexible. Political economists' triumphant view of a clockwork world ticking along powered by humans' selfish desires reached new heights in Spencer's work. "Slowly and silently" the forces of evolution had driven "millions" to factories.[33] And again, there was no alternative to this. In a passage denouncing socialists, Spencer insisted that the desire for private accumulation was "one of the elements of our nature," and that "no change in the state of society will alter its nature and its office"—even though, as we have seen, changes in the state of society have done exactly that.[34] The Benthams sought to remove human will from human work. Spencer argued for removing it from the world altogether.

What made Spencer appealing despite this was the utopian endpoint he promised. As man evolved forward, adapting to new social conditions, he would come to need the state less and less. In the long term, Spencer believed that industrial society was already creating conditions that rewarded cooperation rather than competition.[35] Manners, customs, and habits—all of which could diffuse biologically thanks to Spencer's Lamarckian view of heredity—were evolving beyond competition. For now, the state was necessary to protect men from each other, and Spencer believed it should ideally also prohibit war. But once the perfect man evolved, the state would become unnecessary.[36]

The natural rules that Herbert Spencer claimed to have discovered were in fact social rules that had to be justified and enforced—and the very act of claiming that they *were* discovered helped make this possible through a three-part process of naturalization. First, he made his political beliefs appear to be like natural law. The claim that competition was the order of the universe legitimized unfettered market capitalism. Second, the naturalization of capitalism included an actual alliance with nature. Biology demands that we eat. This does not mean any particular social order is natural. But when you have to sell your labor to someone with capital in order to obtain food, because you can get it only through the market, biological pressures push you to comply with political and economic structures.

Third and finally, the growing influence of market dependence made the laws of capitalist competition function like nature's. Laissez-faire economics and violent competition were increasingly written into the actions and laws of the powerful, as both capitalist structures and political economy's ideas grew in significance. When everyone with a fortune or a seat in Parliament believes private property and free trade are sacrosanct, they are. When everyone else with a factory is exploiting workers and driving prices down, no individual factory owner can choose better working conditions without going out of business.

Only collective action could change this—but of course, Spencer explicitly prohibited that. Spencer was skeptical of intention itself.[37] Individuals in his view were inconsistent composites of passions and instincts, which could not be suppressed or necessarily even distinguished from reason and will.[38] Any imposition of the collective will on individuals, or of the individual's own will upon themselves, was thus doomed to fail. Spencer's behavioral quietism led directly to his belief in competitive evolution. Man could not better himself through intent, only through adaptation—humanity would improve as its emotional constitution improved with conditions, not through conscious action.

Politically, Spencer's competitive evolution resolved a serious problem with Benthamite utilitarianism: how should we actually calculate utility? Bentham had never answered this difficult question, and the stakes were high. Utilitarian calculation as an idea was politically flexible—it could support ideas ranging from bourgeois technocracy to socialism. A great deal depended on who was doing the calculating.

Spencer solved this problem by placing Benthamite utility calculations in the hands of no one. Competition itself would take care of both calculation and execution. Economically, this meant unrestricted markets. Politically, this meant restraining democracy. Biologically, this meant eugenics. Bentham himself believed in the power of market self-interest as a tool to optimize good outcomes. Spencer simply proposed handing everything over to the market economically, and to similar principles of competition more generally. Since there was no need for a central authority, democratic or technocratic, to make decisions about utility, the purpose of the state was simply to protect competitive evolution—to keep the grand competition that was the universe itself running until, at last, the ultimate form of society emerged, bloody from conflict. The ideal society would not be constructed by intent. It would be whittled by self-interest. Beatrice Webb later wrote of this period that "the circumstances of mid-Victorian capitalist enterprise were hostile to any fixed standard of morality."[39] Spencer was a perfect philosopher for this moment.

His ideology was a self-executing version of Benthamite utilitarianism. Why even write, then? Spencer believed that only competitive evolution could produce success, but he did not believe that success was inevitable or that it would appear on a defined timeline. Free will still mattered: humanity might foolishly choose collectivism and thus delay, decay, or doom. The political purpose of Spencerism, therefore, was to discourage intentional action—by rulers, technocrats, or the populace. Jeremy Bentham's Panopticon used the structure of one building to coerce workers. Herbert Spencer believed that the structure of the entire world would do this—as long as we let it.

"The Principles of the Natural Order"

Early modern Japan had its own body of thought on control of the lower classes. Ogyū Sorai, one of the most important intellectuals in eighteenth-century Japan, advocated for combining law and custom as a "subtle technique" by which rulers could control the people.[40] Japanese political thought prominently featured medicinal metaphors in his era, and Sorai used them as well. Like some of his peers in Europe, Sorai was the son of a physician. He referred to human society as a "living thing."[41] But unlike comparable Western thinkers, Sorai did not argue that nature itself prescribed a particular political order. Rather, he insisted, the right way had been created intentionally by wise sages and rulers past. It was a blueprint for society writ large, not a set of individual moral rules.[42]

Japanese intellectuals had spent centuries exploring questions similar to those Spencer addressed, and they had not arrived at the same answers. As Herbert Spencer's student Beatrice Webb explained, Spencer believed capitalism was natural, but any state or trade union action was "artificial."[43] Sorai, in contrast, understood that the social order was an artificial structure of adaptation around natural constraints. His argument for merit-based promotion rather than hereditary succession in government offices, for example, combined a rumination on death and nature with an analysis of socioeconomic class. It was, he wrote, "a general and lasting principle of the natural order that old things should pass away and new things be brought into existence." At the same time, it was "characteristic of human nature" for us to value leaders who have done great work, and to wish for our own family members to live on. Thus, the natural order and human nature were in conflict: we want eternity, and we receive only inevitable death. In neither case could "nature" offer a simple answer about what to do.[44]

Sorai advocated his preferred solution—merit-based promotion—by considering the interaction between human character and power. It was "characteristic of human nature" for elites "reared in the midst of the praise and adulation of their household retainers" to "become conceited," "arbitrary," and to perceive those beneath them as "vermin." Elites were "separated from the common people" by an "unbridgeable gulf." Insulated by social hierarchy, they could never truly come to understand those beneath them, no matter how hard they might try. This meant that elites became not only cruel and oppressive but also incompetent: "members of the upper class become more and more stupid." Since "all human ability is produced by suffering difficulties and hardships," the lower social orders were bound to be more competent than their supposed betters. Accordingly, as the sages prescribed, merit-based promotion was necessary for the health of the state.[45]

Also like Western theorists of control science, Sorai was deeply pessimistic about human nature. Sorai argued that human beings were too unreliable to divine moral truth, let alone make moral choices.[46] But he insisted that ancient sages had produced normative truth in the form of an ideal ethic that promoted "peace and well-being."[47] He likewise endorsed compassion as an ethical principle—treating "the other as if the other is in no way different from oneself."[48]

Sorai was a kind of intellectually curious and practical conservative.[49] He defended the existing political order, in part on the grounds that it was the existing political order.[50] And he did so despite recognizing that social hierarchy was contingent, not natural.[51] At the same time, he was concerned for the health of the state and the well-being of its people, could reject existing interpretations and policies where they failed, and had a pragmatic approach to governance.

On economics specifically, he offered similarly practical and reasonable advice on a particularly difficult topic: money. Rather than narrowly focus on the value or quantity of money itself—a common error even today—Sorai considered its production, distribution, and the role of actual exchange practice in setting prices. He proposed allowing regional lords to coin their own currency because of transportation difficulties, and he criticized the accumulation of gold and silver coins by the rich, since money was useful only insofar as it actually circulated. The philosopher defended credit systems on a natural basis—"it is in accordance with the principles of the natural order that surpluses should be used for the relief of scarcities," and thus it was good for peasants to have access to loans—but argued for artificial, intentional structures including state regulation precisely to make the credit system work better.[52]

Sorai was aligned with the samurai class, which would become one foundation for conservatism in late nineteenth-century Japan.[53] His critics offered a more (again, very roughly) liberal or progressive attitude—that is to say, a political vision that emphasized changes to the existing political order and the fundamental equality of human beings. Nakai Chikuzan, who published an attack on Sorai's thinking in 1785, abhorred Sorai's moral pessimism and insisted human beings, *all* human beings, could come to know moral truth and make virtuous choices. Nakai's moral argument was a defense of commoners—a class that included merchants, who were patrons and pupils at the Kaitokudō merchant academy that his father had founded and that he himself later headed—and their capabilities as political subjects.[54]

We should be cautious in mapping present-day left-right distinctions onto early modern Japanese politics. While both thinkers' politics and class position were connected to their ideas, they did not fully determine them. Sorai's samurai links and conservatism did not keep him from embracing merit-based promotion. Nakai Chikuzan was connected to and dependent upon merchants, but he believed in the moral and educational capacity of all people. And despite vehement disagreements that extended down to the foundations of their respective philosophies, both Ogyū Sorai and Nakai Chikuzan believed that knowledge could and should serve the public good.

This practical character proved invaluable a century later. Historian John Sagers suggests that Sorai's pragmatism enabled later Japanese elites to approach economic matters practically, by prioritizing what actually worked, rather than preexisting practice and norms.[55] Japanese liberals were of course willing to experiment with new economic policy and political structures as well. Flexibility, curiosity, and experimentation were exactly what Japan's mid-nineteenth-century crisis demanded.

"The Very Existence of Our Nation Is in Peril"

The forced opening of Japan, beginning with a coerced treaty signed in 1854, brought economic calamity to the nation. Machine-produced textiles flooded the market, which "ruined" many of Japan's important craft industries.[56] Handicrafts like silk were essential to Japanese peasants' ability to pay rent, and their loss forced many tenant laborers to become wage laborers.[57] Rising imports therefore displaced individual workers and whole communities.

They also produced a permanent external drain: wealth taken from Japan would not circulate back into the country, thanks to the inequalities of trade. This in turn produced shifts in currency, including the issuing of paper money, which had significant impacts on state and private debts.[58] Meanwhile, superior Western production capabilities provided enormous military advantages over Japan. Thus European commerce was a social, macroeconomic, and geopolitical threat. It is important that we understand these events differently from Herbert Spencer: this was not a natural disaster. It was a man-made calamity, one engineered and profited from. The forces unleashed were vast, but they *were* unleashed, and they were human.

Japanese elites refused to let this engineered evolution run its course. The shogunate's decision to accept Western trade, though made at the barrel of a gun, was divisive—and this was a difficult time for political division. The negotiation of the Treaty of Amity and Commerce with the US coincided with the death of the shogun in the same year, 1858. Important noble and shogunate official Ii Naosuke appeared to come out on top, securing both the treaty and his preferred candidate for the succession.[59] But his political opponents began to pull the Imperial Court into politics, in which it had previously played a primarily symbolic role.

Politics divided roughly into two camps represented by competing slogans: *sonnō jōi*, or "revere the emperor, expel the barbarians," and *sabaku kaikoku*, "support the shogun, open the country."[60] The result was a difficult period of assassination plots, purges, and rebellions. When the court-aligned Choshu domain attempted to carry out the "expel the barbarian" part of their political program in 1863 by firing on Western merchant ships, Europeans retaliated in force. On July 16, US ships engaged Choshu forces and sank several ships, ironically including the US-built warship *Daniel Webster*.[61] The following year, a joint Western force overran Choshu.[62]

While expelling the barbarians proved impossible, in 1868–9 imperial-aligned nobles and samurai achieved the other half of *sonnō jōi* by overthrowing the shogunate. This was the beginning of the Meiji era: Japan had a new government for a new age. This new administration quickly began planning modernization efforts to better compete with foreign powers. In 1871, Meiji officials departed for America and Europe on the Iwakura Mission, named after leading official Iwakura Tomomi.[63] Its goals were both diplomatic—projecting the image of the new imperial state and renegotiating treaties—and economic: the ambassadors were dispatched to uncover the material and social foundations of Western economic power so that they could be adapted for and implemented in Japan.

Japan's political economy and culture were markedly different from those of its European rivals in the mid-nineteenth century. It had a stronger administrative state, a politically weaker merchant class, and a samurai class that combined landholding, administrative work, military power, and noble status in a structure that resists easy European comparison. This meant that any adoption of European factory technology would require serious social and political change. The goal of the Iwakura Mission was to carefully judge what might be adapted from Europe in order to resist European empires. When the mission landed in Liverpool on August 17, 1872, it arrived in a rapidly transforming nation characterized by stunning material growth and devastating poverty. Kume Kunitake commented that Europe's "remarkable wealth and prosperity dates to a large extent from 1800, and took a mere forty years to create."[64] This was promising for Japan's own possible transformation, as long as they could bring back the knowledge that that transformation relied on. In September, the Japanese officials visited twenty-eight London factories manufacturing everything from gunpowder to candles. They also sought detailed information on Western government and education.

As they gathered information intended to adapt their economy and society to compete with Britain, they also saw the price Britain's people were paying for those strengths. In the industrialized north, they witnessed poor residents walking around barefoot; in Liverpool specifically, they saw a sky "always darkened by a cloud of coal smoke . . . Our guides pointed out that the people live their lives breathing this blackened air," reducing life expectancy to "just 15 years for the working classes."[65] They visited London's East End, which in the words of Spencer's student Beatrice Webb (who had spent plenty of time there) was defined by the "physical horrors and moral debasement of chronic destitution in crowded tenements in the midst of mean streets."[66] The visiting Japanese officials were stunned: "after seeing that," wrote future Lord of Home Affairs and powerful autocrat Ōkubo Toshimichi, "the whole world appears despicable."[67]

The mission produced divergent views among Japanese elites, sometimes held within the same person. Mori Arinori, for instance, argued for the replacement of Japanese with English, the abolition of sword carrying, and religious freedom—but opposed ending samurai stipends, a critical measure in the shift from the Edo period's hierarchy of nobles and samurai.[68] Kume criticized the American government as inefficient and divided, citing the example of the troubled administration of Andrew Johnson. He wrote that the "Western theory of progress" meant projects being "carried out carelessly and without forethought," with unrealistic expectations and counterproductive results. His vision of progress was more conservative: "By degree there are advances."[69]

Japan's diplomats returned to a country in turmoil. The economy was in chaos because of the collapse of domestic handicraft industries, unable to compete with foreign imports. Peasants could not afford rent or fertilizer, inflation was eating away at government revenue, and political reforms were angering the samurai class, many of whom were also hit hard by the introduction of Western commerce. During the first decade of Meiji rule, there were more than two hundred peasant uprisings, while samurai discontent triggered several revolts, culminating in the 1877 Satsuma Rebellion, which was put down only at great cost in money and lives. All of this explains why Meiji officials prioritized the development of commercial industry over military industry. While Western cannons and rifles were a threat in the future, Western textiles were wreaking havoc now. The stakes of Japan's trade imbalance were enormous: as Iwakura himself put it, "the very existence of our nation is in peril."[70] By developing a consumer economy, Japan would be able to reverse the effects of Western competition and develop industry to employ displaced peasants and samurai—the latter as both workers and capitalists, depending on their economic situation.

It was the Japanese government that took the lead in the establishment of industrial capitalism. This meant that the state took a different role in this transformation than it had in Europe. While the Iwakura Mission was still touring the West, Meiji officials at home were already seeking and implementing Western ideas directly. In 1870, Italian specialists taught European silk techniques in Tokyo, and two years later the government had a large silk mill constructed at Tomioka with French experts' assistance. The effort immediately ran into social problems: the women and girls the state hoped to recruit did not want to travel hundreds of miles for employment. Nor did they want to work with the Europeans meant to train them. Japanese peasant superstitions held that Westerners drank blood and cooked with human fat. Their fears that they would be devoured by industrial machinery were not literally realized, but the underlying accusation was disturbingly insightful.[71]

"This Troubled World"

> To kill a factory girl
> You don't need a knife
> You just strangle her
> With the weight and denier [i.e, thickness] of the thread.

So went one Meiji-era factory song.[72] Cultivating capitalism in Japan meant transforming its people into wage laborers—a process that had taken centuries in Europe. Most people do not want to be *machines that cannot err*. As Herbert Spencer put it, "the acquirement of this ability [to do wage labour]" is "so distressing, that only the severest discipline will force [someone unaccustomed to it] into it."[73] Japanese elites achieved this "severest discipline" by combining market coercion with state funding and force.

As in Lowell, factories began with tolerable, if rough, working conditions. Japanese factory owners had to appeal to peasant families, whose workers had limited but real choices in economic activity.[74] Women in small, local operations during the 1870s had relative freedom of movement, while the larger and more controlling Tomioka Silk Filature offered "nourishing meals, medical care, relatively short working hours with regular rest periods, and days off."[75] Even the harsher cotton industry had a "feudalistic" character somewhat similar to early Appletonian paternalism, though probably more expansive. The combination of recruitment needs and preexisting cultural expectations created a quasi-familial "web of mutual obligations," according to historian E. Patricia Tsurumi, in which owners would not fire employees, nor would employees quit. One cotton mill allowed rest periods and holidays, while its workers "understood that if the mill was busy, holidays might be ignored."[76] This was hardly a just or ideal system, but these mutual obligations limited exploitation.

Still, the paternalism of early factories sat alongside powerful repression. Workers in Tomioka Silk Filature dormitories were unable to leave the factory compound except on holidays and were forbidden from speaking to each other while working. Across the textile industries, workers were categorized by productivity into different classes. At Tomioka, first-class workers were paid 25 yen per month, second-class workers received 18 yen per month, and third-class workers got 12 yen, while unclassified workers received a mere 9. These differentials incentivized competition rather than cooperation, as did the fact that dormitory supervisors were selected from workers of the first class.[77]

Early in the middle 1880s, industrial profit-seeking began to overcome "feudalistic" obligations, just as it had in New England. The enormous Osaka Cotton-Spinning Company opened for business in 1883. Thanks to former Finance Minister Shibusawa Eichi, who raised vast investment capital from merchants and nobles, the firm was several times larger than its competitors. The company ruthlessly pursued profits and chose its location to exploit the urban poor of Osaka and nearby suffering tenant farming families. Taking advantage of their desperation, the firm did not provide housing to workers, offered lower pay, and began night shifts—which came with enormous fire risks.[78]

What made Osaka so successful for investors, and devastating for workers, was the combination of machines and markets. "If an enterprise does not make a profit," Osaka Company representative Akitoshi Monden explained at an 1885 conference of cotton manufacturers, "it will not be a success." He went on to suggest exactly which type of yarn Japan should be focused on producing and working with, and what yarn types manufacturers should try to keep out of Japan. Company records from this same period included detailed sales volume data and considered regional dynamics carefully: "the Owari region ... is another promising market"; "we are not yet selling our products in Shikoku"; "as the Echigo region is one in which the demand for cotton yarn has been large, we are planning to expand our market there."[79] The very architects of this world-altering industrial system understood themselves as following demand, executing on market designs.

As workers followed the machine, executives followed markets. The market for investment further compelled adherence to the market for goods—Shibusawa needed his cohort of private investors to keep their capital in his company, which meant promising them high returns to compete with more reliable alternative options in land and lending.[80] If investors accepted smaller returns, they would fall behind their rivals in economic and political power. Low wages and high volume necessarily followed from this. If Shibusawa had wanted to take better care of workers, that desire would have been irrelevant in the same way as a worker's desire to slow down: the machine would not allow it. Capitalism constrains even capitalists.

Market coercion by account books ordered and intensified mechanized coercion in the factory. Company-wide directives traveled down from administrators to senior supervisors. The junior supervisors under them, who were factory women promoted into this position, could not act in solidarity with the workforce they had come from. Senior supervisors would "make their lives miserable" and even fire them if they failed to meet production targets.[81] Meeting production targets meant maximizing production: each firm was in competition with every other for consumer money and investor capital. None of them could choose some acceptable level of output and deem it enough or decide to go no further. Maximizing production meant brutalizing workers, literally—junior supervisors had to verbally, physically, and financially punish workers to drive production upward. Workers compared managers' supervision to military discipline.[82]

Labor discipline was enforced by the combination of internal discipline systems with the external structure of the market. As at Tomioka, Osaka workers were subject to a ranking classification system based on productivity. In December 1883, the eighty-six women ranked in the bottom nonapprentice pay category were paid at a rate of 7 sen (0.07 yen) per day. The nine women in the next higher rank made 9 sen per day. The two women at the top made 17. Some mills used similar ranking systems for executives and office workers as well.[83]

Japanese mill executives developed a boardinghouse system not unlike those in America and promoted labor education meant to render workers "gentle and obedient." The Kurashiki Spinning Company boasted that within two years, its worker education program had changed employees: "those workers who had never made a bow to company managers [have begun] to pay their respects to them. They used to sing obscene folksongs," perhaps including songs damning the company like those I quoted at the beginning and end of this section of the book, but now "they sang the national anthem in chorus."[84]

Working conditions were horrific. A child silk worker in 1902 explained that she would "get up at four in the morning and work for two hours before breakfast."[85] She stopped work at night, but was not allowed to sleep until 9:00 pm. Contracted for two and a half years, she worked under a twenty-year-old supervisor—the person responsible for ensuring she worked as hard as she could. Older girls bullied younger workers like her if they did not "listen obediently" to them. "[If you] talk back to them they will soon call you all kinds of bad names, treat you dreadfully, and make you do almost impossible jobs." Trapped in a foreign city against her will, afraid of older workers and under the thumb of her supervisor, she longed for home. She was twelve.

A song entitled "My Two Parents" further captures the heartbreak of factory labor. The narrator sings of being "sold to this factory" at "age twelve," upon which her "very heart wept tears of blood." "Mother!" she sings, "I hate the season in the silk plant / It's from 4:00 pm to 4:00 am."[86] She loved and missed her parents, even though they had consigned her to this fate. But her feelings were complicated:

> In this troubled world
> I am just a silk-reeling lass
> But this lass wants to see
> The parents who gave her birth
> Their letter says they are waiting for the year's end.
> Are they waiting more for the money than for me?

If they were, it was not their fault. Everyone in the market had to take everything they could get, because everyone else was. Horizontal competition between capitalists and vertical exploitation by capitalists of workers reinforced each other. The resulting market discipline turned fellow workers into vicious supervisors and parents into child-sellers.

"The God of Evolution"

Japanese political thinkers were in a position to engage with Spencer the moment they either learned English or had his books in translation. Spencer's work was published in dozens of Japanese translations from 1877 to 1900 and discussed in print as well. But because Japanese thinkers had devised different answers for a different social context, they could not immediately conscript Spencer to one particular school of thought, class position, or partisan affiliation. Spencerism did not obviously serve the ends of samurai more than merchants, or of advocates of imperial power more than advocates of democracy.

According to sociologist Michio Nagai, the early Japanese liberal movement read Spencer as a philosopher of liberal freedoms. Important liberal leader Itagaki Taisuke described *Social Statics* as a "text-book of people's rights."[87] Japanese liberals placed central emphasis on his vision of political rights and liberal democracy. Spencer's laissez-faire economics were potentially an inoculation against oligarchic tendencies in the Meiji state.[88] And as a critic of centralized states—if not a liberatory one—Spencer's use for liberal critics of Japan's powerful government was obvious.

Nakae Chōmin's 1887 *A Discourse by Three Drunkards on Government* provides a clear example of the liberal attitude toward Spencerian evolution. Born Nakae Tokusuke, he distinguished himself in spite of his relatively low class (his father was a foot soldier) through academics and traveled with the Iwakura Mission. After returning from France in 1874, he started a newspaper that took the prodemocracy position he would maintain for the rest of his life, in the face of censorship, corruption, and repression, working under the pen name Nakae Chōmin—Chōmin literally translates as "a billion or trillion people."[89] His 1887 *Discourse* took the form of a dialogue in which several characters representing different positions converse. Chōmin's liberal character, the "Gentleman of Western Learning," argued for democracy at home and diplomacy abroad. He believed history is driven by the "god of evolution," by which human society "proceed[s] from an imperfect to a perfect shape, to change from an impure to a pure form."

His evolution was the kinder side of Spencer's, an evolution of manners and emotions in which human desires for freedom drive the world from despotism to constitutionalism and on to full democracy, with no distinctions of rank. The policy implications of this were clear. Japan should establish democratic government, a broad franchise, and free schools, while abolishing execution, censorship, and laws restricting political rights like assembly and speech. This proposal was radical in its day—no nation followed all of its principles yet. The Gentleman criticized Europeans as "blind fools" for ignoring their own ideas of peace and democracy, which he viewed as intimately connected. He exhorted them:

> Cast your eyes, citizens of Europe, beyond your national boundaries. The weapons which your neighbors manufacture are designed some day to kill you with one blast and to burn down your homes in a flash. The warships and torpedoes they build are meant to shake your houses and the trees along your beaches. Today you sleep peacefully, but tomorrow you may become corpses in the field.
>
> Do you really fear that your enemy will some day kill or wound you with a sword, burn your crops and buildings, or blow up your harbors? Then why don't you quickly demolish your guns? Why don't you burn your warships?[90]

And he proposed Japan should do exactly that. Because "everybody yearns for such a garden of moral principles" as his democratic and liberal Japan of free schools and free people, he claimed that "no one would have the heart to despoil it." He argued no nation would likely attack them, but that if one did,

> I would prefer that our people call up no soldiers and carry no bullets, but die at the hands of the invading troops, because I wish to transform us into living embodiments of moral principles and to make a model for future generations. Your theory states that because the other person does evil, I should also do evil. But isn't that the height of barbarity?[91]

Chōmin's idealistic but naive Gentleman proposed out-Enlightening the European Enlightenment: by laying down its arms, the Gentleman's Japan would prove its eternal superiority on Europe's own grounds, embracing liberty and peace in a way Europe never had.

Spencer might have seemed an obvious ally to the liberals that the Gentleman stood in for. But his methods were ill-suited to Japan's situation, and his intentions were fundamentally malignant. "Survival of the fittest" was an awful slogan for commoners who wanted to have more grain instead of to become chaff as Spencer's brutal competition dictated. More well-off liberals threw in their lot with the state thanks to the protection it could offer landowners. Meanwhile, industrialists found traditional social structures quite useful: patriarchy made labor cheaper, while Japan's class structure made controlling the lower classes easier. Facing the cross-pressures of commoner need and capitalist greed, the liberal movement "began to disintegrate," in the words of Michio Nagai.[92] As Nakae Chōmin's drunken mediator character, Master Nankai, warned with a joke, it seemed that "the Asian god of evolution likes aristocrats and dislikes commoners."[93]

It was not Japan's liberals but its conservatives who made the most of Spencer. According to Nagai, Spencer's ideology was "regarded by the liberals as a philosophy" but "considered by conservative intellectuals to be a science."[94] Liberals found him a philosopher of freedom, while conservatives knew him as a scientist of control. The conservative counterpart to Chōmin's Gentleman of Western Learning, the "Champion of the East," argued that war and violence were "an inevitable force in the actual world." Like Spencer, Mr. Champion backed this with appeals to nature:

> It is our nature as animals to love victory and hate defeat. Every living thing between heaven and earth, from the insects to such fierce beasts as tigers, lions, coyotes, and wolves, lives by catching and killing its prey ... Or look at children. Just as soon as they can start crawling about, they will swing sticks to hit dogs or cats whenever they see them, or drag them by their tails, while their round, childish faces are all smiles and joy. Only children who are sick and listless do not do these things ... A quarrel results from the anger of individuals. Those who refuse to quarrel are cowards. Those nations that refuse to fight wars are weak. If anyone says that quarreling is a vice and war an absurdity, let me ask him to consider this: What can be done about the fact that individuals actually possess vices? What can be done about the fact that states act absurdly? In short, what can be done about reality?[95]

His Spencerian arguments about nature's cruelty culminated in the same argument for inevitability.

The Champion was remarkably straightforward about the cruelty of his own vision. He characterized the Gentleman's vision as "living flesh" compared to the "cancer" of his own. To save Japan from the cancer he believed men like himself represented, he proposed an invasion of China. "If we're successful, we will usurp the land, take firm root there, and establish what may be called a 'cancer society.'"[96] The Champion's vision of humanity, like Spencer's, ignored our ethical capacities and our social duties in favor of violent expansion. Cancer's final argument is no argument at all: I am, I expand. *What can be done about reality?*

Real Japanese conservatives likewise took the view that evolution was guiding the world toward a single order, a single answer. In Japan's "first systematic treatise" on sociology, Ariga Nagao argued society was naturally evolving toward a state he called "the world of integration by reason."[97] Nagao's vision was closer to Jeremy Bentham and Helvetius's in one sense, as he imagined a state organizing all matters along rational lines. But it was true to the spirit of Spencer's: the state was supposed to eventually disappear in Spencerian thought only because once man was finally "pure" through social evolution, his free will at last aligned with evolutionary principles so well that no one had to make it do so anymore. "Greatest happiness," in Spencer's words, "is obtained only when conformity to them is spontaneous."[98] Properly orchestrated, the capitalist world of competition produced its own perfect subjects without the "command of any ruler."[99]

Yet while Spencer believed that the rules of competition were natural, he also believed they would need help in the form of state force. Both Spencer and Nagao encouraged adherence to the laws of their respective empires and supported a conservative vision of a powerful state.[100] In practice, their respective visions of adherence to eternal law converged into obedience to human law. Nagao's different view of the state only makes clearer the authoritarian implications already present in Spencer's work by avoiding his gestures at a potential stateless future.

Spencer and Nagao's perfect world was one where every action aligned precisely with their rules. For Spencer,

> the ultimate man will be one whose private requirements coincide with public ones. He will be that manner of man, who, in spontaneously fulfilling his own nature, incidentally performs the functions of a social unit; and yet is only enabled so to fulfill his own nature, by all others doing the like.

Thus, "in the ultimate man perfect morality, perfect individuation, and perfect life will be simultaneously realized."[101] Liberals, believing Spencer's claims about liberty, thought Spencerism meant collective authority would yield to individual freedom. Japanese conservatives recognized that Spencer's constant insistence on obedience to political and natural law was more significant in his thought than his hypothesis that the state must eventually vanish. Spencer's proposals would in fact force individual freedom to yield to collective authority.

The thoughts and feelings of the perfect man would perfectly align with competitive evolution: he would obey Spencer's laws because he was incapable of doing anything else. With his emphasis on individual liberty and hostility to organized intention, Spencer alone might seem an odd choice as a theorist of control. But his ideas proved the perfect justification for coercion by economic power, which required constant defense from the masses anyway—defense Spencer vigorously supported. Influential in its own right and indicative of trends that would develop beyond his own influence, Spencer's thought captures a curious combination of ambition (seeking to understand all humanity) and apathy (primarily using that understanding to justify the status quo) that would come to characterize right-wing economic thought.

Japanese industrialization proves that individualist laissez-faire competition is not the most effective economic strategy even within a capitalist market order. In the pursuit of control science's goals, the Meiji state actually disproved its claims about the economy. Government officials hoping to industrialize Japan did not intend to direct economic development themselves. Why would they, when the European theories they were reading proposed anything but that? They tried to involve themselves in business indirectly at first, but the resulting state attempts to aid private investors through "technical assistance, subsidies, and easy credit," writes Thomas C. Smith, "proved almost entirely ineffective."[102]

This was enough to mechanize silk reeling, but elsewhere the government had to go further and lead outright. Japan did not have a private railway until 1881, and then only because, laissez-faire be damned, the government offered investors exemption from taxes on their land, guaranteed investment returns for years, and in fact *built the railway itself* with government engineers. The state covered the long and difficult terrain of Japan in telegraph lines—carrying more than a million messages per year as early as 1877—while legally prohibiting private ownership of primary lines for security reasons. It invested resources, persuaded (and coerced) the populace, and (through direct state operations as well as subsidization of private ones) created successful mechanized textile industries within a generation.[103]

This was a victory over colonial ambitions but not capitalism. The rapid industrialization of Japan likely saved the country from greater poverty and oppression. But it was also a race to exploit Japanese workers fast enough and well enough that foreign capitalists could not swoop in. The Japanese state went against capitalist orthodoxy to become a contender in capitalism, but become a contender it did, in both capitalism and colonialism. Japan later adopted the Champion of the East's imperialist approach, with grave consequences for all of East Asia. Competing more effectively than the competition was not, on its own, a defeat of competitive evolution as a political and economic paradigm. Only democratic efforts by workers themselves could truly challenge labor control.

"Let's Wrench the Balls of the Hateful Men!"

Japanese history reveals the truth about Spencerism. Herbert Spencer presented his ideology as an objectively true answer to questions of social progress—wisdom that was the only path to prosperity and freedom. In fact, Spencerism was a path to economic ruin and political tyranny. Japanese officials could not take Spencer's economic advice—the state was dragged into the market by the sheer inadequacy of private actors—and those who took his political advice made Japan a more repressive and hierarchical nation.

Mori Arinori, an Iwakura Mission diplomat and later cabinet minister, was one of Spencer's closest collaborators in Japan.[104] In 1873, Mori asked Spencer about political reforms in Japan, which was moving toward adopting a constitution. Spencer unsurprisingly gave what he called "conservative advice," insisting to Mori that the people of Japan "would have eventually to return to a form [of government] not much in advance of what they had" before recent reforms.[105] In part taking his advice, Mori criticized giving parliament any meaningful power. The Meiji Constitution did not go as far as he wanted, but it was "relatively undemocratic," with ruinous results for Japan in the long term.[106]

Even this was not enough for Spencer. In an 1892 letter to Japanese official Kaneko Kentarō, Spencer disparaged Japan's constitution and claimed that Japan was already "experiencing the evils arising from too large an instalment of freedom." He proposed a repressive path to this starting with reliance on the power of "patriarchal organization" with its "despotic power": if only male heads of household could vote, the "electorate would be greatly reduced in number, and therefore more manageable."[107]

In both Japan and Britain, common people fought back against competitive evolution with collective action. Political organizing helped gradually extend Britain's franchise beyond the limits of the 1832 Great Reform Act, to urban artisans in

1867 and finally to a majority of adult men in 1884. British workers won the proper legalization of trade union activity in 1871. In Japan, Nakae Chōmin battled both government censorship and his own alcoholism to argue for representative government in the 1880s. In 1890, during Japan's first national election, Osaka's fourth district selected him for a seat in the Diet.

Workers bitterly resisted Spencerian evolution in the factory. One Japanese factory workers' song announced that "factory work is prison work / all it lacks are iron chains" and expressed a wish that the boardinghouses would wash away, the factory would burn to the ground, and the gatekeeper would die of cholera. The narrator wished for "wings to escape from here."[108] Songs denouncing the "demon overseer" and the "devil accountant" used the language of the malignant supernatural—one runaway sang that the "hateful company" was run by "fiends and demons.[109] Another song invoked the example of a factory worker named Iwataru Kiku, who became a folk hero for stopping what we would now call a serial killer in August 1907. Assaulted by the man while returning from shopping, she yanked on his testicles and fled, then identified him to the police, who were able to capture him before he could strike again. A factory workers' song written about her made her a hero against patriarchal workplace violence as well, exclaiming

> Iwataru Kiku is a shining
> Model of a factory girl
> Let's wrench the balls of the hateful men!
> Mr. Overseer, Mr. Supervisor,
> You'd better watch out!
> There is the example
> Of Iwataru Kiku
> Who dares to say that
> Factory girls are weak?
> Factory girls are
> The only ones who create wealth[110]

Once again: labor was the source of all value, and workers knew it.

This kind of political consciousness served as the basis for collective action. In 1889, workers at the Tenma Cotton-Spinning Company of Osaka went on strike, beginning with a dining hall sit-in and spiraling into a broad work stoppage, with demands including higher wages so that workers could afford food.[111] On October 4, the company asked for reinforcements in the form of police—an 1882 law not dissimilar to Britain's earlier Combination Acts (which Wilberforce had advocated) prohibited strikes. The "free market" was thus maintained against starving workers by state brutality. Despite arrests, the strikers ultimately forced a raise out of their employer. In the long term, a shift back to dormitory living gave employers tight social control, temporarily tamping down strikes. But even this did not work forever: in the 1910s, many Tokyo workers joined the the Yuaikai, or Friendly Society, a union organization.[112]

Japanese worker disputes were driven by more than hunger and individual need. The Tenma strikers focused on arbitrary treatment by bosses as well as wage issues, and its participants denounced the company for refusing to "hear of a wage hike" while "paying out loans on our future earnings."[113] Workers at Tokyo Muslin in 1914 took action after over a thousand of their coworkers were laid off, and the remainder had a 40 to 50 percent pay cut. Their most significant grievance, however, was not their own pay but that of executives: workers were furious that executives and shareholders continued to reap bonuses and dividends during a recession.[114] Ultimately their action was unsuccessful, but workers continued to pursue visions of a fairer economy in Japan and across the world.

Even Herbert Spencer's protégée Beatrice Webb joined them. He was her "closest friend and teacher," yet she could not help but recognize his close-mindedness, and in the 1880s she charted a course leftward. Webb (then Potter; she did not marry Sidney Webb until 1892) read Marx, wondered how Adam Smith's political economy had become "the Employers' Gospel," and inquired into the real conditions of working people.[115] When Spencer pushed back on her criticism of political economy using the theories of political economist David Ricardo, Webb mused in her diary, "as I understand Ricardo's economics, he does not attempt to discover, he merely assumes."[116] She wanted to actually understand the world, not cherry-pick facts like her teacher did.

This honest, empiricist curiosity was a threat to labor control. Asking workers about their lives and examining actual economic conditions was the road to economic democracy, and Webb became an influential advocate of unions and socialism. Even political economists, now beginning to call themselves simply economists, were increasingly turning away from dogma and toward serious social scientific inquiry. Their answers ranged from technocratic regulation to radical egalitarian change. If people could come together and understand the world, they could remake it through collective intention rather than individual adaptation. Herbert Spencer had pretended his philosophy was an inescapable description of reality. In order to remain in power, capitalists would need their science of control to pass as a real science.

6

"In the Past the Man Has Been First; in the Future the System Must Be First": Scientific Management and "Free Enterprise," 1880–1945

Late nineteenth-century American machine shop foreman Frederick Winslow Taylor had a problem: his friends didn't like him. Rather like Samuel Bentham a century earlier, he began his career in a facility defined by working-class solidarity but did not himself come from the working class. Workers in Taylor's shop at Midvale Steel Company collaborated to determine exactly how fast labor in the shop would be. Opposing the market imperative to work faster and faster required workers to cooperate—and supervisors to know their place. When Taylor worked his way up to the low-level supervisory position of "gang-boss," his coworkers, whom he described as his "personal friends," immediately reminded him of his expected role and warned him against exceeding their agreed-upon productivity rates. He responded that he was "now working on the side of the management" and would do "whatever he could to get a fair day's work" out of the machines, and by extension out of their workers.[1]

This began what Taylor called a "war." He wielded every weapon of management against his former friends, from firing workers and reducing their wages to personally teaching new recruits. Workers resisted him with false reports of incompetence, machine sabotage, and especially social pressure—something that worked on new recruits but not on Taylor himself. He wasn't one of them, he had not "lived where they lived," and he was "not of working parents."[2] During his conflict with workers, he found time to win the 1881 US National Championships in tennis as one half of a doubles team—the other was banking heir and future streetcar magnate Clarence Clark, who was also Taylor's brother-in-law. One of their opponents in the finals was Alexander van Renssellaer, whose family fortune went back to seventeenth-century America.[3]

After around three years of conflict with workers, Taylor had succeeded in dramatically increasing productivity and was rewarded with a promotion to foreman of the shop. But this was "in no sense a recompense for the bitter relations" his management activities brought him. When his "workman friends" came to speak with him, he conceded that if he "were in their place," he too would fight to keep productivity down. Ultimately he became determined to "in some way change the system of management, so that the interests of the workmen and the management should be the same, instead of antagonistic."[4]

Taylor set about this task using scientific knowledge, which he felt distinguished him from the craft mindset of the working class. He earned a degree in mechanical engineering through a correspondence course in 1883 and devised a number of new technical and managerial techniques at Midvale in subsequent years. In 1890, he moved on to a paper manufacturer and eventually to independent consulting. A broader theory of management began to come together: like Samuel Bentham, Taylor combined social engineering, technical innovations, and improved accounting practices. Possibly as early as the 1880s, Taylor engaged in "time studies," quantifying tasks with a watch in order to optimize them.[5] When Bethlehem Steel Company became a Taylor client in 1899, it offered special opportunities for testing Taylor's theories, According to Taylor, Bethlehem was in a stronger financial position than previous clients and more open to change. With the help of James Gillespie, who had previously worked with Taylor, and Hartley C. Wolle, a Bethlehem supervisor, he embarked on an important study that later became a famous anecdote in his *Principles of Scientific Management*.[6]

On March 13, 1899, Gillespie and Wolle tasked ten men who they felt were particularly fast workers with moving pig iron as fast as they could. Multiplied across a day, their rate would have been over seventy five tons per day per man. Gillespie and Wolle recognized this pace was unsustainable, though, and so cut it by 40 percent to allow for rest.[7] This was an arbitrary cut, the kind of "rule of thumb" method Taylor loathed—why not 60 percent, or 55? However, his own attempts to calculate a scientific law of human exhaustion were similarly dubious.[8] The utility of science in Taylorism was its rhetorical power rather than methodological rigor: it legitimized managerial tyranny as objectively necessary and ultimately mutually beneficial.

Science also justified Taylor's project of centralizing all decision and thought about work. Under what he called the "task idea," the worker has specified for them "not only what is to be done but how it is to be done and the exact time allowed for doing it."[9] As much as possible, workers were meant to be mere appendages of decision-making managers, components of capital's machinery. The goal was not new, and Taylor's methods were not all that effective in achieving it. The calculations and conclusions of his time studies were remarkably haphazard, and it appears that his organization of physical space and his accounting practices made a far greater material difference for his clients than his worker control schemes did.[10] But Taylor's impact was ideological and political as much as practical. His poorly controlled experiments and confused averages epistemologically distinguished enlightened and rational managers from their subordinates, legitimizing class distinctions.

Whether his methods were properly conducted science is immaterial. What mattered was that Frederick Winslow Taylor could present a convincing and convenient figure for management—approximately 45 tons per man day—and workers could not.[11] Once Taylor and his assistant arrived at this figure, they set about making it a reality. This was no easy task: it was four times what workers were then averaging. The obvious move was to shift workers from day work—pay by day—to piecework, or pay by ton loaded. By setting the rate carefully, they could entice workers to do several times as much work for more pay per time but proportionally less per ton. This was the kind of win-win Taylor felt made his program appealing to workers: in theory, everyone was better off.

In practice, as Taylor himself had written in an 1895 article, piecework schemes were frequently opposed by workers, since the employer could lower the piece rate over time, eventually leaving workers with the same pay they had started with for significantly greater effort.[12] The market race to the bottom encouraged this—why would any employer ever pay more than they had to, especially as increases in output across an industry would naturally lower the price of the goods any company sold? Taylor's article urged employers not to lower rates, appealing to vague principles of justice and insisting that "MEN WILL NOT DO AN EXTRAORDINARY DAY'S WORK FOR AN ORDINARY DAY'S PAY."[13] But ordinary and extraordinary are relative terms. Bosses taking Taylor's advice could interpret these conditions flexibly or simply ignore them. Moreover, Taylor himself clearly defined a "fair day's work" as the maximum amount a worker could perform without long-term physical harm.[14] At best, Taylor's scheme left workers working as hard as they could without injuring themselves; at worst, because it deliberately excluded workers from having any power over the process, it allowed managers to work them even harder.

Naturally, workers resisted: the Hungarian workers that Gillespie and Wolle originally studied immediately figured out what was afoot when they were asked to work by piece on March 16. They refused to work by piece, forcing their foreman, John Haack, to allow them to work by day. Taylor's assistants returned the next day with orders to fire anyone who would not accept the new terms. Once they were fired, Haack's former gang pressured other loaders not to comply, presumably using similar tactics to what Taylor had seen at Midvale. Ultimately Gillespie and Wolle had to rely on seven workers, all of whom were either Pennsylvania Dutch or Irish, meaning they had fewer social ties to Haack's work gang. They assented to work by piece beginning on March 30. Only five of the seven actually showed up, however, and the day after that only three of them did. Only *one* of these was found suitable (and willing) to continue, and though Taylor's team found other workers, he became "the only one who continued with us from the start and at times constituted our whole piecework gang. He worked to his maximum from the beginning and by this means demonstrated that a good day's wages could be made at the existing rates by a good man."[15] His name was Henry Noll.

A warped version of his story became the central example of "scientific management" in Taylor's 1911 *Principles*, in which Taylor recounted his hiring and used Noll as an example of the kind of worker his system could produce. Taylor pitched scientific management as a solution to what was then called the "labor problem"—laborer resistance to management discipline. Scientific management, Taylor claimed, would result in "the elimination of almost all causes for dispute and disagreement" between workers and employers. "What constitutes a fair day's work will be a question for scientific investigation, instead of a subject to be bargained and haggled over."[16]

In practice, worker management was—in the words of historian Daniel Nelson—the "least well-developed" part of Taylor's program, which included the kind of technical innovations that had made him wealthy, as well as the reorganization of work facilities and improved accounting.[17] Making workers into machines was an ambition more than a reality. But labor control was scientific management's best selling point because it was the hardest problem facing any boss. Taylor consistently emphasized the harmony that his system supposedly produced: in *Principles*, he told readers that "there has never been a single strike among the men working under this system."[18]

This was immensely appealing to many, given events at the time. Labor-capital conflict in the United States continued to be bitter and violent during this period. When California manufacturers wielded police and newspapers against ironworkers, they responded with dynamite, including an October 1, 1910, bombing of the *Los Angeles Times* building. The resulting explosion killed twenty-one people and prompted President Taft to propose, and Congress to approve, the creation of a federal commission to inquire into labor–management relations, since they were poor enough that buildings were exploding. In this era of growing labor radicalism and open conflict with capital, Taylor promised docile and happy workers alongside high profits.

He presented pig iron loader Henry Noll, whom he referred to as "Schmidt," as the "first illustration" of his practice in *Principles*. Pig iron loading was not a central part of his practical efforts—this was why he had offloaded much of it to assistants. But politically it offered the ideal example for his purposes. *Principles* includes a dialogue with "Schmidt" that, while entirely fictional, is emblematic of the system, worldview, and political program that "scientific management" represented. It begins with Schmidt being taken aside and asked: "Schmidt, are you a high-priced man?"

"Schmidt" responds in a caricatured accent, and with errors in tense, perhaps to emphasize Taylor's opinion that "he was a man so stupid that he was unfitted to do most kinds of labor work, even."[19] It takes Schmidt a few repetitions to answer the question, and he only begins to do so after an agitated fictional Taylor impatiently explains that a high-priced man receives higher wages. When Schmidt expresses interest, Taylor clarifies in warning:

> A high-priced man has to do exactly as he's told from morning till night . . . if you are a high-priced man, you will do exactly as this man tells you to-morrow, from morning till night . . . Do you understand that? When this man tells you to walk, you walk; when he tells you to sit down, you sit down, and you don't talk back at him. Now you come on to work here to-morrow morning and I'll know before night whether you are really a high-priced man or not.

The real-life Henry Noll was a human being, with hopes and dreams, friends and family. He worked as a volunteer firefighter and may have spent Sundays building his own house.[20] In Taylor's narrative he becomes "Schmidt," a confused and obedient "man of the type of the ox" doing a job an "intelligent gorilla" could do better.[21] This is not just the purpose of Taylor's *story* but also his *method*: what Taylor promised bosses was a world of Schmidts. He infantilized workers, claiming that they could not even properly choose for themselves how long to rest for. Noll's wages did improve, but no doubt so too did his exhaustion—perhaps not coincidentally, he lost both his house and his job a few years later due to alcoholism.[22]

Principles of Scientific Management's success illustrates the utility, and the power, of the *appearance* of empiricism. At best, empirical work in economics or management consulting could identify and address social problems rather than merely justify boss power. But at worst, the empiricism of the growing "efficiency" movement in this period was a sham. Taylorism had the air of science but with few of its qualities. But because it appeared to address complicated problems, scientific management took off. Soon, not only was business a subject for scientific management, in the eyes of progressive elites, but so were schools and even churches and, naturally, cities and nations.[23] Efficiency experts fanned out from academia and the emerging world of think tanks to advise and administer government.[24]

Efficiency's role in politics grew further with the election of former political economy professor Woodrow Wilson to the presidency in 1912. The rhetoric of scientific efficiency and "free market" competition allowed him to *sound* like someone who would pursue change . . . while keeping that change within tightly confined boundaries. As Wilson put it in a 1912 campaign speech, "the whole business of politics is to bring classes together upon a platform of accommodation and common interest."[25] Class conflict could be overcome by compromise. But it could not be ignored. In Wilson's first term, Taft's previously approved Commission on Industrial Relations began its work.

"The Code of Laws Is Above All People"

At ten in the morning on April 13, 1914, Frederick Taylor sat down as a witness before the Commission on Industrial Relations. They were investigating whether scientific management and other "efficiency systems" improved or worsened labor-management relations. By this point Taylor was a wealthy man who could have done whatever he liked, but he chose to continue pursuing his political vision because he believed in it. He claimed to the committee that "as many as a thousand or two thousand men annually come under the principles of scientific management" and "become the best friends that their employers can have. That is to say, instead of being enemies of their employers, they become warm, firm, friends."[26] This was a lie: committee investigators later determined, contrary to Taylor's direct claims otherwise, that several workplaces under scientific management had seen strikes.[27]

After lengthy introductory testimony, Commissioner Harris Weinstock opened with a simple question: "Under this system of scientific management does the worker have a voice in determining the premium he is to receive?" The straightforward answer came first: no, "the worker had no voice in that."[28] Taylor followed this straight answer with a lengthy defense, which included an insistence that his system was not like slavery.[29] Repeatedly, commission members and staff asked or pointed out the ways scientific management disempowered and harmed workers, and Taylor vigorously denied these. When Commissioner O'Connell claimed certain workers under Taylor's system had gone on strike, Taylor quibbled that they were not *truly* under his system, due to failed or incomplete implementation. O'Connell shot back by paraphrasing Taylor on the purpose of business, pushing Taylor to offer the full quote himself: "All employees should bear in mind that each shop exists first, last, and all the time, for the purpose of paying dividends to its owners."[30] He raged against being quoted out of context. The core of his system, Taylor insisted, was mutual benefit.

Workers had no power over the system because they did not *need* a say: scientific management was for their own good.

After the commission returned from lunch, its legal counsel, William O. Thompson, launched into a series of questions about power. He began by asking Taylor how his system calculated and divided work. His answers relied on abstract scientific authority: from their time studies his "investigators" produced "time laws," or average expected work rates. *Who* determined these laws became the focus of subsequent questions by Thompson: "Who hires the investigator?" "Who pays the investigator?" "Who installs the use of your system in the factory?" "If the owner should decide that he did not want your system, it would not be put in"? Taylor squirmed and attempted to evade each question, answering the latter with "I do not know how you can in any way make a man do what he doesn't want to do," which prompted another rebuke from the chair. With repeated browbeating, Taylor was finally forced into short and straightforward answers, and Thompson went in for the rhetorical knockout.

The implication Thompson was attempting to force out of Taylor was this: whether it was mutually beneficial or not, scientific management was autocratic. It gave new powers to bosses and none to workers. It was the boss, Thompson asked, who would select the system his operation followed, correct? "Yes, perhaps," Taylor conceded. And the boss would decide whose advice would be considered on the system? "Yes," Taylor admitted. Could the worker choose the investigator behind this "code of laws?" "No," Taylor replied. "That is all I want now," stated a satisfied Thompson, who then asked: if the worker and the shop owner disagreed over the time studies Taylor's laws were based on, it was the employer-hired investigator who would decide the matter, was it not? Taylor again gave him the runaround, claiming that his team would listen to workers' objections. This led to the following exchange:

> Mr. THOMPSON: But you finally decide whether the workman's objection is well-taken to your ruling, do you not?

Mr. TAYLOR: I do not. This code of laws decides it—this code of laws that has been proved to be right decides it.

Mr. THOMPSON: A code of laws is an inanimate thing and cannot decide anything.

Mr. TAYLOR: There is nothing in the world more powerful than a code of laws. The whole United States is run by a code of laws. This code of laws that has been developed determines, and we ask these men to go to these various shops and see whether it is right. That is our answer. The code of laws is above all people. That is what I want to impress.

Mr. THOMPSON: But the workman does not recognize that code of laws framed by Mr. Taylor and his associates in several shops as ruling human action.

Mr. TAYLOR: It is not framed by us.

Taylor believed there was an objectively correct productivity level that could be ascertained as certainly as gravity. Discovered laws, rather than designed policies, were at work. "These laws are not laid down by me," he insisted, but rather had been produced by "gradual evolution." In line with control science's long-standing naturalization of capitalist hierarchy, and its war on intention itself, this reasoning made employers' and consultants' responsibility to their workers irrelevant. Taylor felt that efficiency could replace goodness.[31]

Thompson, in contrast, kept attention on the human beings behind and beneath scientific management—human beings who had a proper representative sitting in the hall during Taylor's testimony as well: John F. Tobin, Boston-based president of the Boot and Shoe Workers' Union, who sat through Taylor's questioning before testifying himself later in the day.

He probably won over some in the room with a joke early in his questioning. Asked whether he was familiar with "efficiency systems" like Taylor's, he responded to the tired commissioners, who had already sniped at Taylor for being long-winded: "I have tried to study the efficiency systems, but I find the lack of efficiency in presenting them to be an obstacle to understanding them." What Tobin *did* understand was employer self-interest, and he used it to flip Taylor's arguments on their head. In Tobin's view, it was "the employer [who] is the greatest obstacle to the introduction of a rational efficiency system," by refusing to consider workers' interests and rights. Commissioner Delano responded that this ran against Taylor's own stated "principles." Tobin riposted that employer exploitation was "contrary to what Mr. Taylor *claims* for the principles": in practice, employers would resist any effort to respect workers' needs.[32] The commission's final report agreed with him—it found that there was "no reasonable basis" for a wide variety of claims about scientific management's respect for worker health.[33]

Capitalists would have to be compelled to respect workers. Through laborer power, John Tobin offered an alternate path to the "common ground" Delano and the committee were seeking: collective bargaining. Tobin resisted the dehumanizing quantification of control science, stating in an example dialogue with an employer: "the workman has just as much right to decide what he is worth as you have."[34] These were the competing views the commission had to deal with: top-down quantification versus bottom-up negotiation. Tobin's argument was difficult to deny: scientific management was hardly solving the problem of industrial unrest and was probably exacerbating it. When the commission finally concluded, it was unable to come to a consensus on how to achieve labor-management harmony—but the negotiations Tobin proposed saw broad agreement. Scientific management's calculations and accounting, the commissioners broadly agreed, might have some place in the factory. But its political vision did not. Workers needed a voice. The commissioners differed on how this should work, splitting into three broad camps with some overlap and intersection particular issues.

First, Frank Walsh and a number of other commissioners supported Manly's 141-page report, which exhaustively documented inequality and injustice. The Manly report was a landmark call for "industrial democracy." Highlights included proposals for social housing and utility nationalization, a call for legislation mandating equal pay for women (and for state action on their behalf before then), praise for unions for improving the lives of their members, and criticism of union-busting employers' associations as "not only antisocial but even perhaps illegal."[35] Second, in a report of their own, the pro-business commissioners whined that all of this was unfair. Finally, a third report authored by John Commons and wealthy suffrage activist Florence Harriman argued—correctly—that Manly's group wanted unions to be engaged in mass politics rather than just workplace negotiations.[36] Commons and Harriman disapproved. They instead proposed empowering mediating labor boards rather than unions.

This third report evolved out of the "institutionalist" school of economics then dominant in the profession in America. Commons's mentor Richard T. Ely, one of the founding figures of economics as a professional discipline in the US, was originally trained in the German tradition of historical thinking. He and his students, including John Commons, Edward Ross, and President Woodrow Wilson, believed deeply in competition, often in decidedly Spencerian terms. But unlike Spencer, they believed that competition had to be managed and that empirical science could help us understand how to do so. This empiricism made it possible for them to promote relatively proworker policies—like those in Commons and Harriman's report—despite their class status and faith in existing hierarchies. John Commons was a racist technocrat skeptical of working-class power, but his willingness to engage with economic reality made it possible for him to do better than market dogma or narrow class interest.

What was clear to everyone from what came to be known as the Walsh Commission's discussions was this: for all its luster in the eyes of managers and intellectuals, Taylorism did not appeal to workers or the working masses. Regarding such disapproving workers, Taylor's associate Carl Barth huffed during his own testimony before the commission, "It is a false idea among the public, that every man has a right to his opinion. I believe there are very few men who have a right to their opinion."[37] But in America's democracy, those masses mattered.

"You'll Go to Hell When You Die"

Alfred Pritchard Sloan's life is a quintessentially American rags-to-riches story, which is to say that it's a riches-to-more-riches story. After young Alfred graduated from MIT into the 1893 recession's poor job market, he only found a job—at Hyatt Roller Bearing Company—when his father connected him to its owner. Sloan then got his start there thanks to a sales deal to his father's company. He secured his job when the company was struggling by having his father purchase it.[38] From there he rose through a combination of skill, ruthlessness, and mergers to become president in 1923 and, later, chairman of General Motors Corporation.

Sloan developed his own version of scientific management that applied in the boardroom as well as on the shop floor.[39] Like practitioners of control science before him, Frederick Taylor had sought to eliminate workers' intentions from the factory. Alfred Sloan's plan had the effect of minimizing *executives'* intentions as well. At GM he had to contend with strong-willed individuals with their own priorities, including research head Charles Kettering. In the early 1920s, Kettering became enamored with an idea for a cutting-edge air-cooled engine. He believed in it and convinced then-President Pierre du Pont to pursue it, in the hope it would deliver profits—but also because he cared about the invention itself. Kettering pursued his dream engine independent of profits and continued to advocate for it even as it became increasingly obvious that it was not possible.[40]

Similarly, Henry Ford had personally designed his cars with all the experimentation and drama turn-of-the-century invention entailed. The Model T was his baby, and this was reflected in his business strategy: gradually optimizing this single ideal consumer model and building it in vast numbers. Ford sought to personally design his workforce as well, around his vision of a well-behaved man. Like Kettering's engine, Ford's behavioral regulations and single-car vision were intended to produce profit, but they were also clearly motivated by other concerns, from aesthetics to bigotry. Ford and Kettering both certainly convinced themselves that their personal visions were profitable ones. But that doesn't mean that they were. When conflicts between their manufacturing ideals and market demands arose, both frequently chose the former and had to be pushed hard to abandon their visions—it took years for Ford to embrace multiple models and annual updates.[41]

Alfred Sloan, in contrast, understood capitalism properly: cars were a commodity, a form of value, a thing to be sold. Nothing else mattered. As he would later put it, GM was an organization meant to "make money, not just to make motor cars."[42] In a hearing before Congress on early New Deal work legislation, California Congressman Richard Welch asked Sloan when his rapidly growing car empire would reach saturation. Surely eventually America would have enough cars. What then? Welch asked if Sloan "would have an automobile for every person in the United States." The executive joked that every American could have two. The car was a unit of value, nothing more.[43]

Sloan pursued his market philosophy with a highly influential theory of management. He proposed a decentralized corporate structure consisting of semi-autonomous units under a powerful central authority. These units competed with each other, while central management kept that competition within useful limits and set corporation-wide goals. Donaldson Brown, a key collaborator of Sloan's and an architect of this management system, urged the company to consider "return on investment" (ROI) in all its activities—now a standard matter of cost accounting. The contributions that different products and units made to company profit could be calculated and compared to make quantitative, profit-centered investment decisions. GM even tied executive bonuses to ROI.

The company still had to make decisions, but Brown and company had a clever solution to limit how meaningful executives' intentions could be. Instead of making decisions based on what individual executives believed was or should be best, GM would forecast the *future* market so that it could make decisions for them. By gathering sales data from dealers, for example, GM's central administrators could make forward-looking projections and ascertain what the market wanted next year. The future market, not executives' love for an engine or monomaniacal focus on the perfect car or anti-immigrant conception of clean-cut laborers, would determine business goals. Interdivision competition and cost accounting then ensured that GM's executives pursued them. This strategy worked, overcoming Henry Ford's beloved Model T with branding and marketing.[44]

GM administrators would not be *leaders* but *executives*, ascertaining and carrying out the will of the market. This enabled and justified staggering harms—for example, decisions surrounding the GM-developed gasoline additive tetraethyl lead. TEL was a godsend for GM, promising improved performance and reduced engine wear. For the workers who produced it, and subsequent generations of Americans who unknowingly consumed it, TEL was a nightmare. In 1924, these workers began to lose their minds and then their lives as lead fumes misdirected the enzymes in their bodies. An executive with even the vaguest sense of ethics might have tried to do something. Not Sloan.

Not everyone believed in these cold, brutal business calculations. In 1929, the stock market crashed. This was a direct threat to GM's business model: who had the money to buy a car in a depression? GM rapidly adapted with cost-cutting and a new emphasis on cheap models. But market adaptation was not going to be enough. In response to the Great Depression, Americans began to rethink the structure of their country's economy. Franklin Delano Roosevelt crushed President Hoover in the 1932 presidential election. His administration began with technocratic corporatism then turned toward the prolabor policies it has become known for, in part thanks to a series of strikes in 1934.

In response, Alfred Sloan began to mobilize against the government.[45] Also in 1934, Sloan became fundraising chairman of the National Association of Manufacturers. Earlier in the century, NAM had focused its efforts on union-busting, and during this time it began strategizing to manipulate public opinion. Sloan applied his considerable marketing talents to that end as head of the NAM-associated National Industrial Information Council, which semi-covertly flooded the nation's information environment with corporate propaganda. This ranged from billboards insisting "What's Good for Industry Is Good for You" to an afternoon radio drama—*American Family Robinson*—that staged private enterprise's conflict with the New Deal through a small-town conflict in the fictional town of Centerville. It is difficult to measure the extent of the NIIC's concrete impact, but its well-funded efforts reached millions of American voters.[46]

Alfred Sloan also tried to leverage racism against the New Deal. He was a founding participant in the American Liberty League, founded by the du Pont family, which had close ties to General Motors. Sloan, the du Ponts, and other business elites schemed to create an electoral organ that could end Roosevelt's presidency in the 1936 election. The result was the Liberty League, which despite its origins presented itself as, and aimed to be, a cross-class alliance of everyday Americans against supposed government overreach. The Liberty League, and Sloan personally, also offered financial support to the Sentinels of the Republic, which criticized Roosevelt's program as the "Jew Deal." Irénée du Pont proposed collaborating with the Ku Klux Klan.[47]

Despite spending on par with the Democratic Party itself, and even with the potential force of white supremacy behind it, the Liberty League's synthetic cross-class alliance of, as the *Washington Post* put it approvingly, "laborers and farmers, stockholders and bondholders" was less compelling than Roosevelt's message.[48] Ultimately, the Liberty League blew up in Sloan's face. Roosevelt decided to embrace left-populist appeals against "economic royalists."[49] And this wasn't just rhetoric either. What historians often call the "Second New Deal" of his sophomore term was properly left-wing in a way Roosevelt's first term had not been.[50] Class solidarity and human need prevailed over astroturfed fascism.

Roosevelt's leftward turn served him well, and he squashed his Republican competitor in the November 1936 election. A month after his re-election, General Motors workers used the air cover the left-leaning president provided to push a ground assault against capital: they went on strike to demand that GM recognize and bargain with the United Auto Workers (UAW) union. Their legendary sit-down strikes involved physically occupying plants themselves and refusing to work. "[Workers had] seized our properties," Sloan later huffed.[51] He personally intervened with a bitter five-page letter tacked up at all GM factories.

Unconvinced, workers inside his occupied plants sang tunes mocking him. "Old Sloan is feeling blue," went one. Another was set to the vaudeville introduction tune of famous performers Ed Gallagher and Al Shean. Both of their vaudeville personas were buffoonish and ridiculous, and the autoworkers' song loosely cast Sloan as Shean's character, a bumbling incompetent who can't tell the difference between golf and tennis; if it helps for illustration, Shean the performer was the uncle of the Marx Brothers. FDR privately considered Sloan a "low comedy figure," and his striking employees rendered him similarly in their song:[52]

> Oh Mr. Sloan! Oh Mr. Sloan!
> We have known for a long time you would atone
> For the wrongs that you have done
> We all know yes, everyone!
> Absolutely Mr. Travis! [strike organizer Bob Travis]
> Positively Mr. Sloan!
>
> Oh Mr. Sloan! Oh Mr. Sloan!
> Everyone knows your heart was made of stone
> But the Union is so strong

That we'll always carry on
Absolutely Mr. Travis!
Positively Mr. Sloan![53]

Sloan would be forced to give up, but he never did "atone."

The strike reduced Sloan to impotent rage. In an in-person meeting with Secretary of Labor Frances Perkins, Sloan promised to begin negotiating with workers. He called later that night, interrupting dinner with her twenty-one-year-old daughter Susannah and a family friend, to inform her he had changed his mind. The usually reserved, devoutly religious Perkins told him he was a "scoundrel and a skunk" who had "betrayed the men" who worked for him, asked him if he was a "grown man" or a "neurotic adolescent," and warned him, "You'll go to hell when you die if you do things like that."[54]

Sloan went ballistic, screaming, "You can't talk like that to me! You can't talk like that to me! I've got 70 million dollars and I made it all myself! You can't talk like that to me! I'm Alfred Sloan!" He apparently repeated these remarks something like twenty times and then again when he called a friend to vent.[55] The tantrum made it into the newspapers, where Sloan was savaged and mocked. With prolabor Democrats in charge of both the Michigan Governor's Mansion and the White House, even the court injunction that Sloan obtained against the autoworkers was worthless. GM surrendered in February 1937. The company would have to deal with its workers as people, not machines.

In an oral history interview after the fact, Perkins surmised that Alfred Sloan "had never used his mind for the purposes of thinking out a moral problem, a philosophical problem, any problem whatsoever, except a problem having to do with the making and selling of goods." Perkins had "the greatest respect" for the actual minds behind GM's automobiles. She felt Charles Kettering was "tremendously creative." His fellow GM executive William Knudsen, who had a strong manufacturing background, "could build an automobile by hand." "A true manufacturer," she explained, "can make things." Sloan was "not a manufacturer. He was a salesman." He "knew nothing" of manufacturing. *His* inventions were sales tricks, like expanded buying on credit, and a sales model that left dealers "holding the bag."[56]

So when workers went on strike, he was afraid. Human reality had punctured market fantasy. Suddenly he had to think of actual automobiles, of the people who made them, of what was right and what was wrong. "He couldn't really cope with the problems that were before him." He was

> frightened of the world he doesn't understand, of the intricacies of human thought that are not possible to him, because he doesn't have the kind of mind that can think in terms of what's right and wrong, what's good and bad, what's democratic and undemocratic. He had never thought in those terms, and had never been challenged or asked to do so before.

Now he had been forced to think that way, and he had lost. Some people in his place might have had a crisis of conscience or at least for PR reasons felt it necessary to do something unobjectionably good with their money. Alfred Sloan did have a charity—the Sloan Foundation—and he did chart a new course for it after the sit-down strike. But that course was not a new effort at doing good. Sloan directed his charity to begin an indoctrination effort. If he had his way, workers would not be able to make him think about right and wrong, democratic and undemocratic, good and bad ever again. He plotted to change how the public thought—how the public *could* think—about economics.[57]

"Ask the Right Questions"

In the Roosevelt era, American economics was a changing field with multiple traditions and methods. This meant it could be quite critical of capitalists and even capitalism. In his notes, early 1930s Chicago economics student F. Taylor Ostrander recorded economic historian John Ulrich Nef teaching that "the important thing for the economic historian is that he ask the right questions."[58] Sometimes asking the right questions meant answers that could be quite hostile to the economic status quo. Notes from Ostrander's class with Chester Wright, and probably in this case paraphrasing his lectures, describe the modern corporation as "the greatest get-rich-quick devise [sic] ever created—for getting rich at the expense of other people."[59]

The dominant tendency in economics during this period was the "institutionalist" school of scholars like John Commons. Ely's students and the broader historical and empirical approach to economics had won out over classical political economy. Reform-minded but often technocratic, institutionalism used empirical methods to investigate and prescribe solutions to social problems, often including government action. The interdisciplinary and hands-on nature of institutionalist economics limited how much market dogma could dominate, enabling a variety of approaches and political leanings. Economists from the left to the center argued that it was possible to optimize the economy through deliberate government action—and under FDR, America was increasingly doing just that. Outlining FDR's expansion of government power, Wright speculated (in Ostrander's summary), "[It is] unlikely that we will ever go back to extremes of individualism."[60]

Economics had room for people and ideas across the political spectrum and class hierarchy. Ostrander was the son of a logistics executive. His classmate Carl Marzani's father was a mine and railway worker. The Ostrander family had lived in Westchester County, New York, for generations, while the Marzanis were Italian immigrants who fled the Mussolini regime when young Carl was twelve.[61] Carl and Taylor ended up in the same place as undergraduates—Williams College, a cushy New England private institution where they studied economics. Marzani was a scholarship student and worked as a waiter while he was there.[62] Ostrander described him as "one of the most active personalities, although not one of the brightest minds, among his classmates."⁶³ They only overlapped for one year at Williams—Taylor was a senior when Carl was a freshman—and their paths diverged thereafter.

After graduating in June 1932, Ostrander headed off to graduate study at Oxford on a fellowship, and then doctoral studies at the University of Chicago. At the time, Chicago's economics department was not the hub of right-wing "Chicago School" economics it would later become, but as Ostrander wrote in his memoirs, "most of those who made it one were already there," either as faculty or grad students. One important Chicago School figure, Aaron Director, helped Ostrander find a job in government working to implement FDR's New Deal; other Chicago figures like Milton Friedman did as well, putting aside political misgivings for the sake of their careers.⁶⁴

Marzani's career and politics took a different turn. Ostrander and his wife Liesel stopped for tea with him during a short trip to England in 1937. Marzani apparently admitted he was "hardly studying at all," according to Ostrander: politics had taken up all of his time. He was "lecturing to miners," and Ostrander vaguely recalled him possibly saying he was "in the party"—possibly the Communist Party. He even told them he'd briefly served on the Republican side of the Spanish Civil War. The Ostranders doubted this story, but it was in fact true. The couple left with an uneasy sense that Ostrander's former classmate had "gone very far to the left."⁶⁵

Events soon brought Marzani and Ostrander back to the same side of international politics. When Hitler invaded the Soviet Union, the Communist Party shifted away from neutrality toward antifascist alliance with liberal democracies. The party dispatched Marzani to take over a popular front organization called "The East Side Conference to Defend America—Crush Hitler," which rallied community members from labor unions to religious leaders (a wide variety of them, too: a Polish priest, a rabbi, a Black minister) around the cause of crushing Hitler. Always something of a maverick, Marzani was still chafing from a dispute with the party about internal hierarchy months earlier, and he used the organization's creation as an opportunity to leave the party, claiming that he could not "serve two masters."[66] He took to his new work with gusto. When Japan attacked the US at Pearl Harbor in December 1941, he went even further—he sought to help with the war effort directly, despite his wife's fears that J. Edgar Hoover's FBI would keep him out of a job because of his politics. Nonetheless, he persevered: "My country," he later wrote, "needed me. It was as corny as that."[67]

Marzani and Ostrander both contributed to the war effort through their training in economics. The former Communist (but active small-c communist) Marzani went to the new "Board of Economic Warfare" and ultimately ended up working for the Office of Strategic Services, America's new intelligence agency. His work included determining criteria for strategic bombing of industrial facilities, fine-tuning systems for tracking manpower, and developing maps and charts for the Joint Chiefs of Staff. Ostrander, meanwhile, worked on military-industrial economics in the munitions branch of the War Production Board's Research and Statistics Division.[68]

Economics was an applied science that dealt with people and resources, and both the New Deal and the war created a need for experts in exactly those subjects. Economists' star had risen so far that they were making decisions of national importance only a few years out of graduate school. Their field controlled factories, shaped laws, directed bomber fleets, and commanded whole national economies. Depending on who economists were accountable to and what they told the public, economics could further democratic rule by the people, technocratic rule by experts . . . or rule by markets.

"Some Wailing Pressure Group"

The economists of the Austrian School rejected empiricism entirely. They viewed numbers and details as the province of leftists who wished to meddle in the market, including through government price controls.⁶⁹ Methodological individualists and radical subjectivists, they focused on individuals' subjective "preferences" instead.⁷⁰ Austrian School notable Ludwig von Mises devised what he called a "universally valid science of human action" that did not use scientific observation, which he later came to call "praxeology."⁷¹ Exactly like Spencer's social statics, praxeology was (in Mises's words) "a priori, not empirical. Like logic and mathematics, it is not derived from experience; it is prior to experience. It is, as it were, the logic of action and deed."⁷² It was grounded in a radical epistemological skepticism, insisting that experience could not guide the uncertain and complex world of economics, whereas logical reasoning could provide judgments that were certain.

The logical reasoning in question relied on the familiar axioms of control science: methodological individualism, psychological egoism, and market efficiency. In Mises's view we could not know much *except* that markets, consisting of self-interest-optimizing individual actors each possessed of imperfect knowledge, produce efficient outcomes. Where the left saw prices as a power struggle, Mises saw them instead as an exchange of information that resulted in objective truth. "[The resulting] calculation is as efficient as it can be. No reform could add to its efficiency."⁷³ Because markets themselves did this calculation, an efficient socialist economy was a logical impossibility—public ownership made it impossible to make economic calculations at all. Likewise, government intervention in a capitalist economy could only disturb the functioning of the market machine.

Another cluster of economists—the germ of what would become known as the Chicago School of economics—took a similar approach to the Austrian School. Already in the 1930s, some of Ostrander's professors at Chicago were part of a "neoclassical" tendency that, against institutionalism, stressed the efficiency of "free" markets and argued for a laissez-faire approach that left as much to the market as possible. Among them were Aaron Director and Charles Hardy. The latter viewed

FDR's National Recovery Administration (in the words of another economist, Robert Dimand, describing Hardy's position) as an "attempt to substitute centralized authority of one sort or another for what is left of free competitive enterprise."[74]

Two central figures in this early iteration of the Chicago School were Frank Knight, an acerbic specialist in entrepreneurship, and his imperious colleague Jacob Viner, whose pedagogy included mocking students and hurling chalk at them.[75] Despite or perhaps somehow because of this behavior, certain Chicago students took to neoclassical ideas like religious converts. One, Milton Friedman, called a course taught by Viner "unquestionably the greatest intellectual experience of my life."[76] Another, James Buchanan, claimed that he saw the light as a graduate student of Frank Knight's at Chicago and experienced a "full-blown intellectual conversion" to free market economics.[77]

The gospel they were converting to was something called price theory, or "the price system." It was a solution to the problem of alternatives. We can apply our energies, individually or collectively, to all sorts of things, but how do we decide among competing alternatives? Do we build more shoes, or more houses? Grow more food, or craft more dishware? We could answer this with democratic decision-making—but to the Austrian and Chicago Schools alike, this "planning" was a loathsome Soviet solution, inherently tyrannical. Markets were a self-regulating alternative. Ludwig von Mises's associate Henry Hazlitt described them with the same metaphor—steam engine governor devices—that gave a different kind of science of control (cybernetics) its name.[78] Prices, according to price theory, act as signals, distributing information throughout the economy so that individuals could act on it.

The genius of the price system was that it coordinated activity through the principles of the structure itself, without the meddling of "bureaucrats [who] do not understand the quasi-automatic nature of the market" or "some wailing pressure group," in Hazlitt's words.[79] This (in price theorists' view) made it both more just and more efficient. Milton Friedman argued that the "magic of the price system" was accomplished through two functions of prices: they transmit information, and they determine how much each person gets to spend. He insisted that these functions could not be decoupled, despite government efforts to do so. If prices did not determine individuals' wealth and well-being, they would not have coercive force and would not work. Price theory, then, was ultimately a justification for the maximal application of the mute compulsion of economic power.[80]

This was the latest innovation in control science. Historian Jennifer Burns has called price theory an "architecture of mind," writing that "it boasted the clarity and precision of mathematical concepts, but it was not math."[81] Their framework was a new form of control science's collapse of the normative into the positive. Methodologically, it drew on the "marginalist" ideas of late nineteenth-century economists. Philosophically, it was Spencerian: it promoted constant competition, denigrated cooperation and democracy, relied on methodological individualism, and backed all of this up with anti-empiricist "science." Price theory was *mathlike*, but it was not math.

Still, not all price theorists rejected numbers and rigorous analysis the way the Austrian School did. Milton Friedman and Anna Schwartz, for example, popularized the quantity theory of money with a careful empirical study of the US money supply.[82] But while Chicago economists could use numbers, they used them quite differently from the institutionalist economists they displaced. As Jennifer Burns puts it regarding Friedman's dissertation on wages in medicine—and here it's worth noting that her biography is very sympathetic to him—it "seemed to Friedman's critics that he was not testing his theory with facts but using facts to confirm his theory."[83] This was how price theorists tended to use facts.

Price theory offered an elegant, almost geometric argument for the inherent efficacy of markets over government action. Because that argument was rooted in rationalist logic rather than empiricist fact, it could be applied almost anywhere. In an age of expanding government, "neoliberal" advocates of a return to nineteenth-century capitalism were useful to businessmen like Alfred Sloan because they shared their fears of state action. Writing in 1933, Mises asserted that nothing less than "the fate of mankind" was at stake in economic debates. We could choose either "progress on the road that Western civilization has taken for thousands of years, or a rapid plunge into a chaos from which there is no way out, from which no new life as we know it will ever develop."[84]

"Facts Helpful to the Public"

Unfortunately for his cause, Ludwig von Mises was a dismal messenger, at least in terms of popularizing right-wing economic ideas. Anyone who feels their argument is absolutely logically certain risks writing in a way that repels skeptical readers. Mises's prose in particular rings with so much arrogance that it's hard to imagine how he lowered his chin enough to look down at his desk and write. And his ideology itself was one that many then and now found both repellent (bow to the market!) and inconvenient (stop trying to fix recessions!).

But Mises made an ally much better equipped for public communication than he was: journalist Henry Hazlitt, then the economics editor at the *New York Times*. Hazlitt helped popularize the work of Austrian School economists like Mises and his colleague Friedrich Hayek. He also made his own contributions to right-wing economic literature, which often consisted of translating ideas like Mises's into a simplified form for a popular readership. His 1946 *Economics in One Lesson* claimed that the central rule of economics was that different policies affected different groups differently—a borderline tautological claim that he wielded as an argument against interventions in the market.

Among the most popular and influential works of right-wing economics was Friedrich Hayek's *The Road to Serfdom*. Like Herbert Spencer and Ludwig von Mises, Hayek preferred evolution to design, and his book was an attack on the idea that, as he put it, "our economic life should be 'consciously directed.'"[85] Any kind of planning by government was both inherently tyrannical, as it restricted liberty through coercion, and invariably the road to greater future tyranny, as in Nazi Germany. Only the spontaneous competition of individuals expressing their liberty was valid economic activity. Hayek's account offered numerous arguments to support this: the limits of direct democracy, the personal character of individuals who rise through a totalitarian party, the attitudes welfare supposedly encourages.

While Hayek did periodically gesture at examples, his account was primarily rationalist, deriving conclusions from reason and first principles rather than observation. This could lead him to strange places, like claiming that British state pensions would lead to concentration camps for the elderly.[86] Still, Hayek's prose and tone were far more persuasive than anything one found in Mises. For example, where Mises presented socialism as a stupid delusion, Hayek's readers were instead told it was a well-intentioned mistake; where Mises appealed to geometric reason, Hayek offered a kind of common sense backed with gestures at current events. While Mises's praxeology texts would become weird scriptures only for the truly invested, *Road to Serfdom* served as a gateway drug to right-wing economics, conveniently printed in more polemical form in the magazine *Reader's Digest*.

Hayek, Hazlitt, and other popularizers of right-wing economic thought were helped along by big business, including Alfred Sloan himself. While the Sloan Foundation had been formed in 1934 for narrow charitable use, Sloan began seriously investing in it after the Flint sit-down strike. The foundation's board of trustees made the decision to focus "exclusively on American economic education and research," and as its reports clarify, those research efforts were themselves focused on "facts helpful to the population at large in formulating judgments on nationally important economic issues."[87] Alfred brought in his brother Harold, an economist, to head up the foundation.

Since the Sloans were interested in winning the next political war, not just the current one against the New Deal, their efforts extended to public schools, higher education, and think tanks as well as propaganda. Schools were central from the beginning. The public, they felt, was not educated in the lessons of economics. Their 1938 report condemned a "total disregard of scientific knowledge in some expressions of popular opinion, in general approval of certain social procedures, and in no small amount of legislation," an obvious if vague reference to the sweeping economic intervention of the Roosevelt era.[88] Alfred wrote to Irénée du Pont that his new outreach program was meant to "get across to the people of the United States, the fact that they can not get something for nothing."[89]

Sloan's plan for doing so was a multifront education campaign. A 1944 graphic in the foundation's report summarized the program it had put together over the preceding few years.[90] First, it targeted the estimated 15 percent of the population it believed could "provide economic leadership." These individuals were targeted with public forums, the relatively intellectual University of Chicago Round Table radio program, and tax analysis training programs at the University of Denver. This all dovetailed with broader education efforts, including fellowships at MIT, as well as funding for research in economics.

Meanwhile, the broad masses—"about 50% of the population"—needed to be prepared to accept the 15 percent's economic leadership. The foundation aimed to achieve this by presenting "objective facts" to the public through education.[91] One part of the foundation began a film program meant to present "simply and entertainingly . . . significant elementary relationships in our economic life concerning which there is believed to be widespread misunderstanding."[92] This culminated in the creation of a single short film, initially called *The Challenge* and later *The Machine: Master or Slave?*[93] Through a quarter-hour of dismal acting and vigorous montages of America's humming industry, the film presented the problem of workers losing their jobs to machines and strongly suggested that capitalism would fix this itself through economic growth. While Sloan's film efforts fizzled, he was more successful in radio. Alongside the Chicago program, and presumably coming off the earlier success of the housewife-targeted *American Family Robinson*, his foundation also funded the production of more colorful works like *Keeping Up with the Wigglesworths*, which aimed to teach right-wing economics to the youth through the antics and adventures of teenage Snuffy Wigglesworth.[94]

In 1938, Sloan funded a $50,000 "study of the American capital market." Published in 1940 as *Capital Expansion, Employment, and Economic Stability*, it railed against government deficits. It argued that long-term capital investments, like building factories, were faltering due to fears of taxes and debt. Specifically, capitalists feared "the *will* to check the growth of public indebtedness no longer exists." Government would continue to grow and thus to tax; fearing this, capitalists were making fewer investments. The report previewed what would later become a common threat by capital against the state: the threat of losing *investor confidence*. Its authors claimed that the government had to do what they proposed or "no restoration of confidence," on the part of investors, could happen—and therefore capitalists would not start investing properly in the economy again.

This trope was not powerful enough, yet, to kill FDR's programs or his powerful political coalition. Moreover, by the time the report was published, war had broken out, and shortly thereafter America entered it. As in World War I, this put the brakes on much of the capitalist antigovernment program, as the state conscripted industry into the war effort. The New Deal and government intervention had to be accepted—for a time.[95]

Sloan, however, was playing a long game. His foundation plan was implemented *after* it was clear he had already lost the first battle over the New Deal, and it began with long-term "experimental" investigation into education. In the short run, the New Deal might be accommodated, but Sloan—and the broader business community still working its influence in politics—could have the last laugh by shaping the institutional and ideological conditions of American economic thought.

Thus, American capitalists showered the Austrian School and other market ideologues with cash. The William Volker Fund—built on a Kansas City furniture fortune—bought Hayek a professorship at Chicago. It paid for Ludwig von Mises's salary when he couldn't find a permanent position and propped up Aaron Director's career when he proved unable to actually finish a book.[96] The Volker Fund, like the Sloan Foundation, aimed to influence popular—not just academic—understandings of economics. Sloan's outfit sold 2.5 million pamphlets in 1944—enough, they reported with a memorable graphic in their annual report, to make twenty-five stacks as tall as the sixty-six-story Radio Corporation of America building at 30 Rockefeller Plaza.[97]

Yet still they ran into trouble from insufficiently right-wing economists. In 1945, Henry Hazlitt wrote Alfred Sloan—who had long admired his work as a columnist—to warn him that his foundation was giving money to the wrong people. As part of his economic education efforts, Sloan was funding the Public Affairs Committee (PAC), which was dedicated to the dissemination of economic research in popular pamphlet form. PAC leadership was mostly liberal (in the American political sense, not the economic and ideological sense), and drew heavily from Columbia University, where institutionalism reigned supreme, in contrast to the neoclassical nexus developing at Chicago.[98] Among its publications were *Workers and Bosses Are Human*, which argued for cooperation with labor unions, and *There Can Be Jobs for All*, which supported economic planning in favor of full employment.

Hazlitt wrote urgently to Sloan when he came across the latter pamphlet. The committee's work aligned perfectly with what Sloan said he was doing with his economic education efforts—but quite poorly with what he actually intended to achieve. When the foundation claimed to be offering "facts helpful to the public," he hadn't meant *these* facts. Purely by accident, Sloan had actually engaged in the kind of well-meaning education efforts he had claimed he was, rather than the indoctrination he meant to bankroll. Horrified, he pulled any further funding to the PAC and asked Hazlitt to investigate his own foundation and make sure nothing else like this would happen.[99]

The following year, Friedrich Hayek's *Road to Serfdom* came under fire in a discussion on the Chicago Round Table radio program. One of the participants, socialist economist Maynard Krueger, insisted that Hayek's dreaded "planning" could be democratic and that some freedoms in fact had to be compromised for the sake of liberty and equality. "One of them," he explained, was "the freedom to own privately and to control for profit the means of life which are essential to others." If we did not restrict private property, "liberty is simply going to be a word in 'Liberty League,'" Krueger snarked, holding up the defunct far-right business front to denigrate Hayek's vision of "freedom" as plutocracy.[100]

Sloan was decidedly displeased—he himself had helped fund the Liberty League and perhaps remembered it as an embarrassing failure. Now his money was being used to platform a socialist maligning exactly the kind of right-wing economist whose work he hoped to amplify. Sloan threatened to cut his financial support to the program and dispatched his brother Harold, director of the Sloan Foundation, to Chicago to complain that the program did not give conservatives enough time or weight on the show.[101]

Those who wished to promote "free enterprise" economics needed their own ecosystem altogether. Hazlitt advised as much—he had taken Sloan up on his request to review the car magnate's foundation, a task he undertook with the help of failed grocery wholesaler Leonard Read. A creature of business lobbying, Read had made a name for himself in conservative economic circles through his work with the Chamber of Commerce, where he had taken a succession of jobs selling business interests to the public after he failed to succeed in business himself.[102] In the resulting report, Read, Hazlitt, and economist Leo

Wolman argued that the foundation should produce content directly instead of funding outside groups who might be interested in education rather than indoctrination. Their proposal soon became the backbone for a new organization: the Foundation for Economic Education, which was firmly focused on propaganda.[103] Another of its founders was Donaldson Brown, who had helped design Sloan's management system and now hoped to make its underlying principles popular across the nation. A right-wing network dedicated to a decidedly partisan vision of "free enterprise" was coming together.

"Do Not Be Afraid of Large and Bold Schemes"

Yet this right-wing economic movement was unable to stop the rise of an opposing approach to economics: Keynesianism. Published in 1936, British economist John Maynard Keynes's *General Theory of Employment, Interest, and Money* provided what became the dominant economic paradigm of the postwar era. Epistemologically speaking, Keynes was not an empiricist, but his theories offered room for empiricist intervention, in contrast to the right's rationalist arguments for restraint.[104] He argued that, contrary to price theory, markets could be quite inefficient. There were millions of people in wealthy economies who could not find jobs, and, in recessions, millions of goods that could not find buyers. The solution to this obvious wastefulness was government action.

What became known as Keynesianism offered a solution to the boom-recession "business cycle" that had been plaguing capitalism: during a downturn, the government had to stimulate the economy by spending money. "Let us not submit to the vile doctrine of the nineteenth century that every enterprise must justify itself in pounds, shillings and pence of cash income," Keynes urged in a 1942 BBC address. "Anything we can actually do, we can afford." By this he meant that economic limits were a product of real resources, not money or markets—and the state could close the gap between the two. Whereas Hayek called planning dangerous, tyrannical, and ineffective, Keynes urged listeners "not [to] be afraid of large and bold schemes." Grand government efforts could make use of what markets wasted and discarded, including workers themselves: "With a big programme carried out at a regulated pace we can hope to keep employment good for many years to come. We shall, in fact, have built our New Jerusalem out of the labour which in our former vain folly we were keeping unused and unhappy in enforced idleness."[105]

Some of his followers took this even further than he did. In 1941, F. Taylor Ostrander and a number of other economists working in government had dinner with John Maynard Keynes in Washington, DC. According to Ostrander, Keynes argued that America should be careful not to spend too much during the war, to prepare for inevitable inflation afterward. Two American liberal economists—Ostrander was not among them—argued that by Keynes's own theories, such restraint would make it harder to tackle unemployment. Their debate continued until Keynes stood up and huffed that they were "more Keynesian than I."[106] Big spending proved popular with politicians and the public as well as economists. To governments facing the vast task of fighting the war and then rebuilding after it, Keynesianism was immensely attractive, and Keynes himself contributed greatly to the architecture of the postwar economic order.

Dismayed, right-wing economists from the Chicago and Austrian Schools joined forces against Keynesian interventionism. Advocates of these economic ideas claimed that their vision of economic freedom made them truer "liberals" than the Democrats who went by that name in mid-twentieth-century America. These right-wing economists instead called themselves *neoliberals*. Friedrich Hayek schemed to hold a conference for "all those who have become gravely concerned about the chances of preserving a free civilization," in order to challenge "dominant beliefs and misconceptions" that threatened to "drive us ever further in a totalitarian direction." The Volker Fund and the Foundation for Economic Education helped provide the necessary money, and the conference was held in spring 1947 in Switzerland. After the conference, they formed the Mont Pelerin Society—an academic network dedicated to restoring nineteenth-century competitive evolution and defeating twentieth-century collective intention.[107] World War II had ended, but a war for the capitalist world's economic future had just begun.

7

"A Fantastic Fairyland": Factory Discipline and the Postwar Right, 1946–67

After the end of World War II, America entered into a new war—a war at home, over prices. After years of New Deal programs followed by wartime mobilization, the American economy was anything but an unrestricted market. The Office of Price Administration ran a rationing and price control system covering everything from meat to tank components. This was exactly the kind of "planning" Austrian economists hated—but even Chicago economists were involved: F. Taylor Ostrander, for instance, worked on "price stabilization" in the defense industry.[1]

Now Roosevelt was dead, and the war was over, but the OPA remained active, and many American workers still hoped to realize his dream of a "Second Bill of Rights": economic rights to housing, healthcare, education, and a job. *Deadline for Action*, a 1946 film made in collaboration with the United Electrical, Radio and Machine Workers of America (UE), cast the postwar labor struggle as an extension of the Roosevelt program.[2] Prices were at the center of that struggle. Like many other unions after the war, the UE asked for a wage increase—in this case, $2 a day—from employers like General Electric. Companies insisted they couldn't pay due to price controls. The UE said otherwise, offering refrigerator pricing and productivity data as a counterexample: a graphic broke down the $169 production cost of the fridge. Only a little over 10 percent of that came from labor costs.

In the eyes of the UE, prices were a question of power, not just market information. Inflation, the phenomenon of broad price increases across an economy, exemplifies this. According to the UE, business's other argument against wage raises was that they would "cause inflation, because the workers, with their war bonds, would have too much money." The idea here is simple enough, captured by the common phrasing "too many dollars chasing too few goods." In practice, the relationship between wages and prices is decidedly more complicated.

The politics of inflation have a tenuous relationship to the reality of prices and the factors that shape them. When we say "inflation" we frequently mean a generalized increase in prices of important goods—for example, during a crisis like a major war, or especially disruptions to the energy supply, prices for *all* goods can increase. But even these increases are not perfectly even, nor are they experienced evenly across society. As a political term, "inflation" often means "price increases I don't like." What workers call wage increases, bosses describe as wage inflation, as well as wage-*driven* inflation.

Every dollar workers capture as a wage increase is a dollar that cannot be pocketed as profits. Capitalists have class interests as well: more prosperous and secure workers are more difficult to control, for example, with threats of firing. While a healthier economy of higher wages and lower unemployment should lead to more profits in absolute terms, as economist Michał Kalecki put it in 1943, "'discipline in the factories' and 'political stability' are more appreciated than profits by business leaders."[3] After all, control of workers is what makes them business leaders in the first place. The stakes of postwar labor-management conflict were higher than money or profits— this was a conflict over power, and it went far beyond the UE. While the UE was a particularly left-wing organization—it was closely associated with the Communist Party—its postwar economic demands were not atypical of American unions. In 1945 and 1946, US workers organized the largest wave of strikes in the country's history. Central to their case, and their philosophy, was "ability to pay": General Motors *could* pay more without raising prices, so it should. This argument was infuriating to GM, and to Alfred Sloan personally. When the head of the fact-finding board appointed by President Truman indicated ability to pay was among the facts they would be finding, GM walked out.[1]

Postwar conflict between workers and capitalists was, in the UE's view, part of an international struggle to determine who would prosper from peace. *Deadline for Action* described General Electric as part of a vast international business conspiracy to drain wealth from workers around the world. The film presented American big business as a new empire seeking "colonial rule," linked to and directly succeeding earlier empires. "Bill Turner," the film's worker figure—a UE man from Lynn, Massachusetts—gazes at the newspaper and sees a headline indicating Britain's use of recently surrendered Japanese troops against Indonesian independence fighters opposing Dutch troops sent to reoccupy the country. His brother writes a letter from China asking why the hell they're still fighting there—implicitly, though he doesn't say it, on behalf of an unpopular government against a popular communist movement that had recently been an ally. Was this, the film asked, what millions died for? Would this be the "century of big business" or the "century of the common people?" *Deadline for Action* called for mass voting as an electoral strategy complementing strikes.

That strategy was not enough. The strikes were, in the words of historian Nelson Lichtenstein, a "pyrrhic victory."[5] When Congress let price controls lapse at the end of June 1946, meat prices skyrocketed. Truman then reimposed meat price controls in August, infuriating meat suppliers, who unleashed a capital strike by withholding their cattle. With an election looming, the indecisive Truman once more lifted price controls in October. Sloan's bet on consumer economics proved prescient: American voters caught between high prices and shortages blamed Truman for both. The despondent president wrote, but did not deliver, a speech in which he accused voters of "deserting your president for a mess of pottage, a piece of beef, a side of bacon. You've gone over to the powers of selfishness and greed."[6]

As the UE predicted, the new Congress sought to crush the left after World War II just as capitalists and the government had done after World War I. They dismantled the OPA and passed the Taft-Hartley Act, which restricted union activity, over Truman's veto. Taft-Hartley also had a clause requiring unions to disavow communism—a problem for the communist-linked UE. For both ideological and internal political reasons, the CIO (Congress of Industrial Organizations), the nation's leading union federation, followed. The UE resisted, which prompted the CIO to create a competitor union called the IUE.[7] McCarthyism came for universities as well as factories, and left-wing and left-leaning economists were purged from the American academy. Among those who suffered was an economist outside academia at the time: Ostrander's Williams classmate Carl Marzani, who turned the filmmaking skills he had developed in the Office of Strategic Services to making left-wing documentaries. His Union Films outlet, run with a few fellow left-wingers out of a brownstone in New York City, was behind the UE's *Deadline for Action*.[8]

Marzani also produced films for Henry Wallace's 1948 third-party presidential campaign, which likewise emphasized internationalist cooperation, rather than competition, with the Soviet Union. Like Roosevelt, Wallace was no Marxist, but the left could make common cause with him on both domestic and foreign policy issues. Again, the UE's neo-Rooseveltian dreams were hardly niche. But communism, and Wallace's willingness to accommodate it abroad, was not popular. The right hounded leftists, and many liberals abandoned them. General Electric discussed Marzani's film *Deadline for Action* at a meeting sponsored by the National Association of Manufacturers, probably planted stories about it in the press, and sent the federal government after Marzani. His earlier evasion of FBI surveillance provided an excuse: the government charged and imprisoned him for three years because of his previous membership in the Communist Party. While McCarthyism soon burned out, the damage to labor was lasting. The post-Roosevelt Democratic Party still accommodated unions, but it did not champion workers, and its agenda more broadly was far less ambitious.

Though American liberals did not want to make the postwar era the "century of the common people" in the way the UE wanted, they also did not necessarily want it to be the "century of big business" either. America's economic and political structure from the end of World War II to the mid-1970s can be characterized by three terms. First, "Keynesianism." John Maynard Keynes's prescription for social spending and state stimulus was popular national policy in the postwar era. Second, "corporatism." Not to be confused with "corporate" as in "corporation," "corporatism" refers to a political system in which the state governs through negotiation between different interest groups, like unions and business. Third, "Fordism": an economy of mass consumption and mass production.

Each of these terms reflects a compromise. Postwar Keynesianism used government spending to stabilize and grow the economy, as well as to achieve some social goals through welfare, but it did not guarantee "economic rights" of the kind Roosevelt once gestured at—in particular, full employment. Corporatism tried to hold class struggle at bay via negotiation. Fordism promised women and children material prosperity but within the male-dominated family, particularly the white family, given employment discrimination and business's success in keeping unions out of the South. These compromises were good for capitalists, but they wanted more. And as before, capitalists' efforts to discipline labor helped them find the political and intellectual strategies necessary for getting more. The postwar era's compromises persisted until the early 1970s, but, the entire time, a subset of America's capitalist elite was scheming for a new order.

"We Are Being Invaded"

Lemuel Ricketts Boulware was promoted to head of employee relations at General Electric in May 1947. Like the rest of big business, GE was loathed by many American workers—as

Boulware put it, employees and the public "distrusted and disapproved" of the American megacorporation. A former marketing consultant, Boulware approached this as a marketing challenge. General Electric already had "the best of intentions" and "the best practices known."[9] The company was hated, he believed, because it had failed to explain its benevolence to the public and its workers.

In 1947, GE printed Boulware's rules of engagement for a PR war on labor: thousands of copies of a spiral-bound blue booklet stretching just over 100 short pages. Boulware's team had spent months surveying and investigating workers and now presented to factory supervisors the fruit of its labors in the form of this *Supervisor's Guide to General Electric Job Information*.[10] Boulware's booklet was part anti-Communist political vision, part marketing strategy, and part corporate policy structured and formed by the problem of labor control.

Lemuel Boulware is well known to historians as a political figure who connected workplace negotiation with economic thought. His *Supervisor's Guide* reveals the factory floor roots of this political program: it was written for managers who supervised five to twenty-five workers. The bulk of the guide is a point-by-point refutation of every worker complaint Boulware's team felt was worth mentioning. When a worker came to a supervisor with grievances, or a supervisor suspected they were harboring them, Boulware's booklet guided the supervisor's response. General Electric workers, even if one were judging only from the complaints in this booklet, had a sophisticated political consciousness and understanding of their interests as a class. One of Boulware's first tasks was to disrupt this political consciousness.

To that end, Boulware invoked familiar rhetoric of mutual benefit and necessity. Some workers claimed that technological improvements at GE facilities did not benefit them, only the company, which received increased profits.[11] Boulware asserted that the worker "benefits because his job is more secure" with new technology. Only GE's "constant ingenuity and diligence," via technological improvement, kept consumers preferring their products. This was an argument for technology but not on its own an argument against also improving worker pay with productivity.

But like Alfred Sloan, Boulware was hostile to the "ability-to-pay theory," which he called "a fallacy that runs counter to the whole concept of the free choice of jobs."[12] Pay should be determined by the market. In Boulware's words, "When technological changes occur, it is necessary to change job rates," so as to "distribute properly" the savings that technological improvements resulted in. That proper distribution came through the price system. The "system of passing the fruits of technological improvement through the price structure to the consumer," Boulware wrote, "has been one of the most important factors in producing the high standard of living Americans enjoy." Through the magic of the market, the employee thus "benefits as a *consumer* [emphasis in original]" rather than a worker.

Lemuel Boulware was a close friend of Friedrich Hayek's ally Henry Hazlitt, and the GE manager leveraged the economic journalist's "one lesson"—all economic matters affect multiple groups, and differently—toward their shared right-wing political goals.[13] He encouraged workers to see themselves as consumers, not workers. The booklet instructed managers to explain to the GE worker that Taylor-style time studies benefited them by "reducing costs and making work easier, thus resulting in more goods for consumers like himself."[14]

To a worker, a speed-up driven by new technology and/or time studies was a source of stress and injustice. But to a consumer, it could be a source of joy: behold, marginally cheaper refrigerators. Boulware wanted them to think of the latter and not the former. Similarly, his insistence that technology produced security through GE itself tied workers to the company, first and foremost, rather than each other. By refashioning workers as "consumers" and "employees"—he almost exclusively uses this term instead of "workers"—Boulware sought to reshape class itself as a social category, and in so doing reshape politics.

This was consistent with other efforts across American industry, initially with only limited success, to redefine the employee-employer relationship. General Motors, for example, had separate divisions for "industrial relations," which negotiated with its unionized workforce, and "employee relations," which sought to promote a competing pro-company orientation for employees. Boulware's own Employee Relations Department at GE took both roles. In 1947, GM's ER department ran a popular "My Job and Why I Like It" competition, which offered "more than $150,000 in new cars and kitchen appliances."[15] This was a precursor to the present-day's office pizza party, but competing with a large and successful union required better prizes than pizza. GM's competition united form and content effectively: by centering consumer goods, it encouraged identification with consumption and the firm rather than production and the union.

GE's employee relations approach was not all discipline, tyranny, and manipulation. In Somersworth, New Hampshire, GE jobs were considered good jobs. The company offered promotions, pensions, and Employees' Association Christmas parties. Working at GE was a desirable privilege—among the alternatives was a shoe factory.[16] General Electric supervisors and managers genuinely listened to worker grievances, within limits, and met certain needs. When GE workers complained of feeling powerless, "Pushed Around by Powerful People," Boulware suggested two paths depending on the cause of this sentiment. "If it is actually the actions of local management, [the supervisor] must see that the situation is corrected." But if "this attitude is a feeling of resentment born of insecurity and belief in personal insignificance, the supervisor must help the person develop his confidence, pride, and sense of well-being."[17] Throughout the booklet, he insisted that supervisors should deal with real issues. But it was supervisors who decided whether a worker's complaint was legitimate and thus whether it was worth engineering or therapy. Both were top-down.

What defined Boulware's vision—and ultimately distinguished the HR approach from industrial relations—was the refusal of meaningful worker *power*. For Boulware, workers' complaints were useful insofar as they pointed to real issues, and it was necessary to begrudgingly deal with them as a labor relations problem, but workers should have no say in whether or how their grievances were addressed. In response to complaints about lighting, Boulware wrote: "Is condition wrong from scientific standpoint? If so, the supervisor should try to correct it. If not, he should show why it is correct." Likewise, if the plant was not "cheerful" enough, supervisors should ascertain why and then either implement solutions or, "if remedies are impractical, he should show the employee why."[18] Management could be sure of the objective truth of their judgments—"the procedures now followed by General Electric were slowly and painstakingly developed over a long period of time," as Boulware put it regarding time studies.[19] At no point should workers themselves have any actual decision-making power.

The negotiating philosophy that Boulware became known for meant not actually negotiating. Prior to bargaining with unions, General Electric examined the facts with careful research and put together a "fair" deal for workers entirely on its own. As with individual shop floor grievances, GE's deal was not necessarily bad in material terms, especially compared to conditions at other workplaces. But it was GE's deal. The company offered it in take-it-or-leave-it form, refused any meaningful negotiation, and used mass communications, a "veritable avalanche of publicity," to force its deal through.[20] GE under Boulware did not negotiate, it decided. His enemies called it "Boulwarism." He called it simple common sense.[21] Thanks to the preceding centuries of psychological egoism and market thought, Boulware wasn't the only one who found that characterization credible.

Rather than deal with unions, Boulware went directly to workers. GE peeled off support by calling individual workers to scab, drew on its vast media channels and carefully cultivated notables like clergy and local officials to trumpet the value of its deal, and demoralized anyone who did not believe in it by making clear they could not get a better one.²² Boulware was hostile to collective action, and in the guide's second section he focuses on reasons workers "don't like to give the skill, care, and full day's work expected." He broke this grievance into two problems: first, workers who believed spreading work out, especially over time, would help them individually. Working at maximum rates all the time, some workers perceived, was a part of the same short-term and profit-focused thinking that denied them annual pay guarantees and reliable job security.

GE workers believed the company could provide both by distributing work with an eye toward their own needs, not just immediate market concerns. To this problem, the first cited in the relevant section, Boulware responded mostly with the same cool and detached economic rhetoric the booklet largely consists of. He informed supervisors that they should explain economics to workers: slower work means higher-cost products, which increases the price of goods. The worker should be reminded that "he is not only injuring his buying power as a consumer, but also his own job security."²³ Only the unassailable price system could regulate workers' actions.

A second reason for slowing work caused Boulware to erupt dramatically: workers who (as the subheading puts it) "Want to Spread the Work in Interest of Fellow Employees"—rather than only themselves. While self-interested slow-walking was inefficient, Boulware felt collective-minded slow-walking was something worse. It was "almost treason" against the United States, in his view,

> for a man deliberately to produce less than his machine and a reasonable day's work will permit. The more he shirks, the fewer pieces he produces. His action causes costs to rise on what has been produced. It means more of his fellow Americans must do without.
>
> We would all be horrified and rush to arms if some outside, destructive power were to invade our country and shut off what we want and could otherwise have.

Yet we are being invaded.

Certain ideas which have been tried without success in foreign countries are being urged upon us. Each time any of us deliberately sets out to produce less than his reasonable share of goods per day, we are allowing ourselves to be enslaved by these false ideas.

Workers existed to serve the consumer, and even inefficient service was communist sabotage. Ironically, this mirrored Stalin-era Soviet rhetoric about work. Boulware's rhetoric was unhinged, but it was based on an accurate insight that Marxism recognized and the Russian Revolution had depended upon: workplaces are sites of intellectual and ideological production.

"Sound Economic Teaching and Practices"

In June 1949, Boulware gave the commencement speech for Harvard Business School. Entitled "Salvation Is Not Free," the speech painted a dark picture of America and the world. Businessmen in "country after country" had been "gradually weakened and then displaced." Along with them had gone "freedom—for all the people—freedom and any hope of human dignity, plenty, and the good life."[24] Lying "government planners" were "debauching and corrupting" America and the voters whom they tricked into supporting them. The business class had provided a "fantastic fairyland" of consumer goods, "raising the standard of living through voluntary action inspired by the incentive to save and to compete." But it had failed to defend the merits of this consumer paradise in the political arena.

Success, he warned in terms that infantilized the laboring masses, would not be easy: like "parents facing up finally to telling the truth about Santa Claus," they would have to deal with tears. Boulware proposed forming a political coalition of "managers, farmers, stockholders, bond holders, insurance policy holders, savings bank depositors, pensioners, and any other upstanding citizens with an interest in keeping the value of money honest" to promote "sound economic teaching and practices by their representative in government, in unions, even in education and the clergy, as well as in business."[25] Boulwarism as factory-floor managerial politics had to be extended up to the level of the nation and the world. He gave the speech to this influential class of future businessmen and again and again on future occasions for years.[26]

Boulwarism included and extended two right-wing economic ideas. The first was the same market philosophy that economists like Ostrander and Milton Friedman picked up from Chicago faculty in the 1930s—price theory. Second, Boulwarism included an early version of what came to be known as monetarism. It was rooted in an older basic principle known as the quantity theory of money, which held that the total amount of money in circulation determines how prices across the economy change—thus, as Milton Friedman later put it, "inflation is always and everywhere a monetary phenomenon."[27] More money in circulation means less value for money. Quantity theory was popular in the same 1930s Chicago circles as price theory, and Friedman ultimately expanded it into a broader approach to the economy writ large.[28]

Price theory and quantity theory (and then monetarism) served parallel purposes: the former was a microeconomic argument against state regulation, and the latter became a macroeconomic counter-theory to Keynesian stimulus. Rather than managing demand across the economy with state spending and investment, monetarists held that governments should optimize the total amount of money in circulation via central bank action. This was convenient for capitalists like Boulware, who relayed and made similar claims even as monetarism was still forming.

In his 1949 speech, Boulware narrated a worker entering the grocery store and finding high prices. Upon doing so, Boulware's worker "concludes that the grocer—and his own boss" are a hostile ruling class."[29] In Boulware's view, this was a lie: inflation is the result of the government spending too much money. Workers only believed otherwise, Boulware argued, because of what they have been "told by the agents of those very ones who have been doing the diluting of the money and causing the high prices." Evil liberals were pushing wasteful spending, causing prices to skyrocket, and then blaming businessmen—who were not only innocents but victims.

The GE manager had stern words for workers about inflation. Another worker grievance subheading in his pamphlet for supervisors read:

> Don't Have to Give the Skill, Care, and Full Day's Work Expected—Government Will Take Care of Me, and Can Print Money to Do So. Government Better than Private Business in Giving Job and Other Security to Underdog. I Don't Fear Inflation. I Like It So Far.

Boulware's advised response included an insistence that *"real wages increase only when over-all production increases."*[30] The italics are his. Boulware was insistent because he was lying. There is another way real wages could increase: when workers took from capitalists' profits. Unions achieved this directly by bargaining up wages. Inflation could as well, by eating away at the value of saved money—something the wealthy had plenty of and the working class did not. "I like inflation" was a reasonable position for workers: government spending and wage increases that contributed to inflation benefited them more than their employers, while inflation itself harmed them less.

If inflation truly were always monetary and always bad, the politics of macroeconomics would be simple enough: it would be both practical (just control the amount of money!) and desirable for everyone to prioritize avoiding inflation as much as possible, as Boulware and his ilk advocated. But inflation is not always bad. It is not always bad for all people. It does not always follow from government spending, and other factors can cause it. Perhaps most importantly, accepting inflation is often preferable to the alternative. "Price stability" trades off with important other social goals, like unemployment, workers' bargaining power, and even economic growth itself. Thus questions of inflation became central in postwar politics: How much inflation is acceptable? What causes inflation? What should we do about it?

Boulware drew on proto-monetarist ideas and price theory because they offered convenient answers to these questions—answers convenient for big business. Price theory and monetarism combined to make a case against government spending and thus government economic action. Under a monetarist paradigm, the Roosevelt legacy and subsequent Democrats' more limited Keynesian agenda were dangerous, a "diluting of money" by increasing the total supply of it. In theory, a monetarist response to the New Deal could mean increasing taxes instead of reducing spending. But price theory ruled this out: such a policy would displace the efficiencies of the price system with the inefficiencies of government—the evils of "planning." When Boulware's summarized surveyed worker declared, "Government Better than Private Business in Giving Job and Other Security to Underdog," Boulware replied that this was a trade of "economic security in exchange for political slavery."[31]

Proto-monetarism and price theory were useful to capitalists not merely because they proscribed particular policies capitalists did not like. Rather, down to the level of fundamental principles and methodology, neoclassical economics was against democratic decision-making itself. The democratic public mattered in Keynesian policy-making practice: it was their elected representatives, after all, who would determine where and how to engage in economic stimulus.

In contrast, monetarist macroeconomic policy placed authority in the hands of technocratic central banks, tasked them with only ensuring price stability, and argued that they could do so merely by optimizing the amount of money in circulation. Price theory, meanwhile, insisted that the deliberate political decisions of the democratic state were always less efficient than the impulsive economic motions of the market. Anti-empiricism and anti-democracy supported each other in neoclassical economic thought: the simple conclusions that followed from its reductive and abstract approach left little room for collective intervention.

Postwar right-wing economics thus continued the crusade against human and especially worker intention as a political force, in favor of Spencerian evolution and Hayekian spontaneous order. Ludwig von Mises praised the "consumers' democracy" of markets.[32] Ideally, democracy is defined by formal political equality—one person, one vote—and collective deliberation—you discuss with your community and together vote for the world you want to see. Mises's vision included neither feature. Votes in his supposed democracy were made with unequally held dollars rather than evenly distributed ballots. "As a producer," under capitalism, "a man is merely the agent of the community and as such has to obey. Only as a consumer," Mises wrote, "can he command." Furthermore, consumers could command only through their individual economic impulses—*I want or need this product*—not their collective political intentions—*we believe in this kind of world*.

Foundation for Economic Education founder (and failed grocery wholesaler) Leonard Read neatly articulated this paradigm in a classic and popular presentation of price theory, later made famous by Milton Friedman: the 1950 essay "I, Pencil."[33] Written from the perspective of a pencil, the piece described the coordination of Sri Lankan graphite miners, California sawmill workers, and Indonesian oil cultivators necessary to form the ubiquitous writing implement. Read insisted that no one person knows how to make a pencil, nor does anyone direct its construction:

> Neither the worker in the oil field nor the chemist nor the digger of graphite or clay nor any who mans or makes the ships or trains or trucks nor the one who runs the machine that does the knurling on my bit of metal nor the president of the company performs his singular task because he wants me. Each one wants me less, perhaps, than does a child in the first grade. Indeed, there are some among this vast multitude who never saw a pencil

nor would they know how to use one. Their motivation is other than me. Perhaps it is something like this: Each of these millions sees that he can thus exchange his tiny know-how for the goods and services he needs or wants. I may or may not be among these items.

People are motivated, brought together, by market exchange: each person involved knows their wages can be used to satisfy their own desires. Millions are summoned to work for something they don't even want.

Read's pencil was made possible by workers who were not so much trading "tiny know-how" for wants as they were selling much of their waking life so that American kindergarteners could write. Forests were cut down to surround the graphite; canola oil plantations were erected in Indonesia, likely from razed forests, so that they could erase. No one had decided that this state of affairs was how things should be—it was a result of the aggregation of market impulses. Economist Wilhelm Röpke, who was a Mont Pelerin Society member like Hazlitt and Read, wrote that "the modern economic system, an extraordinarily complex mechanism, functions without conscious central control by any agency whatever."[34] In the eyes of neoliberals, this was freedom, and it had to be maintained and expanded.

An "Anti-Statist Tradition"?

Lemuel Boulware picked up and propagated these right-wing economic ideas because of their utility in managing workers. Neoliberals, conservatives, and capitalists disagreed on plenty, but they agreed that labor had to be constrained. To make the ideas of writers like Hayek and Mises into reality—he owned copies of their books—Boulware expanded his employee relations program into a broader propaganda and coalition-building machine.[35] He leveraged four national-level GE publications and local plant newspapers to spread his message. Each week, he sent out a newsletter to GE's thousands of managers, and it and other publications often commented directly on political issues, offering the GE company view on subjects like defense spending. In time, the mailing list grew to include clergy, entertainment figures, teachers, and academics.[36] He even paid for an economics class for General Electric's hundreds of thousands of employees.[37]

Also among the measures Boulware took to promote Boulwarism were company book clubs featuring conservative economics texts. Boulware's memoir, *The Truth About Boulwarism*, mentions eight selections from these clubs. Both the books and their publishers are telling. Two of the eight were published by the Foundation for Economic Education. Boulware's choice to rely on the FEE, which grew out of anti–New Deal efforts and included Henry Hazlitt and Sloan associate Donaldson Brown as founding members, was an obvious one. Another two books came from Regnery Publishing, which was established in 1947 as a conservative publishing house. Regnery was part of the "fusionist" architecture of the conservative movement, which combined social conservatism with laissez-faire economics and hawkish foreign policy.

Lemuel Boulware's selections from the Regnery Publishing portfolio included *Prosperity Through Freedom* by marketing man Lawrence Fertig and *Economics of the Free Society* by Wilhelm Röpke. Both were frequent and important participants in the meetings of the Mont Pelerin Society, which the latter led for a time in the early 1960s before departing due to a feud with Hayek. Fertig's book defended the "spiritual" value of economic liberty in its opening. Röpke, meanwhile, argued that neoliberal market order could only be sustained with attention to the "natural order"—conservative social hierarchy—and a strong but "impartial" state to safeguard capitalism.[38]

Within the new conservative movement, Lemuel Boulware's program aimed to serve the business class by remaking the working class. And GE hired a very specific spokesperson to front this: a struggling actor named Ronald Reagan.[39] His job included hosting a television program called *General Electric*

Theater, touring plants, and making speeches. Reagan entered GE as a Democrat—two years before he started he had called himself "a New Dealer to the core."[40] But as he pitched materials from Boulware's conservatism-in-a-box program, he came to believe in what he was selling. And Boulware came to believe in Reagan's ability to sell it.[41]

Both Reagan's contact with right-wing economics and the strategies he later used to spread its good news to the nation came from his time at GE, a job he called a "postgraduate course in political science." In his 1990 autobiography, Reagan boasted that contrary to his younger liberal self's "inherent suspicion of big business," "[GE] left it up to me to decide what to say" and never began "trying to write my speeches for me."[42] They didn't have to. GE chose Reagan—in the words of the aide who GE had accompany him, the firm wanted a "good, upright kind of person" with no reputation for "social ramble." At the time he was struggling economically, and probably eager to please the "ultra-conservative" corporation. That aide, Earl Dunckel, who accompanied Reagan on every plant tour, was a self-identified "arch-conservative" and constantly threw right-wing talking points at him.[43] General Electric and Lemuel Boulware gave Reagan his platform, his audiences, and his words.

Adherents to right-wing economics like Chicago price theory and Hayekian neoliberalism frequently described it in terms akin to religious conversion—now Reagan was undergoing one himself. On long train rides across the country, he read and memorized Boulware's pseudo-nonpartisan, highly readable literature. He honed an important and very Boulware-esque script later known as "The Speech"—which he characterized as a "sermon."[44] Reagan noted that his speeches evolved over time because of the "swiftly rising tide of collectivism"—something he feared because of Boulware.[45]

In his future political career he quoted most of the economists you have met here, and he worked closely with the postwar conservative political ecosystem. As a politician, he leveraged both the content of Boulwarism—Hazlitt's economics, for instance—and Boulware's campaigning strategies, like moving public opinion between elections, according to Thomas Evans, who wrote a book on Reagan's relationship with Boulware. Reagan became the perfect standard-bearer for American bosses because his political ethos was their own, learned on the very factory floor tours that initially made up one-fourth of his job for GE.[46]

But American capitalists did not yet have everything they needed to impose neoliberalism on their country or the world. Propaganda was only one part of their strategy. They also relied on economic power: market forces, multinational corporations, and the global monetary system. There were not only millions of Americans but billions of people around the globe who would never accept anything like Boulware's vision of the world. And as decolonization continued over the course of the 1960s, those billions asserted more and more economic and political power.

Former colonial possessions were breaking free of their European overlords, by ballot and by force. Many of them were rethinking capitalism as well. The right was horrified at the resulting threat to economic and racial hierarchy. In a 1965 letter, Wilhelm Röpke compared the global spread of democracy to rabies.[47] An April 1967 article in the libertarian magazine *The Freeman* denounced liberals for trying to "[cure] poverty in Africa, Asia, Latin America, Appalachia, Harlem, Watts, and other slum areas."[48] Collective action could not be allowed to remake the world anywhere. Decolonization raised questions similar to the UE's *Deadline for Action*. As anticolonial movements pushed back empires, would the breakdown of formal political rule by colonial states mean a similar retreat by the economic hegemony that had come with it? Was this going to be the century of big business or of the common people?

8

"The Interdependent World We Have Tried to Build": Multinationals, Macroeconomics, and the Road to Reagan, 1967–80

In the early part of the cool dry season (May–August) of 1962, a visitor arrived at Roan Antelope Copper Mine in Luanshya, in what was then Northern Rhodesia and is now Zambia: F. Taylor Ostrander, acting in his capacity as an agent of the mining firm AMAX, which owned part of the company that ran the miles-deep mine.[1] His tour took him to a "control room" using numbered boards that tracked the performance of individual workers. The control room, and Ostrander's visit to it, were both part of transitions for the mine in an age of political turbulence.

AMAX was a prime example of a new political-economic form rising in the postwar era: the multinational corporation (MNC). As empires fell, the corporations that had once stretched across them now straddled political boundaries. The MNC was an international economic entity in a world of nations. Decolonization placed MNCs at the center of some of the most important political conflicts of the age. AMAX's mining investments on what had very recently been British imperial territory were now split across, among other political territories, the Federation of Rhodesia and Nyasaland (which included Northern Rhodesia), the increasingly isolated apartheid regime of independent South Africa, and present-day Namibia, then occupied by South Africa.

In this business environment, economists like Ostrander were useful, even necessary. AMAX's business could be disturbed by anything from macroeconomic change to new regulations to local politics. FTO, as he was often referred to in company paperwork, had experience with all of these—he'd worked at the US Treasury, then as an administrator of the postwar price control regime in Germany.[2] The dual character of economics, as empiricist social science and rationalist market philosophy, helped it serve both functions of control science: optimizing labor control and justifying it. While right-wing economists often ignored or abandoned empirical methods when making broad pronouncements like those of price theory, the discipline's mathematical and social-scientific methods remained part of economists' training and toolkit, even at the University of Chicago. In other words, most economists were not Ludwig von Mises: they could and did engage with reality and do math.

Still, we should not overestimate the power of postwar economists. The fact that AMAX wanted an economist in FTO's position speaks partly to their usefulness but also simply to the reputation and social position of the discipline. While he appears to have been a competent administrator, or at least navigator of institutional politics, nothing in Ostrander's biography seems relevant to labor relations or Africa specifically. He had the power to offer influential opinions on the management of Northern Rhodesian mineworkers because of the institutional authority of economics and the broader political economy of multinationals.

The "control room" Ostrander visited in the spring of 1962 was part of a broader vision of "personnel administration"—a vision that highly impressed the economist. Roan personnel manager Bob Menzies, according to Ostrander, used the control room to tell

> exactly which Africans are working for each European and what the African's group numbers are, what his training has been, and even whether he is doing well or poorly. The important innovation here is to consider the African employee as a personality whose progress can be observed and which ought to be observed.

This goal might have been panoptic, but the architecture at Roan was quite the opposite. Menzies encouraged wide open spaces. Next to the administrator's office, Ostrander found a conference room for union-management discussions that he called "one of the most comfortable such rooms on the Copperbelt." In most of the region, African workers seeking to deal with the company lined up "outside various wicket windows in small shacks," according to Ostrander—but at Roan Antelope, they instead sat indoors in a large corridor, on steel benches opposite a long counter of clerks. This comparative improvement on other workplaces, Ostrander felt, was indicative of Menzies's broader attitude toward Africans. The economist claimed that Menzies's subordinates were all "imbued with his philosophy of nondiscriminatory treatment of Africans as human beings."[3]

Nondiscriminatory did not mean equal. In 1953, Rhodesian Selection Trust (RST) executive Ronald Prain explained that "equal pay for equal work" was impossible—"on those terms no-one will employ the African." He instead suggested "a formula approximately that of the type adopted in the [neighboring] Belgian Congo," which worked out to Africans making 30 percent of what an expatriate might earn doing the same job.[4] The resulting savings were one reason that RST committed itself to the progressive "advancement" of African workers. It didn't hurt that this allowed them to position themselves positively with rising local nationalists and international liberals, rather than with increasingly isolated white minority regimes. But African advancement risked the ire of expatriate white workers in the mines, which prompted strong resistance. The company overcame them: in 1955, RST forced white mineworkers to concede "the elimination of all racial restrictions in theory."[5]

In practice, this first round of "advancement" affected only a small number of workers. The company then sought to split these workers from the existing African Mineworkers Union (AMWU) into a smaller group, the Mines African Salaried Staff

Association (MASA), in order to separate skilled potential leaders from the class interests and institutions of most workers.[6] Menzies's decidedly Benthamite control room board and Boulware-like program of ventilated facilities were (like both Bentham and Boulware's own efforts) part of a system of worker control.

Not unlike General Electric and the right in America, RST and the Federal Party in Northern Rhodesia sought to neutralize working-class radicalism by manipulating class politics. The mining companies had already used this strategy to split expatriate supervisors from their union, and they now pursued the same goal with African workers. The Federal Party, meanwhile, hoped to cultivate a Black middle (not working) class that might support the existing Federation of Rhodesia and Nyasaland rather than Zambian nationalism, which most miners were in favor of.

Union miners struggled against the staff association on the grounds of both national and labor politics. They shunned those who chose to join MASA, aimed to intimidate them out of doing so, and went on strike in 1955 and 1956. Even children participated: the children of union workers mocked children of MASA members. In resisting the staff association, union miners contested class structure itself and with it the class politics that elites hoped to realize. The mining companies and the government perceived the strikes as an attack on the Black middle class and on Africans who supported the Federation. Striking workers, for their part, called for the dissolution of both MASA and the Federation.[7]

While the strike was put down by the government, miners' class consciousness and nationalism remained.[8] Miners joined the radical United National Independence Party (UNIP), while staff association members were more likely to support the rival moderate nationalist African National Congress. At stake in political conflict over independence was nothing less than who would benefit from the mineral wealth of the nation.

On June 1, 1962, a day after summarizing his Roan visit, Ostrander wrote a confidential memo outlining recent developments in Zambian politics that concerned RST and AMAX.[9] While waiting in the lobby of the Ridgeway Hotel for a meeting with UNIP leader Kenneth Kaunda, an organizer for ANC ran into Ostrander and cornered the surprised and embarrassed economist into a chat. The organizer explained that he'd left UNIP after a short membership because of policy disagreements. Kaunda offered a different explanation: the man had been kicked out of UNIP because he was a police informer. Apparently happily taken in by the ANC, he had just been bribed with a brand-new American car. The bribe, Kaunda explained, came from a powerful opponent of UNIP's: the British South Africa Company (BSA). Thanks to an unusual arrangement from its colonial past, BSA—not the state—had control over Northern Rhodesia's mineral rights. The ruling United Federal Party (UFP) and its leader, Roy Welensky, had already chipped away at that arrangement, which meant any future nationalist government would have both every right and every reason to do so further.

With decisive elections approaching in the fall, BSA had marshalled its resources and connections against UNIP. It was not-so-secretly funding the ANC—whose leader pledged a government with the UFP—in order to weaken UNIP. Kaunda believed that BSA had secretly pushed the money from London through Katanga—a breakaway region of the former Belgian Congo whose Belgian-backed regime probably assassinated UN Secretary-General Dag Hammarskjöld. Ronald Prain, whom Ostrander also met on this trip, claimed that BSA had made ANC an outright and open gift rather than relying on "subterfuge."

Either way, the scheme was as ludicrous as it was offensive: ANC was apparently spending so much money that it would run through its BSA slush fund before the election, at which point it could blackmail them for more. Prain "couldn't understand how any management could have been so stupid as to put itself in this position." Kaunda now had a needle to thread: he had to attack BSA for its support of the ANC-UFP alliance, but he had to do so without spooking investors or alienating mining firms in general.

RST's and UNIP's fates were tied together by Northern Rhodesia's dependence on copper, and they would remain bonded through it. Ostrander's company was betting on a UNIP victory, but it didn't want to put all its eggs in one basket. By announcing the opening of a new mine at Chambishi *before* the fall elections, Prain and Ostrander believed, RST had won the gratitude of "the African side" by signaling that they were happy to invest in a country soon to be ruled by its Black majority, but also "lulled the European side," who erroneously believed that any company investing in Northern Rhodesia would do so only if it believed white minority rule remained. Kaunda, for his part, urged the RST officials not to perceive his attacks on BSA as an attack on mining in general—he "thoroughly appreciated" the Chambishi opening as continued investment in this important industry. And in the elections in late 1962, Kaunda won. BSA had been even more "stupid" than Prain imagined: their bribed allies' loyalties were not just expensive, they were worthless. ANC formed a coalition with UNIP, which took the nation out of the Federation and into independence.

RST and AMAX took a pragmatic approach, working with rather than against the nationalists. They had little other choice—Zambian independence seemed inevitable—and decided against the embarrassing flailing of some of their competitors. Independence did not end the class struggle between labor and capital—high politics did not resolve labor conflicts, because political conflicts were also labor conflicts. Despite the nationalist sentiments of many miners, there were tensions between AMWU and UNIP. The union called off a 1962 strike to help UNIP win the election, but it did so reluctantly. UNIP believed that the union—and everyone else—should be pursuing the national interest, which was not the same as workers' interests.[10]

"The Interests of the Mining Industry Are the Interests of the Whole Nation"

Not long after UNIP took power, state rhetoric and actions began to resemble those of managers rather than workers. A 1967 press release by the government partly blamed workers for recent accident fatalities, claiming that they were unwilling to listen to their supervisors.[11] In 1968, mining minister Lewis Changufu sent a letter to the mining companies regarding contract negotiations for expatriate workers, in which he also opined on the matter of wages more generally.[12] "As you are aware," he informed the industrialists, "the interests of the mining industry are the interests of the whole nation." The government believed neither expatriates nor "local workers" could receive wage increases. Any rise in wages "increases copper production costs and reduces our competitiveness in the world market." Wage increases would also reduce investment and cut into public revenue, they warned. Accordingly, they urged the companies not to raise wages.

Still, this was in service of national objectives rather than profit, and in this same period UNIP resolved to nationalize the mines. Since the nation could not afford to lose access to global capitalist markets, this was going to happen by negotiation. In 1969, Zambia's negotiators reached a partial nationalization deal, and a good one, all things considered. The nation would receive nearly 90 percent of all profits.[13] For a comparison we can look to Chile, which in 1969 signed its own nationalization deal to acquire a majority of Anaconda Copper Company. For this, Kaunda explained in an October draft memo to his cabinet, they paid the equivalent of eight years of mine earnings. The equivalent statistic for Zambia was four years. Zambia paid in bonds, which it had the option to repay faster (to avoid interest expense) if it had the means. While they guaranteed that taxes on mines would not increase, that tax rate was already a hefty 73 percent.[14]

The plan was to use Zambian copper for the good of all. A speech Kaunda gave on nationalization insisted that "our society must be kept man-centered," in line with the more general "Zambian Humanist" vision he deemed the philosophy of his rule.[15] Ideally, Zambia could use mining profits—as it already did less directly through tax revenue—to subsidize its economic development, making copper serve the nation's people rather than international investors. Moreover, it could make important investments and expansions that foreign corporations were reluctant to move forward with.[16] By investing in new facilities that AMAX would not have built, it could spur the development of new jobs, new markets, and new growth in Zambia.

At least in theory, this was Boulwarist efficiency in the mine and Zambian humanism at the level of the nation. A message from mining minister John Mwanakatwe to mine workers, probably dating from early 1969, offers a useful comparison with Boulware's messages to workers in the US.[17] Mwanakatwe explained to workers that "employment in the mining industry" came with a "responsibility to the whole country." The relationship between Zambia's mines and its general national welfare was more direct and substantial than GE's with its own country. Copper mining, Mwanakatwe explained, made up half of government revenue. "If you as a miner do not do your job to the very best of your ability, it means in real terms that one rural clinic might not be improved; one primary school might not be finished; one co-operative society might not get a loan." Nationalization meant RST's wealth could, and should, flow out across Zambia.

But following nationalization, the government itself continued to think more and more like a business. Now that it was the owner of a major mining corporation, the Zambian government had to prioritize profits in the mines it controlled. When copper prices fell in the early 1970s, the need to support the heavily indebted mining sector froze the very national development plans it was supposed to fund.[18] Ultimately, nationalization left AMAX with a pile of money and Zambia with liabilities. The multinational corporation, as a form, was so embedded in the global economy that it could swallow whole states with different ideologies.

There were of course problems with Zambian mining that weren't reducible to global capitalism—corruption, mismanagement, Kaunda's decision to move to one-party rule. His successor, Fredrick Chiluba, began to guide the country toward multiparty democracy but then attempted to consolidate power himself. In a retrospective with an American think tank, the Brookings Institution, following Chiluba's death, Mwangi Kimenyi and Nelipher Moyo warned that "without strong institutions that place effective constraints on leaders with self-seeking behaviors, Africans cannot hope to sustain democratic leadership."[19] At least as important as the absence of these institutions, though, was the *presence* of strong institutions that would place constraints on the pursuit of the common good—institutions like multinationals, global markets, and ultimately the International Monetary Fund, to which the country became heavily indebted. In 1997, the Zambian government privatized the mines once more.

American investors neutralized Zambian organized labor and left-wing politics by wielding market forces and international institutions against them. Where control through direct planning and intervention had failed, control through abstract market forces succeeded, resoundingly. Rather than taking direct action in the workplace, capital could use markets to discipline national governments. Worker beliefs could become irrelevant if the state believed its economic fortunes depended on acting in concert with capital. By using Boulwarist economic ideas, capitalists could create a political environment in which workplace Boulwarism was no longer necessary.

And at this moment, Boulwarism had to ascend beyond the workplace, because back in the United States it had just been declared illegal by the National Labor Relations Board.

"The Interdependent World We Have Tried to Build"

From 1946 until 1968, there was only one strike at General Electric—an effort by the IUE (the CIO's less radical alternative to the UE) in 1960 that collapsed in the face of Boulware's trademark intransigence. Although Boulware crushed the strike, his hardball tactics came under the scrutiny of the National Labor Relations Board, ultimately leading to years of litigation. In 1969, this was settled with a federal court decision ruling that Boulwarism was a violation of workers' right to collective bargaining. Later that year, the IUE and the UE came together and organized a three-months-long strike. They won.[20]

By the 1970s, the postwar order was faltering. Macroeconomically, growth was slowing. The US entered a period of "stagflation," or inflation without increasing employment. Deindustrialization—which had already begun by the late 1960s in general and earlier in specific regions—started to speed up, disrupting industries that were the economic foundation of whole communities and even regions. Confronting this changing global economy, Republican President "Tricky Dick" Nixon was willing to violate free market orthodoxy if it helped his re-election prospects. In August 1971, he imposed price controls, using broad powers granted by the Democratic Party–written Economic Stabilization Act of 1970. Horrifying to free marketeers, price controls were meant to protect the economy after Nixon's suspension of the ability of foreign central banks to exchange their dollars for gold.

This ability had been central to the global monetary arrangement known as the Bretton Woods system, in which the US dollar served as an international reserve currency, with exchange rates between it and other currencies fixed, and the dollar itself anchored by a fixed price to gold. The system was shaky from the beginning: the supply of dollars increased faster than the supply of gold. For much of the 1960s the US and cooperating economies kept the open market price of gold aligned with the fixed conversion rate by selling their reserves in order to close the gap, in what was known as the London Gold Pool. This kind of fiddling was emblematic of the Bretton Woods system, which operated in full only from 1959 (when it was completely implemented) to 1968, after which the London Gold Pool collapsed, and the system began coming apart. President Nixon's closing of the "gold window" was only the latest step in this unraveling, and it would not be the last.[21] Both this measure and price controls were meant to be temporary. Only the latter actually were.

Decoupling money from gold expands the capacity of the state to act. Under a metallic standard, the amount of money the government can produce is artificially restricted by the supply of the relevant metal. Released from those constraints, the government can spend far more money. There are three ways for the state to spend: taxes, borrowing, and monetary finance (also known as debt monetization, or "money printing").[22] With the gold constraint removed, it becomes possible to do either of the latter two at a far grander scale. Neither are inherently the harmful options they are often made out to be. Unlike that of individuals or households, governments' incomes and spending are linked. If I cut my spending by a quarter, I get to save extra money. If the government cuts 25 percent of its spending, the country's economy will suffer gravely and tax revenues will go down. Likewise, while personal spending increases can cause spiraling debt, government deficits contribute to economic growth.

On three occasions, the United States broke with metal standards and unleashed the full power of money against a military threat: first against Britain's Atlantic empire in the 1770s, then against the Confederate slaveholder state during the Civil War, and finally against fascism in World War II. Each time, America printed money without the false security of gold backing. Each time, the nation achieved remarkable things by spending beyond the limits a metallic standard would allow. And each time, when the threat passed, economic elites overcame popular resistance and sealed the full power of money once again in a tomb of gold (and sometimes silver).

With his 1971 suspension of gold convertibility, Nixon had unsealed the tomb again. The possibilities within—a spirit of collective action, of cooperation, of *deliberation* rather than spontaneity, of dreaded "planning"—threatened to escape. Citizens might realize they didn't need the fear of Nazis to come together and grow the economy through democratic action by dramatic state spending. What good was faith in market self-optimization if the very basis of exchange itself could be manipulated by a powerful state? If workers might decide inflation was acceptable, eroding the very basis of wealth? If they realized government debt was a good thing? That money was not a fixed resource but a resource allocation mechanism they could potentially wield to their own ends? Capitalists thus had two tasks. They had to create a new monetary regime that worked for America and the world, and, simultaneously, they had to shape political conditions so that this new regime could not be used by the laboring masses for their own benefit.

In March 1972, a succession of technocrats and businessmen from the US and the European Economic Community (EEC) gathered in Versailles at the historic Trianon Palace Hotel, a short walk from the sprawling Palace of Versailles itself. Attendees included Prince Guido Colonna di Paliano, an Italian aristocrat who had bounced around various diplomatic roles for several decades; William Blackie, head of the Caterpillar Tractor Company; David Rockefeller, chair of Chase Manhattan Bank; Wilfrid Baumgartner, a French chemical and pharmaceuticals executive; F. Taylor Ostrander; and his boss Ian MacGregor, chief executive of AMAX.[23] This was the first US-EEC Businessmen's Conference. On the agenda was nothing less than the fate of what the US delegation called "the interdependent world we have tried to build."[24]

Specifically, as William Blackie's opening address explained, attendees were concerned with three things: "international trade, international investment, and the international monetary system required to promote and facilitate the same." The latter was critical. In Blackie's words, international exchanges "have to be resolved into a price, and this immediately brings into the computation the rate of exchange between the involved currencies." Bretton Woods had offered certain and stable rates. Now that system was on the ropes. Facing the resulting problems, Blackie insisted the conference should not only be "one more exercise in the dialectics of free enterprise economics—stimulatingly informative, educationally beneficial, and socially enjoyable" but also a platform for "constructive action."

For William Blackie and his audience, the multinational corporation (MNC)—not the national state—was the answer to the profound questions of their era. In his words:

> What organization other than the multinational corporation could be more constructively appropriate or even available to be the vehicle for carrying material progress through and beyond the present level? International business is not the business of any one country; it is the creature of a world which is crying out for a scheme of things in which there shall be an allocation or reallocation of resources into a more productive and more widespread combination. That cry had better be heeded!

Blackie admitted that this was a choir he did not need to preach to but nonetheless praised the MNC to them as "the most constructive agency for the propagation of material good ever known." And anyway, what other option was "even available"? Naturally, the future therefore demanded a more limited role for government and an expanded role for multinational corporations. Blackie explained that government officials had intentionally been kept out of the conference, partly as an expression of the view that "business itself should contribute more to the determination and direction of political economics" and policy. Governments needed to know their place.

A paper by the conference's working group on investment (headed by Ian MacGregor, probably with Ostrander's input) echoed price theory notions of market efficiency (over "non-economic decision-making" by governments) and implied that the ideal relationship between corporations and nations should be more like the relationship between corporations and cities—which they were free to leave as they saw fit. The working group paper suggested three paths for achieving this vision in the face of economic challenges and political resistance.

First was "self-discipline, leaving fewer real abuses subject to attack." Of course, this conveniently vested power in the hands of MNCs themselves. Beyond self-regulation, the paper—and Blackie—promoted "international codes of behavior covering all the various aspects of international economic activity." William Blackie had praised the General Agreement on Tariffs and Trade (GATT), an existing treaty regime that had helped lower tariffs, but felt it had to be extended because governments were relying increasingly on "nontariff devices" to engage in protectionism and throw up barriers to international business. Finally, to the extent that direct regulation was necessary, the paper suggested business could "cooperate" and ensure that it was "sensible and acceptable."[25]

International business found useful collaborators in academia and government—particularly economist George Shultz, whom Nixon appointed treasury secretary in 1972. The son of a New York stock trader, Shultz had gotten his start as an economist at MIT, studying industrial economics and then teaching industrial relations—both disciplines concerned with labor control. After a stint in the Eisenhower administration, he moved to a professorship in industrial relations at Chicago's Graduate School of Business, where he became a close ally of Milton Friedman. As head of the Treasury Department, George Shultz unsurprisingly collaborated with business on the matter of changes to money. He appointed William Blackie, along with a number of bankers and multinational heads (for example, General Electric chairman Reginald Jones) to an advisory committee on monetary reform in 1973, when, Shultz explained, "negotiations for world monetary reform" were reaching "their definitive stage."²⁶ As "experienced and expert members of the private financial and business community," the committee would "help assure that reform is realistic, practical, and effective."

With the advice of these "experts" and his friend Milton Friedman, Shultz pursued a new monetary agenda. While gold convertibility was dead, the other pillar of Bretton Woods, fixed exchange rates, was not. Negotiations to repair the Bretton Woods system were ongoing, and plenty of people who mattered—most notably Arthur Burns at the Federal Reserve and Secretary of State Henry Kissinger—wanted to keep some version of the old system of fixed exchange rates. Shultz and Friedman instead proposed "floating" exchange rates: currencies would be traded like any other market commodity, with no defined or regulated rates at all. Their proposal was not immediately embraced, but it helped legitimize the idea, and when the oil shock of 1973 threw the global economy into chaos, Shultz and Friedman got what they wanted.²⁷

Floating rates brought Spencerian competition, Hayekian spontaneous order, and Friedmanite price theory to the mechanism of currency exchange itself. Historian Jennifer Burns's biography of Friedman characterizes floating exchange rates as "the ultimate extension of price theory." With "the price of money itself" determined by market forces, nations would be "forced to compete in an international market, compelled to offer political stability, desirable products, and attractive opportunities for capital investment."²⁸

Just as Ian MacGregor and Ostrander had hoped in 1972, nations would have to relate to business more like cities did. International business was achieving other goals outlined at the US-EEC Businessmen's Conference as well. Ostrander worked on policy for the 1973–1979 Tokyo Round of GATT revisions. They ended up including business "codes" and measures targeting nontariff trade barriers—just what William Blackie and other businessmen's conference attendees had called for in 1972.²⁹ International capitalists were making progress on their first goal: the international monetary system was saved, and an international trade regime even more friendly to MNCs was coming together. Now it had to make sure that the newly supreme dollar was not wielded against it through the power of democracy.

"The Market Gives Them That Choice"

On October 8, 1975, representatives of US and European capital assembled for the second annual conference of the US-EEC Businessmen's Council, which had formed out of the 1972 conference. Former Nazi steel executive Hans-Günther Sohl, now chairman of the Federation of German Industries, warned that a "deep shadow" was haunting Europe: the shadow of recession and inflation. The reasons for this were complicated—and numbering high among them was oil prices—but Sohl had a simple answer. He blamed workers, in two senses. First, they had pursued the politics of a "magic formula," sold in the "ideological guise" of social justice and equality, consisting of "less and less work and higher expenditures." Second, workers engaged in "redistribution struggles" had placed "excessive strain" on resources. The result was inflation. A man who had once supervised forced labor on behalf of a fascist regime now lectured the world's billions for not working hard enough and for fighting for economic equality.[30]

For Sohl and the international business community, both the problem and the solution lay in money. In summary remarks at the end of the conference's third plenary session, MacGregor claimed that Sohl had "touched the fundamental problem" of the ongoing economic disturbance, "the reconciling of consumption with savings and investment." This raised the question of by whom and how savings and investment would be prioritized over the masses' economic demands for consumption. Immediately following that summary of Sohl's ideas, MacGregor asked "whether it is possible for free societies to reconcile their freedom with the essential discipline that brings needed savings and investment." Earlier in the session, he had offered a potential answer when he praised floating exchange rates as a "form of free market mechanism" that could "impose discipline and stability."[31]

While businessmen like those at the US-EEC conferences were devising new schemes to insulate business from government, they were also hard at work developing new political coalitions and the rhetoric needed to realize them. A report in the 1972 conference materials spoke positively of "the efforts of many American multinationals who are countering the 'exporting US jobs' and other charges of organized labor by aggressive advertising and in-plant educational campaigns."[32] Also in 1972, business interests assembled a group called the Business Roundtable, cofounded by the head of GE out of foundations including the previously existing Construction Users Anti-Inflation Roundtable.[33] Organizations like the Business Roundtable and the American Legislative Exchange Council, along with business media and Republican politicians, pursued what sociologist Melinda Cooper has called a "business-led tax revolt."[34]

Like Boulware's efforts, the tax revolt sought to make workers think of themselves as consumers and savers instead of workers. Through rhetoric like Reagan's claims of "welfare queens," the right linked their vision of spending, inflation, and taxes to racial and gendered animus, casting the economic turmoil of the age as a conflict of hardworking men against greedy women, and white savers against Black spenders.[35] The business press more generally, in Cooper's words, presented wage inflation as a "feminine malaise."[36]

Democrats seemed unable to solve it—thanks in part to the new international monetary system. Beginning in 1977, Democrats controlled the presidency and much of the government. While newly elected President Jimmy Carter was a relatively conservative Democrat, he nonetheless proposed a strong international response to the economic stagflation of the age. Carter's administration planned a coordinated international economic expansion with West Germany and Japan. All three nations would spend more money and grow their competitive economies; together, they would pull the global economy back into growth. But exactly as neoliberals hoped, international cooperation was difficult—Germany and Japan were not interested.[37] When it pursued expansionary policy on its own, the US incurred the ire of the market: investors began fleeing the dollar for the yen and the mark (something that cooperation could theoretically have prevented). Its value relative to them dropped by about half.[38]

Hans-Günther Sohl's earlier insistence on the necessity of confidence was a threat. If the US did not get inflation down and deal with its external deficits (outflows of money to other nations), investors would take their ball and play somewhere else. Investment capital would rush out of the United States. President Carter chose to give in. On December 9, 1978, he gave a speech promising budget cuts to tackle inflation.[39] Business was pleased. AMAX's chairman Pierre Gousseland wrote a letter to the White House declaring "AMAX supports your efforts" and that they pledged their "best efforts to assist," including advice on reducing costly environmental and occupational safety regulations—an implicit call to compromise workers' health so that AMAX could lower its prices.[40]

The following year, Carter appeased markets by putting Paul Volcker, well known as someone who took a hard line against inflation, in charge of the Federal Reserve. Volcker wielded the Fed's authority over bank reserves and later interest rates to engineer an artificial recession. If spending went down, eventually prices would have to follow. The price was American jobs and growth, but that was a price Volcker was willing to pay.[41] Americans had spent too much and saved too little—Ian MacGregor's *freedom or discipline* dilemma would now be resolved in favor of the latter, using the force of the central bank. Volcker sacrificed millions of jobs at the altar of price stability.[42]

Meanwhile, Milton Friedman began delivering right-wing economics into American homes through his popular ten-part television series *Free to Choose*. Carried, ironically, on America's public broadcaster PBS, *Free to Choose* was a distillation of "free market" thought into ten watchable one-hour episodes, split between a documentary segment led by Friedman and then a roundtable of debate. The greatest hits of capital's science of control in general, and postwar "free enterprise" thought in particular, are all there. In the first half-hour alone, Friedman retells Leonard Read's pencil story from the university Adam Smith lectured at, and glosses Nock and Spencer's argument for unrestricted consequences: "most important of all," he said of the relatively unrestricted market activity of Hong Kongers, "if they fail they bear the costs."[43]

Free to Choose presented a curious idea of freedom. Frequently and intentionally, Friedman conflated political rights like the freedom of speech with "economic freedom"—which includes the right to sell your labor at any price someone will buy it at, the freedom to work in a poorly ventilated workplace, and, as socialist Michael Harrington put it during the debate section of the first episode, "the freedom to die from the lack of medicine" without Medicare, a program which Friedman opposed. The Chicago economist described workers in Hong Kong as "free—free to work what hours they choose, free to move to other jobs if they wish. The market gives them that choice. It also determines what they make." Workers have a choice, but it is not a choice in the sense we tend to think of it or desire it. They can choose what the market allows. The purpose of economic "freedom" is to execute the price system's grand design.

Friedman had offered an effective pitch to many Americans. The one actor with some actual freedom under price theory is the consumer—and the middle class in the US had been increasingly encouraged by men like Boulware to see themselves as consumers. Their power in that role had grown rapidly enough in the preceding few decades to make consumption feel like a right, before slowing enough in the 1970s to curdle that sense of right into resentment. Rhetoric like Friedman's economics encouraged Americans to blame this slowdown on government: while the state could fail, the market could only be failed. Right-wing economics had brought the mid-century Keynesian order to the chopping block. Lemuel Boulware's protégé stepped up to swing the axe. *Free to Choose* ran during the 1980 election year, and Jimmy Carter's Republican opponent was Ronald Reagan.

"Thrifty Americans Like You"

For Carter, inflation was a complex problem. For Reagan, it was a simple sin. Forget carefully crafting economic policy—we simply had to throw the bums out and cut taxes. Reagan's paradigm was much easier to campaign on. In early October 1980, with Election Day mere weeks away, the Republican and Democratic candidates for Indiana's fourth congressional district visited fifth graders at Aboite Elementary School in Fort Wayne, Indiana. A newspaper reporter for the local *News-Sentinel* relayed the views of the assembled children on inflation. Young David Wendell correctly blamed oil prices and reported he would vote for the Democrat if he could. His classmate John Morrow blamed "foreign countries [who] are out-producing us," while J. J. Foster indicated he had witnessed inflation in orange juice prices. Many of the children told stories about parents laid off by truck and tractor manufacturer International Harvester, an important local employer embroiled in costly strike negotiations. The kids feared for the future.[44]

Ronald Reagan spoke to those fears in an October 24 speech on the economy, delivered on television. The "mighty music" of American economic growth, he exclaimed, had been replaced with "eerie, ghostly silence." Toward the close of the speech, he relayed an anecdote about one of the kids from that Fort Wayne classroom, a girl named Andrea Baden. Andrea wanted a pair of roller skates, "so, in the Great American tradition, she saved her allowance until she had the money to buy them." But to her shock and dismay, the price had gone up while she was saving. She saved more—only to find it had gone up again. "It's just not fair," Reagan cried, quoting Andrea.[45]

"Well that's right," he reassured her. "What Mr. Carter's done to this country's economy just isn't fair. It just isn't right." Inflation hurts, and Reagan was going to stop it. He called for help from "thrifty Americans like you" against the free-spending government and its greedy allies. This formation encouraged middle-class families to identify as and with virtuous savers—Boulware's coalition of small and large capital, "managers, farmers, stockholders, bond holders, insurance policy holders, savings bank depositors, pensioners, and any other upstanding citizens with an interest in keeping the value of money honest"—rather than other workers.

Thrifty taxpayer identity encouraged laid-off International Harvester workers to identify less with laid-off Black manufacturing workers and more with people like Andrea Baden's father Ron, who as far as I can tell was a successful accountant.[46] In 1976, voters in Fort Wayne's Allen County had chosen the Republican over the Democrat by a margin of less than 8 percent. In 1980, they went for Reagan by nearly 20 percentage points.[47] With their help, Ron Reagan would make sure ten-year-old Andrea could afford roller skates. She reported a "happy feeling" when Reagan relayed her story on national television. What ten-year-old wouldn't have felt happy?

She might not have if anyone had told her who was going to pay: people like her classmates' laid-off parents. President Reagan devastated the American working class, particularly in unionized manufacturing. In Reagan's America, capital captured the power of fiat money for itself by running up vast deficits through tax cuts—giveaways to the rich—while keeping wages down through monetary policy, domestic spending cuts, global competition, and union-busting. A post-postwar economic settlement began to emerge: assets like housing and stocks would be allowed, indeed encouraged, to appreciate in value. Wages would stay down.[48] This was the price of price stability. *Deadline for Action* had been right on two counts: prices were political, and with conservatives at the helm, only the prices they wanted to go up would do so. Stock prices would rise. Wages, for the most part, would not.

President Reagan was guided, and indeed created as a political figure, by right-wing economics, the latest iteration of capitalism's science of control. The United Kingdom's new prime minister, Margaret Thatcher, was an adherent of the same discipline herself. Like its earlier practitioners, Reagan and Thatcher sought to remake the masses as political-economic subjects. "Welfare queens" was a racist and misogynist reiteration of Joseph Priestley's rhetoric of the undeserving poor. Priestley had proposed forcing the poor into individual savings accounts (not pensions or something like social security); Reagan's economy meant fewer and fewer Americans had pensions, causing more and more of them to turn to Individual Retirement Accounts, which Ron Baden rightly characterized in a 1987 *Fort Wayne News-Sentinel* article as "forced savings," since account-holders are penalized for early withdrawal.[49]

Thatcher became known for saying, "there is no such thing as society" (Herbert Spencer's methodological individualism distilled) and "there is no alternative" (Spencer verbatim). Those who were not convinced of these statements could be made to accept them with the force control science's practitioners had always used. In 1984, Thatcher's handpicked head of the National Coal Board orchestrated the repression of a national strike. He was Ian K. MacGregor, formerly of AMAX.

Economics could have been better. The discipline entered the postwar era with a rich empirical tradition that supported considerable political diversity. But McCarthyism chased anything too left-wing out of the profession while promoting business-friendly economics within universities, corporations, and ultimately the public square. America rewarded working-class leftist economist Carl Marzani's wartime efforts on behalf of his country with prison. His shipping scion classmate Ostrander got to run an international business.

Economics also entered the postwar era with an anti-empiricist tradition—the Austrian School and its American connections, both with links back to Spencer. Ludwig von Mises and company's hostility to reality made it impossible for them to manage the capitalist system they defended—you can't run a global economy without real numbers. What they could do, with the help of businessmen like Lemuel Boulware and Alfred Sloan, and popularizers like Henry Hazlitt and Ronald Reagan, was build an activist base and public support for a "free enterprise" system in place of the negotiated corporatism of the postwar era. Milton Friedman finally combined both traditions into a package pragmatic enough to govern. Control science had become mainstream economics.

9

"Economics Represents the Actual World": Popular Economics, 1981–2008

Retired Federal Reserve chair Alan Greenspan "spent his extraordinary career reckoning with how the world really works," according to a 2006 announcement of his upcoming memoir. A year earlier, the bestselling book *Freakonomics* promised wisdom for those who wanted to understand "the actual world." *How the World Really Works* is also the title of a 2025 book by the scientist Vaclav Smil; in it he describes decarbonization by 2050 as impossible, a fantasy. In 2010 Smil published *Energy Myths and Realities* with the right-wing think tank AEI, which was praised by one Robert Bradley for its free market description of "energy reality." Bradley is an expert in energy falsehood; he spent sixteen years at Enron, an energy company that imploded due to multibillion-dollar fraud, and now peddles climate change denial on behalf of the oil industry.[1]

"How the world really works" is control science's rejection of morality distilled into five words. In them ring Lemuel Boulware's assertion that American workers' sympathies for government action made them like children who still believed in Santa Claus, and Helvétius's claim that in order to love mankind, you must lower your expectations. This is how the world *really works*, and there is no alternative. "We have no sensible choice other than to let markets work," Greenspan wrote in that memoir. "Market failure is the rare exception," he promised, "and its consequences can be assuaged by a flexible economic and financial system."[2]

A year after Greenspan published his book, the global financial system he had shepherded for twenty years imploded, shattering millions of lives. The cynics who tell us *how the world really works* are in fact describing how they *want* it to. But having defeated the left in the 1940s and put an end to the postwar order in the 1980s, practitioners of the science of control had a freer hand than ever to remake the world according to their vision.

"Charts for Charles"

Like the families of so many other figures in this book, Charles Koch's family made it easy to believe the world was a selfish and competitive place. His father, Fred, was a cold and resentful man. A childhood friend described the family patriarch as a "stiff, calculated businessman" whose "interest was not in his kids, other than that he wanted them educated." Koch biographer Daniel Schulman writes that Fred "was the type of father, one Koch relative said, who taught his children how to swim by throwing them into the pool and walking away."[3] One family friend speculated that Fred's harsh parenting came from a sense that he had made his eldest son Freddie gay by being too affectionate. Determined not to do this again, Fred was stingy at best in disbursing love to his three other children—Charles, who was the second oldest, and younger twins Bill and David. Freddie ultimately escaped the family business for a life in drama and arts. It fell to Charles to take over the family business.[4]

Charles learned well from his father. His younger brother Bill said all of the siblings fought for Fred's love, and in turn, Charles himself set Bill and David against each other, according to Bill, who recalled him as a bully.[5] Charles learned from his father's politics too. A vehement anticommunist and founding member of the extreme-right John Birch Society, Fred Koch self-printed an anticommunist pamphlet in 1960. It denounced communism as a "disease of the mind," one he warned "the children of the very rich are far more susceptible to" than those of the poor.[6]

Charles was apparently not among them. He joined the John Birch Society himself, and on a blind date while he was in his midtwenties Charles once went off about communism, discussing Bircher propaganda materials, at such length that his date left early.[7]

Like his father, Charles became enmeshed in the American libertarian-conservative political network. One important influence on him was F. A. "Baldy" Harper, a founder of Leonard Read's Foundation for Economic Education (FEE), a founding member of the Mont Pelerin Society, and a one-time codirector of the William Volker Fund. In 1957, Harper published a short book with FEE called *Why Wages Rise*, an accessible free market tirade of the kind Boulware distributed to his workers and managers.[8] Its primary argument was that wages rose because of productivity increases rather than unions. It raged against inflation as a hidden tax, and it insisted on the supremacy of the market over the government. When Charles Koch first read *Why Wages Rise*, he explained later, he "had what [psychologist] Abraham Maslow called a 'peak experience'"—in Maslow's words, "secularized religious or mystical or transcendent experiences," that "have to do with the nature of reality" and can transcend "distinctions between good and evil."[9] Harper's book, Koch said, convinced him "that it was possible to understand and help improve the social world, just as it was the physical world."

In 1973, Koch delivered a eulogy at Harper's memorial service. He explained to those assembled to grieve that the late Harper's writings "on morality were possibly the most profound." He cited in particular Harper's belief that "there is a force in the universe which no mortal can alter," a line from his 1971 article "Morals and Liberty."[10] This force, Harper explained, was sometimes called God, or the Supernatural, or Natural Law. For Harper it was simply "Truth," "a force which rules without surrender to any mortal man." Causality itself—"the rule of cause and effect"—and with it science, relied on this force. "[The] Law of Gravity is one expression of Natural

Law," which is part of a broader "Truth" that man must obey. All mankind is "subject to the superior rule of Natural Law of Moral Law." Just as "someone walking off a cliff" will meet "death because of his ignorance" of the Law of Gravity, "violation" of the Moral Law has caused "the downfall of individuals and civilizations." Counterintuitively (again) for an article that insisted that morality must come before practicality, Harper was engaged here in the same collapse of the normative into the positive as earlier practitioners of the science of control.

The foundations of Harper's Moral Law were the Golden Rule and the Ten Commandments. For him, the Golden Rule was central because it "serves the necessary function of impartiality." But, he warned readers, the Golden Rule was not "sufficient unto itself." After all, it could be used for various ends: "the thief may argue that if he were like the one he has robbed, or if he were a bank harboring all those 'ill-gotten gains,' he would consider himself the proper object of robbery. Some claim that justification for the Welfare State, too, is to be found in the Golden Rule." Accordingly, further rules, "such as the Ten Commandments, or perhaps the Cardinal Sins, are necessary."

His article focused on two in particular: "thou shalt not steal" and "thou shalt not covet." The target of his ire was the "Welfare State," which manifested as programs like Social Security, the New Deal's Tennessee Valley Authority, and public education; rhetorically, "fair prices," "reasonable profits," and "the living wage" were all labels of welfare state thinking according to Harper. Though these programs claimed to have "laudable objectives," they were unethical, because all taxation was theft.

"Moral laws," Harper wrote, "are strict. They know not the language of man; they are not conversant with him in the sense of compassion." Like others in the American libertarian movement he was aligned with, Harper spoke in the language of racial anxiety as well. "Slavery," he wrote, "might be described as just another form of Welfare State." The government of the United States, Harper contended, was evil. It promised white slavery, it undermined "self-restraint" and "compassion," and it spread "Moral Decay." Its practices were a cosmic violation of the very laws of the universe itself.

This was the ethical and economic program behind Charles Koch's management philosophy. He believed that human behavior was a kind of fractal: rules that described individual human action applied at any level. Principles derived from those rules could therefore be scaled up to corporations, governments, and even the world. In the 1960s, fresh out of a short career in consulting, Charles brought in concepts like opportunity cost and the sunk cost fallacy in order to make better decisions.[11] After implementing basic market concepts at his company by informally bringing them up in meetings, Koch soon became "intrigued by the potential power of more advanced concepts and derivative models."

Among these was the "continuous improvement" model of W. Edwards Deming. Deming was popular in the 1970s and 1980s thanks to a reputation for helping rebuild Japanese industry after the war.[12] To Americans terrified of Japan's growing manufacturing capabilities and economic power, "Made in Japan" labels were a threat—one they could keep at bay by listening to the American who supposedly deserved much of the credit for this situation. In fact, Deming was a better salesman than a management consultant. A scathing 1996 article in the *Journal of Japanese Studies* suggests that "the greatest achievements of Japan's quality control did not so much derive from the guidance of W. Edwards Deming as emerge in spite of it."[13] But his statistics and his philosophy were good enough for Koch, particularly his idea of "continuous improvement."

Applying economic principles on a broader scale was no easy task, despite the role American business had played in developing and popularizing those principles. Koch faced particular resistance in the early 1970s when his firm tried to take control of Pine Bend Refinery in Minnesota. Koch took over Pine Bend because it had a unique profit-making feature: as one of only a few refineries that imported oil from Canada, it bypassed caps on oil imports, allowing it to bring as much cheaper imported oil into the US market as it desired. Moreover, according to Koch biographer Christopher Leonard, this enabled it to take advantage of additional government subsidies. Taking over Pine Bend meant taking over a money printer. But to do so, Charles Koch had to break Oil, Chemical, and Atomic Workers' Union Local 6-662.[14]

The union forced managers to follow considerations other than profit. For example, if management wanted a worker to stay late, they needed to give at least two hours' notice or pay that worker extra. For parents who cared about picking up kids or making it to their baseball games, this was rational. But for Koch, it was an inefficiency. In Baldy Harper's paradigm it was nothing less than a breach of moral law itself: the union forced anyone who wanted a job at Pine Bend to work under these generous rules, thus violating the "moral right [of the individual] to be free to choose his work," including under worse conditions.

Perhaps Koch told himself this; it is equally likely that he simply saw dollar signs. When the union went on strike, Koch's handpicked union-busting henchman, Bernard Paulson, flew scabs over OCAW's picket line, hired a private security firm, and devised a parking lot transfer scheme that allowed Teamsters drivers to *technically* observe the picket line while still making deliveries to the refinery. Ultimately, they broke the strike.

Not even law could hold back men like Koch—because in the 1970s, wealthy capitalists and right-wing economists began to take over the American legal establishment. The groundwork had already been laid. In part because of his inability to finish a dissertation or anything publishable, Aaron Director ended up working not in Chicago's economics department but at its law school. Here he pioneered the development of the subfield known as "law and economics."[15]

The application of economic thought to law produced conclusions that ranged from seemingly anodyne, even useful, to straightforwardly right-wing. In a 1968 article, economist Gary

Becker categorized crime as an economic activity rather than irrational evil. Comparing the economic value of prison time and fines, he observed that fines are perceived as unfair to poorer defendants because small fines tended to be associated with comparatively long prison sentences, which defendants nonetheless had to "choose" because they did not have the money to pay the fine. But by the same logic, Becker reasoned, prison sentences were often unfair to the wealthy, since they deprived them of more income than the same sentence would for a poorer convict.[16]

This was the kind of reasoning Henry Manne sought to popularize in the American legal establishment. He initially faced enormous resistance. Recalling matters many years after the fact, Manne whined that his early law and economics work was "ignored" and "ridiculed" by "the leading law professors" in his field. He claimed that he was met with "intense hatred," as were other "defenders of private property and free markets. "Chicago Economics" was, he believed, practically a slur among academics, legal academics included. But Manne, a self-described "full-time missionary" for his cause, was determined to change this.[17]

To do so, Henry Manne used the most powerful weapon in the arsenal of right-wing economics: money from rich donors. Manne began a summer seminar program at the University of Rochester for law professors and paid them a then-sizable $1,000, plus expenses and "very fancy meals." The money came from around a dozen "large corporations, most of which were concerned about antitrust matters." They funded the program because—by Manne's admission—they found Chicago School economics useful in their own lawsuits. Chicago economists had long offered a dissenting approach to antitrust law—price theory held that the market itself solved competition issues, and so the state rarely needed to intervene. To make his program intellectually appealing, Manne attracted top legal minds from illustrious institutions.[18] Everything about the summer program was orchestrated to create a successful legal field out of nothing.

With the help of the Liberty Fund, which is what it sounds like, Manne's Law and Economics Center expanded to a seminar program, and in 1976, its "Summer Camp" extended to federal judges.[19] A 2022 paper by Elliott Ash, Daniel L. Chen, and Suresh Naidu quantitatively examines the impact of law and economics seminars on attending judges' decisions. The results are striking. Attendees on average voted (federal judges rule as panels) against labor and environmental agencies 15 percent more often, decided in conservative directions on cases 20 percent more often, and imposed prison sentences 4 percent more often and 13 percent longer. This was exactly the kind of effect Manne's wealthy backers were hoping for.[20]

In 1986, Manne's Law and Economics Center found its long-term home: Virginia's George Mason University, where Charles Koch lavishly funded the development of right-wing economics.[21] Koch was not a hands-off funder. When Murray Rothbard, working for Koch's Cato Institute think tank, criticized the Koch-backed Libertarian Party presidential candidate in 1980, Koch had him fired. Charles fancied himself a man of ideas—and while his own writing doesn't suggest much in the way of deep thought, he had the money to make up for it. His wealth helped fund the expansion of "law and economics," the advancement of free market ideology in economics, and its diffusion to the public through campaign work, publications, and astroturfed political movements.

The "Science of Liberty"

While Charles Koch worked to develop his "science of liberty" in politics, he was co-developing it alongside a science of control in Koch Industries workplaces. Though he was able to sideline unions, other difficulties implementing his vision quickly arose. On a trip to an Oklahoma gas liquids plant in the mid-1980s, Koch found electricians "spending a large portion of their time measuring activity and drawing charts instead of doing electrical work. Our people referred to this as 'charts for Charles.'"[22]

Other difficulties arose from the rote application of models without understanding the philosophy beneath them. "Misapplications such as these," Koch wrote, "put us in the same trap as the government's wasteful approach to regulation, mandating the exact methods to be used, rather than setting and enforcing science-based standards."[23] According to Austrian economics, optimal results could be achieved only by enforcing rules that created the conditions for Hayekian spontaneous order to arise, not by seeking to direct matters from above. Yet this emphasis on local latitude created its own issues. He wrote that on some occasions, "employees have used the local knowledge model to rationalize their desire to do whatever they want without supervisory challenge."[24] Labor control schemes were not easy to create.

One person corporate America leaned on for lessons in worker control in this period was Jack Welch, who took over as CEO at General Electric in 1981. This was a new era for the company. Industrialization was declining in the United States, and with it so was manufacturing, long the company's core business. That same year, Reagan had brutally crushed a strike by air traffic controllers—one of the few unions that had supported his election—when they tried to demand a shorter workweek on account of their stressful line of work.

Both the game and the rules of the game, so to speak, were changing. In the 1950s, the standard American workplace was the factory. By the 1990s, it was the office—cubicles, performance reviews, profound alienation. Just as most Americans were never factory workers—manufacturing employment peaked at over one in five workers, in 1979—the platonic ideal of the office never described most jobs either.[25] But it described many of them. Moreover, the CEOs at the head of corporate America were public figures and political players just as their manufacturing titan predecessors had been.

Welch remade General Electric. It remained a vast conglomerate, but Welch changed the composition of that conglomerate by reducing its manufacturing divisions, spinning off parts of the business, and expanding its finance operations. He cut one in four GE workers—more than 100,000 jobs. Welch became known as "Neutron Jack": like a neutron bomb, he eliminated people while leaving buildings intact. While shrinking the company's manufacturing footprint, he expanded its financial services division, GE Capital. In a few short years the share of GE profits coming from the Capital division more than doubled, to one-sixth, and it later peaked at fully half.[26] GE sold turbines and appliances, but it also acted like a major bank.

GE's business had become, in effect, business. Welch's memoir includes a lengthy anecdote about a scheme for Capital to buy auto loans in Thailand, which would "make us the owner of one of every nine cars" in that country. Welch was initially skeptical. GE Capital's Thailand head, Mark Norbom, had a plan, though. He had contracts ready to go for the 1,000 employees required to manage the loans and promised they would pay off. "A car is among the most prized possessions in Thailand. People would give up almost everything else—would even sleep in their cars—before losing them for nonpayment of a loan," he explained, presumably salivating. Welch was convinced, and he approved the deal.[27]

A new company and a new economy meant new philosophies for management. One favorite, and famous, policy of Jack Welch's was what he called "differentiation." Welch split workers into As, Bs, and Cs. As, the top 20 percent of performers, were defined by their passion and hard work. They were rewarded with raises and stock options. The humble Bs, the middling 70 percent, received periodic raises, but only half or a third of what the As got. "Cs," Welch wrote, "must get nothing." "You can't waste time on them." They should be fired, in a policy that came to be known—to his ire—as "rank and yank."[28] He preferred the term "vitality curve."[29]

The political and practical demands of corporate management produced a library of such schemes. Some of them, like Six Sigma, were quantifiable ideals with real potential benefits. Others, like "rank and yank," had a kind of profit logic to them, even if their practical application could produce questionable results. Still others were more nebulous, at best philosophies rather than policies. Welch's GE had the four Es of leadership, *energy, energize, edge, and execute,* "connected by one P—passion."[30]

Vacuous alliterative devices like this were an obvious result of the circumstances they were made for. Managerial advice like this had to be broad, apply to all kinds of business, and be easily memorizable so that it could be learned by busy executives and invoked briskly like magic words. Yet the four Es were quite serious. At periodic "Session C" HR meetings, during which executive performance was reviewed and graded, the Es served as important grading criteria for a three-by-three grid of "performance/potential" that could determine whether an employee stayed.[31]

This was part of a viciousness that stretched to the top of GE management culture. One outdoor retreat for GE's corporate management in the 1990s had them construct rafts and race. During such a competition, labor negotiator (with, not for, labor) Dennis Rocheleau, irritated by the splashing oar of a GE Plastics executive named Jeff Immelt, threatened to "stick that oar so far up your ass your tonsils will pop out." According to journalists Thomas Gryta and Ted Mann, this competitiveness was the "fiery vibe that Welch liked."[32] In his memoir, Welch boasts of examining photographs of executives during Session C meetings, identifying anyone who looked too tired, and performatively shouting for them to be fired, in order to spur hard conversations.[33]

The boisterous threats, "war" to cut employees, scream-inducing raft races, and stale mnemonics were all part of a corporate management philosophy with political as well as economic utility. "Rank and yank" simultaneously imposed discipline—work hard or else—and conferred legitimacy—if you remain, you're the best of the best!—on corporate employees. It undermined solidarity between workers: the company was permanent—all else was transient, subject to constant change. And it served important political, psychological, and philosophical ends by reinforcing a meritocratic self-image of executives. Politically, corporate America had spent generations rejecting charges of economic royalism. Particularly in and after the 1980s "greed is good" era, they had to make clear to others, and had to believe for themselves, that they were not aristocrats living high on the hog. America's growing executive class began to work hours no union would ever have allowed on the shop floor.

In addition to justifying their power in an increasingly unequal economy, harsh corporate culture was an extension of market logic. If executives ran the company according to their own ethics or whims—mercy for workers, a desire for green energy, even mere interest in pet projects—that would be interfering with the work of the market. Executives *had* to be cogs in a machine. Unsurprisingly, financial markets rewarded Welch handsomely. During his tenure, GE's share price skyrocketed. Trained originally as a chemical engineer, Jack Welch gained a reputation for having, in Gryta and Mann's words, "somehow transformed the day-to-day tasks of managing a business into something resembling a hard science."[34]

Charles Koch had a similar ambition with his own labor management system. "Systematic study of classics in history, economics, philosophy, psychology, and other disciplines," in Koch's view, "reveals certain laws that govern human well-being."[35] He had learned these from the work of mid-century right-wing economists like Ludwig von Mises, whose *Human Action* he cites today as one of the four books in which he "learned how the world works."[36] Koch believed the Austrian economist's "Science of Human Action" could be "applied in an organization."[37]

The result was something he called Market-Based Management® (Koch consistently, in his own book, includes the trademark; in contrast, please feel free to use the term "control science" widely). Like Welch's management philosophy, Koch's MBM gives us a variety of lists and letters again: his *Science of Success* explains the five dimensions of MBM (vision, virtues and talents, knowledge processes, decision rights, and incentives), the six "core capabilities" of Koch Industries ("Market-Based Management®, Innovation, Operations Excellence, Trading, Transaction Excellence and Public Sector"), and psychologist Howard Gardner's largely bogus eight types of intelligence (musical, bodily-kinesthetic, interpersonal, intrapersonal, linguistic, logical-mathematical, spatial).[38] Beneath and within Koch's lists is the value system of right-wing economics. Charles adapts the right's oversimplified version of Adam Smith, including his concept of "comparative advantage." Institutionally, MBM and Koch's thought more broadly are founded in Hayek's concept of *spontaneous order*—organizational structure that evolved through adaptation and relied on bottom-up agency instead of top-down intention and design.

Right-wing economic principles already urged keeping workers in their place, and Koch made sure they would continue to do so when he adapted them into a management scheme. MBM's fourth "dimension," "Decision Rights," aimed to "replicate the beneficial roles of property rights in society" within a firm.[39] In right-wing economics, property puts power in the appropriate hands and gives powerful incentives for that power to be wielded efficiently—as Koch's science of liberty put it, the principle of decision rights meant "clear, dependable property rights earned according to the value created and comparative advantage." But at the level of the firm, in MBM itself, this could not mean *actual* property rights. Koch Industries is private. Charles firmly opposed the general public owning any part of his company—he certainly did not want his employees having a piece. The most radical interpretation of Koch's emphasis on property rights would be a worker's cooperative. Staying well clear of this, Koch instead transformed property rights within the firm into "decision rights," which are really just guidelines defining workers' sphere of authority.

As a whole, MBM was three things. First, boilerplate motivational poster rhetoric—its first "dimension" was "vision."

Second, an excuse for keeping workers in their place. Its fifth principle, "incentives," supposedly meant "rewarding people according to the value they create for the organization."[40] Judging from Koch Industries reviews on the employer review website Glassdoor, in practice this was usually wielded to blame workers for their own low pay rather than reward them for hard work with performance bonuses. Third, and typical of labor management schemes since Samuel Bentham, the most concrete and perhaps most impactful component of MBM was changes in cost accounting. One example Koch used concerns an asphalt plant in Iowa. A sales rep heard that a business was looking to build a casino in the area. Koch Materials Company did the math and realized they could sell the plant's land for more than the plant itself was going to make, so they did.[41]

In 1995, "a breakthrough came with the MBM Toolkit" which apparently "demonstrated that the five dimensions must be in harmony and applied holistically," though he does not explain exactly how. Koch's identification of bland management language as a scientific breakthrough was ludicrous, but no one was in a position to tell him that.[42] With unions in decline and management ideology like his increasingly popular in and beyond the workplace, capitalists like Charles Koch had greater power to shape the way Americans think and talk about work.

While Koch was building up Koch Industries and imposing MBM, he was also building a political infrastructure to spread his ideas more broadly. For a time, Charles and David Koch flirted with the tiny Libertarian Party—David was its nominee for president in 1980—before settling on influencing the Republican Party instead. Koch's interventions in government were motivated by the political equivalent of MBM, what Koch called the "science of liberty." His political machine's purpose was to realign the federal government, and ideally global governance, with the science of control, just as he had realigned his own business.

The government, for Charles Koch, was an enemy. Though the deregulation era began in the late 1970s, there were still plenty of laws Koch Industries had to follow. Koch whined in *Science of Success* that "it took years and repeated setbacks to build an effective compliance program" for the company because of "all the complex, confusing, and ever-changing government mandates."[43] Koch Industries' failures of "compliance"—some settled with fines, others buried with political influence—include the following: stealing millions of dollars' worth of oil from the Osage Nation by falsifying measurements, contaminating wetlands with hundreds of thousands of gallons of jet fuel, filling Texas air with toxic benzene fifteen times over the limit set by the Clean Air Act, and running explosive butane through a pipeline that had corroded into what the pipeline industry calls "Swiss Cheese."[44]

In 1996, that leaking pipeline caused teenager Danielle Smalley and her friend Jason Stone to burn to death before the eyes of her father Danny. For him, this was the end of the world. For Charles Koch, it was a tick against a fortune. Charles puts on a kind of smiling grandpa act in videos and interviews. Behind that facade is a man who would accept the incineration of children to make a buck, then bug the office of a grieving father's lawyer when he dared to sue over it.[45]

"When faced with laws we think are counterproductive, we must first comply," Charles Koch wrote in *Science of Success*. *Then* one could undermine those laws, first by trying to capture regulators—"a dialogue with regulatory agencies to demonstrate alternatives that are more beneficial"—and then by "using education and/or political efforts to change the law."[46] Koch's funding of "law and economics" was part of this; Koch lackey Ron Howell even set up an organization that graded judges based on their adherence to right-wing economics, then published these rankings in local opinion pieces. Judges upset about this were offered free seminars that doubled as vacations—at a mountain ski lodge, or a beach resort.[47]

President Clinton's EPA administrator Carol Browner was right when she claimed that Koch Industries "did not believe the law applied to them."⁴⁸ Beyond Koch's specific hostility to "political" power, this attitude followed naturally from MBM's own principles. If the company operated according to the objective Science of Human Action or to Harper's divine Truth, why should it have to follow other rules? Certainly, Koch admitted, MBM was imperfect, and imperfectly applied, something he always sought to improve. But its principles were sound, objective, and true, unlike the capricious mandates of Uncle Sam.

A "Shareholders' Nation"

In June 1993, President Bill Clinton gave a speech to the Business Roundtable. The organization's foundations were in the 1970s tax revolt that had helped elevate Republicans to power, yet Clinton's speech was anything but hostile. On the contrary, he praised the assembled executives as "among the most enlightened leaders of our nations in any walk of life" and thanked them for making "American companies" "once again the wonder of the world." He personally thanked the CEOs of firms like Ford and Xerox, as well as industry associations like the Homebuilders' Association, the Realtors' Association, and the Electronic Industry Association for supporting his economic plan. And Clinton himself made clear that he was thinking like a businessman—he compared voters to stockholders and boasted of financial markets' positive reaction to his economic plans.⁴⁹ Democrats had embraced neoliberalism—Clinton axed planned investments in education and infrastructure, let Alan Greenspan and Wall Street advisors bully him into budget cuts, and passed the North American Free Trade Agreement, or NAFTA, over widespread opposition from workers and the public.⁵⁰ What mattered here was not just policy—NAFTA's effects were complex, and included real economic benefits—but who got to make it: economists and executives, not workers.

The post-postwar economic consensus had firmly taken shape: wages were stagnant, and asset prices were ballooning. Alan Greenspan began to fear the "irrational exuberance" of the stock market, which was inflating stock values to impossible prices that had to come down eventually. But publicly bemoaning this irrational exuberance—with that phrase—did nothing to stop it. Nor did an interest rate increase in March 1997, which the market effectively laughed off. Greenspan gave up: "we never tried to rein in stock prices again."[51] Since markets could not be controlled, Greenspan came to believe that all the Fed could do was pick up the pieces after bubbles imploded.

This meant protecting investors from their own mistakes instead of letting markets punish them. In 1998, for example, Greenspan's Federal Reserve helped rescue investors in a hedge fund called Long-Term Capital Management. LTCM used leveraged investment—investing with borrowed money—to make investments far beyond the value of the capital it actually held. At its peak in early 1998, with only around $5 billion in equity, LTCM held more than $100 billion dollars in assets bought with borrowed money, as well as positions in complicated financial instruments known as derivatives worth more than $1 trillion, several times the entire American military budget that year. When LTCM collapsed in August due to Russian debt default, the Federal Reserve stepped in to save the fund's investors from their own risky bets. Greenspan's Fed also cut interest rates to juice the economy and kept them low until mid-1999.[52]

The LTCM intervention was one instance of a broader tendency that became known as the "Greenspan put."[53] It was named for a put option, a contract that gives someone the right to sell a security at a particular price within a particular time frame. Investors often use puts to protect themselves from risk: you pay for a put so that you can sell an asset later if its value goes down. Like an ordinary put option, Greenspan's Fed swooped in on multiple occasions to keep markets from declining—hence the term "Greenspan put." Unlike actual put options, they didn't even have to pay for this.

Under Greenspan, in Melinda Cooper's words, "financial asset holders were assured that they could only fail up."[54] Greenspan's policies contributed to the "dotcom bubble" of the late 1990s, in which frenzied speculation drove stocks with internet associations to ridiculous prices. Pets.com achieved a valuation of over $80 million while losing money on every single sale. A survey of individual investors, carried out in 2000, found that only 16 percent of them knew they were not insured "against losing money in the stock market or as the result of investment fraud."[55] Technically speaking, they were not protected. But as a whole, the Fed *was* committed to keeping asset prices from going down. People apparently stopped Greenspan on the street to thank him for their 401(k). "America was turning into a shareholders' nation," Greenspan reflected.

The Fed could discipline workers on behalf of the market, but did not see the need to discipline the market or even let the market discipline itself. Workers could not be protected from economic competition or change, but LTCM's investors had to be protected from risks they had chosen to take. This meant increasing wealth for investors, who were now largely protected from their own decisions, and stagnation for everyone else. The "Greenspan put" socialized risks and privatized gains.

From the 1980s until 2008, American economic policy was defined by two commitments: keeping asset-holders from suffering meaningful losses and keeping workers from making meaningful gains. The former goal, asset price inflation or asset appreciation, was secured by policies like the Greenspan put and tax cuts (which, again, from an accounting perspective are tax expenditures). Policymakers achieved the latter objective, wage stagnation, through union-busting, the threat of another Volcker shock, and trade liberalization, all working in tandem with deindustrialization. Asset appreciation and wage stagnation were a fantasy, a dream that capital could reap the benefits of market efficiency and extraction without handing any of it to workers or losing much of it to the business cycle.[56]

Part of that vision was a bipartisan commitment to deregulation. The federal government killed airline route and fare regulation beginning in 1978, the Environmental Protection Agency's noise control program in 1982, price regulations on trucking in 1980 and 1994, and caps on radio station ownership in 1996.[57] Deregulation was both a product of and a reason for the American and global economy's move from the mid-century Fordist economy of intention and negotiation between states, large firms, and labor to a market economy of organization among firms, with states facilitating rather than regulating exchange, while deliberately sidelining labor. While deregulation never went as far as Chicago price theorists and Midwestern libertarians wanted, it was a victory for their vision: deregulation was meant to replace government intention with the Hayekian "spontaneous order" of markets.

The deregulation of finance was a key development in this process. In 1999, President Clinton signed the Gramm-Leach-Bliley Act into law. It repealed New Deal–era regulations that had separated commercial bank activity, like personal checking and savings accounts, from investment banking and insurance. This made it easy to aggregate home loans into mortgage-backed securities, which offered better interest rates than the bond market, while promising more stability than the stock market. As these securities grew in popularity, America's housing market increasingly served two purposes: it met physical demand for shelter, but it also met financial demand for high-return assets across an increasingly interconnected global financial system. From above, this was indeed a "shareholders' nation"; an "ownership society," in the words of President Bush.[58] As long as you didn't look at the condition of workers, things were going swimmingly.

Like earlier practitioners of the science of control, Alan Greenspan tried to argue that there was no alternative to this economic regime. In his 2007 memoir, Greenspan insisted that the increasing complexity of corporate activity and the speed of financial transactions made regulation impossible. "Effort to monitor and influence market behavior that is proceeding at Mach speeds will fail." This was the reasoning behind his aforementioned argument: "We have no sensible choice other than to let markets work. Market failure is the rare exception, and its consequences can be assuaged by a flexible economic and financial system."[59] The market could not fail—it could only be failed. With a ballooning share of American wealth linked to financial markets, they could not be *allowed* to fail.

The Principles of Freakonomics

The public, meanwhile, was being taught the same faith in markets. There is a difference between economics, a fractious and often empirical field of practitioners with a diverse range of views and methods, and economics, the gospel truth of abstract and simplified graphs and right-wing "common sense." But the latter is a real part of the former, and a particularly influential one. N. Gregory Mankiw's 1999 textbook *Principles of Economics* offers both. The book is named after its titular ten principles. Principle one, "people face tradeoffs," is certainly obvious enough—Mankiw gives the example of a family saving for vacation or for college. We then jump right to tax policy: "society faces" a tradeoff between "efficiency," or "getting the most it can from its scarce resources," and "equity," or "distributing economic prosperity fairly among the members of society."[60] Mankiw explains,

> When the government redistributes income from the rich to the poor, it reduces the reward for working hard; as a result, people work less and produce fewer goods and services. In other words, when the government tries to cut the economic pie into more equal slices, the pie gets smaller. This is the one lesson concerning the distribution of income about which almost everyone agrees.

Principles thus presents as a fact the claim that redistribution harms overall economic output. In fact, it is debatable at best—in a 2021 critique of Mankiw, German economist Peter Bofinger claimed there was "no evidence for this" at all.[61] Inequality hampers efficiency—a thriving middle class drives more economic growth than a few oligarchs who have run out of things to purchase. And as we have seen, government spending can promote investment, growing the pie rather than shrinking it. Society is limited by resources, but this has a complicated relationship to how the state is limited by money.

With principle four, "people respond to incentives," the influence of Chicago economics on Mankiw's textbook becomes particularly obvious. The principle itself—in just those four words at least—is difficult to argue with. But from this unassailable position Mankiw moves to an extended example about laws mandating wearing seat belts, which he argues shift "the cost-benefit calculation of a rational driver. Seat belts make accidents less costly for a driver because they reduce the probability of injury or death. Thus, a seat belt law reduces the benefits to slow and careful driving." Accordingly, drivers choose to drive less carefully and thus cause *more* accidents, including fatalities, since seat belts do not protect pedestrians.

Choosing to drive more dangerously because you are wearing a seat belt is not behavior most of us would call "rational," but for Mankiw it is exactly that, and he asserts that we should expect this behavior. He backs up his conclusion with a 1975 study that found exactly the result he expected, done by Chicago-trained economist Sam Peltzman. A 1977 follow-up using Peltzman's own data found his conclusion "unwarranted" and his model "not supported empirically."[62]

The fourth principle's introduction illustrates a common feature of Mankiw's book and of right-wing economics more generally: a jump from tautological principles to contested or outright inaccurate descriptions of reality. Mankiw says that "people respond to incentives" but implies that "people respond meaningfully to all incentives in a market-like manner." By presenting "seat belts are bad" as a necessary and logical extension of the obvious and bland "people respond to incentives,"

Mankiw's readers are led to believe that an idea that is controversial at best is both a consensus view among economists and an unambiguous fact of reality.

This is the same error he makes throughout the book. The fifth principle is "trade can make everyone better off"—obviously it *can*, but when? Principle six, "markets are usually a good way to organize economic activity," is a slightly softened version of price theory, hedged by the *usually* and introduced with a lengthy and laudatory explanation of Adam Smith's "invisible hand." Principle seven, "governments can sometimes improve market outcomes," offers room for government intervention, but whenever Mankiw speaks of government actions he begins warning of perverse consequences and tax costs. Principle eight, "a country's standard of living depends on its ability to produce goods and services" is true, but even here Mankiw smuggles in a highly debatable characterization of budget deficits as invariably bad for productivity. Principles nine, "prices rise when the government prints too much money," and ten, "society faces a short-run tradeoff between inflation and unemployment," present monetarist macroeconomics as a consensus view when it is anything but.[63] Usually his analysis leads from a straightforwardly true principle through muddled hand-waving about debate to, finally, a Reaganomic conclusion—for example, instead of a minimum wage, Mankiw prefers "wage subsidies" from the government that allow employers to pay workers less.[64]

Among Mankiw's most obvious substitutions of market ideology for reality comes in chapter 11, on public goods. Here he invokes the infamous "Tragedy of the Commons." Popularized in a 1968 article of the same name written by eugenicist ecologist Garrett Hardin, the titular "tragedy" claims that when a resource like water or a field is shared, everyone has an individual incentive to take from it, and no one has an individual incentive to preserve or save it. This is frequently described through the prisoner's dilemma.[65] Based on economic self-interest, the conclusion is ironclad: "the commons" must always collapse beneath self-interest.

But this is empirically wrong. Through rich study of the actually existing commons in places ranging from Japan to Spain, political economist Elinor Ostrom demonstrated that communities are capable of collective stewardship of their resources.[66] Ostrom's work is not obscure—she won the Nobel Prize for Economics in 2009. She was hardly a radical—Ostrom herself identified with the political legacy of Smith, Hayek, and Koch collaborator James McGill Buchanan, and she gave a lecture named for Hayek at a right-wing British think tank shortly before she died. But political economist Derek Wall has pointed out that she drew on institutionalism as well, and her work exemplifies what empiricism can do for an economist: dispel myths and cut through flawed armchair analysis by engaging with the real world.[67] Garrett Hardin, meanwhile, was a eugenicist crank backed by the Pioneer Fund, a racist nonprofit that has spent decades funding bogus research claiming that Black people are biologically inferior to others.[68]

Yet Hardin's "tragedy of the commons" is widely known to the public, and even regarded as common sense, while Ostrom's work—though popular in academic circles—has had no such impact on how the broader public thinks about collective action and property. Instead of citing Ostrom and considering the reality of the commons, Mankiw paraphrases Hardin and cites Aristotle of all people against it.[69] Simple models diffuse faster than complicated truths. This is especially true if those models fit the basic political assumptions of our society or appeal to the wealthy and receive widespread support from them.

Mankiw's book is the best-selling economics textbook in the United States and is commonly used in introductory courses at universities. By reading it, Mankiw assured students, "with practice, you will become more and more accustomed to thinking like an economist." This could mean discarding basic ideas of right and wrong: after a section explaining how traffic engineers put a financial value on lives, one end-of-section "quick quiz" in *Principles* asks students to consider whether poorer people's lives have less value.[70]

Mankiw, it must be noted, was not a Chicago or Austrian School ideologue, nor were most of the other reigning voices in academic economics in this period. A one-time advisor to George W. Bush, the Harvard economist did not reject empiricism, though his introductory textbook certainly did little to suggest empirical research was necessary. Macroeconomically, he was what's known as a New Keynesian, part of a broader neoclassical synthesis of the Keynesian approach with the classical economics understanding of markets. He could and did present his arguments with a nuance and care that the neoliberals generally lacked; unlike them, he could and did advise government intervention and engage with facts.

This let him present what were often *their* arguments that much more persuasively—price theory, monetarism, faith in markets. In policy terms, the fact that Mankiw was not a wild-eyed gold standard advocate looking to blow up the economy, a loathsome sophist whose research only ever justified his original assumptions, or a sycophantic incompetent like the economists the Trump White House would later bring in, does matter. Things could be worse and would get worse. But his mainstream nature makes clear how far right orthodoxy in American economics had drifted—and how cruel and cynical it had become.

Popular economists' rejection of ethics was even clearer in another widely read book: the 2005 bestseller *Freakonomics: A Rogue Economist Explains the Hidden Side of Everything*.[71] A smug and decidedly self-satisfied "how the world *really* works" screed, *Freakonomics* was born from the minds of economist Steven Levitt—at the University of Chicago—and journalist Stephen Dubner, who profiled the Chicago economist for the *New York Times Magazine* in 2003. Levitt, he explained, was a different kind of economist. The Chicago professor confessed "I just don't know very much about the field of economics. I'm not good at math, I don't know a lot of econometrics, and I also don't know how to do theory." Dubner even said Levitt "fear[ed] calculus. But Levitt didn't need math or theory—what made him special was the questions he asked. Levitt was valuable because he was the kind of person who, upon seeing a homeless man while driving through Chicago, wonders "how does a homeless man afford $50 headphones" rather than whether he's okay.[72]

Steven Levitt's research questions were often similarly misguided. The first chapter of *Freakonomics* focused on teachers who cheated to help their students get ahead on high-stakes tests that determined funding for their schools—rather than on why they didn't have sufficient resources in the first place, or the decision-makers who forced schools into brutal competition with each other to try to get funds. In a 1998 paper, he argued (though he was careful to say this was not sufficient for a policy recommendation) that tough-on-crime policies work effectively on children.[73] What kind of person, when granted all the resources of American Ivy League institutions to investigate any social problem they wish, chooses to spend months or years pursuing teachers in poor school districts and incarcerated kids? Levitt's research agenda suggests an expert in dismissing problems, blaming victims, and asking the wrong questions.

Dubner called Levitt a "rogue economist." As a description of his place in economics, the label was ludicrous. The entire reason for the profile and thus the book was that Levitt had won the Clark Medal, a prize that meant he had been "deemed, at least, by a jury of his elders" the "most brilliant young economist in America," to quote the very beginning of Dubner's profile. Levitt had been admitted into Harvard's prestigious Society of Fellows earlier in his career, thanks in part to the intervention of libertarian philosopher Robert Nozick, as the profile recounted.[74] Today he is the director of the (Gary) Becker (Milton) Friedman Institute at Chicago, which is what it sounds like. Ideas like Levitt's were so mainstream that most of the federal judiciary had been taught them at seminars funded by some of the wealthiest men in America. Politically, Levitt was more a creature of the establishment center than the partisan right—which demonstrates how influential right-wing economic ideas had become by the 2000s. The rogue economist was such a rogue that he said exactly what the ruling class was already saying.

Levitt's "rogue economist" act was just a posture based in his gleeful rejection of "political correctness" and ethics. "If morality represents an ideal world," Dubner and Levitt scoffed, "then economics represents the actual world." Specifically, the economics of "people respond to incentives," the same meaninglessly broad observation as Mankiw's fourth principle and the fifth "dimension" of Charles Koch's MBM, smuggling in the same psychological egoism and noxious cynicism. Unlike some of the more extreme psychological egoists, and like most economists by this point, Dubner and Levitt conceded in principle that not all human action was self-interested or incentive-based. But they still believed they could use incentives to study all human action: "Since the science of economics is primarily a set of tools, as opposed to a subject matter, then no subject, however offbeat, need be beyond its reach."[75]

This was a license for Levitt to overturn "conventional wisdom" in any area he saw fit; the book proper is a series of case studies about, as they put it in the beginning of the book, "how the world really works."[76] *Freakonomics* presents a world where child car seats in automobiles are a mostly worthless ruse by Big Car Seat; your doctor lies to you; your kid's teacher cheats; your real estate agent is taking advantage of you (this one was true but also probably not a surprise to anyone); and you can trust no one but yourself. While "they" do not want you to know the truth, the rogue economist will help you seek it. Only if you apply numbers rigorously (something Levitt, notably, did not do!) while always keeping in mind the selfishness of mankind, trusting no one, can you find the truth. This was a recipe for political cynicism at best and conspiracy thinking at worst.

The actual cases in *Freakonomics* have been criticized and indeed debunked. One chapter confidently makes the argument that "legalized abortion resulted in a massive drop in crime." The data suggests otherwise: the Romanian case study they base part of their argument on found that Romania's 1967 abortion *ban* correlated with an improvement in education and job outcomes, while the data did not allow for a similarly meaningful comparison of crime. And no responsible social scientist could confidently offer such a monocausal analysis of a complex and difficult-to-measure phenomenon.[77]

But Levitt and Dubner were not responsible social scientists. They were polemicists. The book is more interested in making inflammatory claims than making accurate ones. They knew their claim would "inevitably lead to explosive moral reactions," which was great for them. That was the "rogue" economist's brand. Loud rejections of morality were where their authority came from. "Freakonomics-style thinking simply doesn't traffic in morality," which was why it was trustworthy. In a world where every other incentive-motivated human was trying to take advantage of you, ethics were for suckers, and Levitt and Dubner's cynicism was merely honesty about how the world *really* works. The inevitable controversy and the collection of easy-to-spread *well actually* stories that came with this approach certainly didn't hurt sales either.[78]

Like Mankiw, Levitt and Dubner asserted authority as disinterested observers by insisting that they were not making normative statements, which in fact meant asserting the supremacy of ostensibly positive economics over normative ethics. You should trust an economist to make good decisions, not your own unreliable conscience, let alone the morals of others. They wrote in *Freakonomics*,

> The typical economist believes the world has not yet invented a problem that he cannot fix if given a free hand to design the proper incentive scheme. His solution may not always be pretty—it may involve coercion or exorbitant penalties or the violation of civil liberties.

They continued, "But the original problem, rest assured, will be fixed." Levitt and Dubner could have been describing themselves when they said: "*Experts use their informational advantage to serve their own agenda.*"[79]

And at least a dishonest real estate agent knows they're dishonest. Levitt and Dubner appear to have genuinely believed in what they were selling. *Freakonomics* recycled control science's reductive psychological egoism, blinkered methodological individualism, proud rejection of ethics, and market thinking into an airport book of superficial dinner party anecdotes. This made for a bestseller in part because it matched the preconceptions the neoliberal world itself encouraged. Americans in the 2000s thankfully didn't all—or probably even mostly—believe in the sneering amorality of *Freakonomics*, but they didn't have to. Control science was the language their boss spoke, their children were learning in school, their journalists were parroting in magazines, and politicians from both parties were giving speeches in. Right-wing economics ruled the world in the 2000s.

But it could not ignore either reality or morality forever.

"Somebody's Gonna Have to Start Raising Money for *Us*"

The unholy trinity of deregulation, asset price inflation, and wage stagnation eventually produced consequences that could not be easily ignored or pushed onto workers. Asset price inflation sent housing prices upward. Wage stagnation made it increasingly difficult for working people to pay those prices. Deregulation encouraged risky lending practices to bridge the resulting gap. Eventually, the market value of homes exceeded the real capacity of buyers to pay for them. When hedge funds' desire for high returns via mortgage-backed securities outpaced what struggling workers could actually generate (as both builders and buyers), calamity resulted. The popularity of those securities made the entire world's financialized economy vulnerable to the resulting cascade. What followed was an artificial global calamity: the 2008 recession. Unemployment in the US doubled.

Under President Obama, the Democrats referred once again to the Keynesian wisdom that the 1970s tax revolt had tried to vanquish. President Bush had already pushed a massive $700 billion stimulus program that bought up "toxic assets," and Obama expanded this once he took office with another $787 billion in stimulus. Among the Obama administration's efforts was a program called the Homeowners Affordability and Stability Plan. By enabling struggling homeowners to refinance, working with lenders to modify mortgage payments, and paying loan servicers for each such modification, this comprehensive multibillion-dollar program aimed to save millions of homeowners from foreclosure.[80] Macroeconomically, it was also a well-reasoned intervention to keep the economy from eating itself alive: by disturbing the lives and annihilating the credit of evicted and indebted homeowners, every foreclosure was a hit to the American economy.

But right-wing economics abhors complexity, and the simpler lesson on "incentives" that Greg Mankiw (in business schools), Jack Welch (in corporate culture), and Levitt and Dubner (in airport books) had helped popularize in the 2000s suggested a different interpretation. "The government is promoting bad behavior!" howled a belligerent CNBC reporter, Rick Santelli, from the floor of the Chicago Mercantile Exchange in February 2009. Did America "really wanna subsidize the *losers*' mortgages?" We could instead buy them and give them to people who could "actually prosper down the road, and reward people that could carry the water, instead of drink the water!" The traders behind him erupted in cheers. "How many of you people wanna pay for your neighbors' mortgage, that has an extra bathroom, and can't pay their bills?" he asked. Boos followed.[81]

On air, Santelli proposed a "Chicago Tea Party" revolt akin to the Boston Tea Party of 1773, in which Bostonians protested British tea taxes by boarding East India Company ships and dumping their cargo into the harbor. The Chicago Mercantile Exchange sells derivatives—financial instruments that helped create the crisis in the first place—and Santelli was a hedge fund trader before he was a reporter. From one of the scenes of their crimes, the perpetrator class jeered at the ambulance sent for their victims.

The threat of an actual protest was merely symbolic—Santelli half-heartedly joked about dumping derivatives into Lake Michigan instead of tea—but the CNBC reporter's tirade gave a name to the rising coalition of the resentful that would engage in mass protest: the "Tea Party" movement. Gesturing to the trading floor, a swaggering Santelli preposterously blustered that the derivatives traders behind him were "a pretty good statistical cross-section of America, the silent majority." This was ridiculous—but they were a substantial minority. Numbering in the millions, Tea Partiers rallied across the nation, pulled the Republican Party to the right, and immersed themselves in a right-wing media ecosystem that assembled itself to meet their interest.[82] They saw themselves as patriots resisting illegitimate taxes just like the "Founding Fathers," whom Santelli said were "roll[ing] over in their graves."

The Tea Party movement did echo America's early history, but in a different sense than it believed. Prerevolutionary agitation in New England ports was driven by an uneasy alliance of merchants opposed to taxation and maritime workers, farmers, and artisans opposed to surveillance, policing, and corruption.[83] After the revolution, when the latter sought to share the burdens of war debt and promote local growth and economic needs through inflationary policy, the merchant elite cracked down with force, violently suppressing debt-ridden farmers and writing limits on democracy into the Constitution itself. It was this political tendency—property-holder backlash—that the twenty-first-century Tea Party extended. The economic rescue policies that Rick Santelli and company loathed, including debt relief on personal land and housing specifically, were the kind of policies many ordinary Americans fought and died for after the Revolution. *How many of you wanna pay for your neighbors' farms?* The small business owners of the Tea Party and their big business allies engaged in downward-punching class warfare while calling themselves oppressed underdogs acting in the name of liberty. The Tea Party movement was similar to the Founding Fathers—just in their capacity as antidemocratic oligarchs after the Revolution rather than anti-aristocratic insurgents before it.

From almost the moment of its birth, Americans debated whether the Tea Party was "astroturfed"—an artificial construct of corporate money—or "grassroots." American politics was an expensive arena, and certainly any movement like the Tea Party would want money. When one of the other CNBC talking heads jokingly asked if Santelli had raised money for recently impeached Illinois Governor Rod Blagojevich, Santelli shot back *"someone's gonna have to starting raising money for us."* And someone had. The Kochs' Americans for Prosperity and FreedomWorks outlets offered logistical and organizing support for the Tea Party while amplifying its message.[84]

But the movement was not literally created by Charles and David Koch, soon known nationwide as the sinister "Koch brothers" thanks to a *New Yorker* article published by Jane Mayer in August 2010.[85] America's commitment, from the Volcker shock onward, to growth in capital gains and stagnation in wages created what economic historian Yakov Feygin has called a "deflationary coalition" of asset-holders who demanded deflationary policies well beyond macroeconomic necessity.[86] The economics were simple: if wages were flat, asset prices and capital gains were the only opportunities for growth. Housing in particular—the most expensive asset most Americans own—*had* to appreciate. The financial well-being of millions of well-organized assetholders, like the profits of American business, depended on housing becoming increasingly inaccessible to working people. "Subsidizing losers" was a threat to the entire wealth structure of many Tea Partiers. The same economy that ensured that millions of homeowners shared corporate America's interest in keeping wages down sidelined the most obvious counterforce to this deflationary coalition—unions—and ensured that business had massive piles of cash to fund political agitation.

The Tea Party movement was the product of late-twentieth- and early-twenty-first-century economic thought as well as practice. It drew directly on both high (academic) and low (airport books) versions of 2000s free market rhetoric, the ideology of the 1970s tax revolt, the anti-inflation discourse Lemuel Boulware developed to protect General Electric from wage increases, and the "free enterprise" propaganda GM Chairman Alfred Sloan devised in response to the New Deal. American capital had worked hard to create Reaganite neoliberalism, and the Tea Party tried to protect its logic—even though it had led to catastrophe. The Great Recession prompted Americans of all kinds to develop escape routes out of neoliberalism, from experiments with a return to Keynesian stimulus by technocrats in Washington to the occupation of Wall Street by a fractious coalition of leftists and libertarians. What the Tea Party did was try to bar the doors.

10

"No Space to Be Human": Dreams of Exit, 2009–24

In the spring of 1982, during the early years of the Reagan Revolution, Miami Palmetto Senior High School valedictorian Jeff Bezos gave a graduation speech explaining his plan to "get all people off the Earth and see it turned into a huge national park," as a local newspaper put it.[1] This vision followed him from high school in the 1980s to the heights of financial success as one of the richest men in the world thirty years later.

It was inspired by utopian science fiction, in particular the American television series *Star Trek* and the "Culture" novels written by Scottish author Iain M. Banks, both of which feature decidedly left-wing post-scarcity societies.[2] Science fiction of this era offered more pessimistic visions of a galactic future as well. In a 1985 novel, Isaac Asimov had one of his protagonists irradiate Earth to make humanity leave, kick-starting the creation of a Galactic Empire—an act presented as a necessary evil.[3] In an influential film released three years later, Yoshiyuki Tomino's iconic villain Char Aznable sought to force humanity off Earth for the *planet's* good by smashing asteroids into cities.[4]

Utopia and calamity feature in twenty-first-century spacebound billionaires' dreams of exit. While Jeff Bezos wanted a "huge national park," another spacebound billionaire, Elon Musk, has insisted that space colonization is necessary to protect humanity from itself. He has told the mothers of his children to hurry up and recruit more so that he can have a "legion" before the "apocalypse."[5]

Those oligarchs who fear society will collapse before we can make that escape proposed a nearer alternative, for themselves and their entourage alone—New Zealand, where Paypal founder Peter Thiel and OpenAI head Sam Altman plan to flee in the event of catastrophe.[6] Some among the super-wealthy have even constructed complex underground bunkers to wait out Armageddon.[7] All this from the same billionaire class that promises utopian multiplanetary societies, artificial intelligence catering to our every whim, and technological solutions to all our problems.

One might expect these men to be celebrating rather than plotting escape routes. Capitalists have achieved unprecedented political dominance and economic success. After four centuries of development, their science of control—philosophies and practices for controlling labor—has remade law, social science, common sense, and even the language with which we speak of money and power. But that remaking threatens to unmake societies, Earth's climate, and the very markets in which it urges faith.

Many workers, too, dream of exit—of an escape from the wreckage of neoliberalism. Some leave their countries in favor of economic prosperity or simply physical security elsewhere. Others demand via mass protest that their countries leave neoliberal international institutions like the World Trade Organization. From migration and Grexit to New Zealand bunkers and imagined moon bases, the clashing visions of workers and capitalist raise questions. Who will get to escape the consequences of capitalism? On what terms? And how far will they have to go?

From Bentham to Bezos

Even capitalists want to escape competition. If you open a South Indian restaurant and "think your naan is superior because of your great-grandmother's recipe," Peter Thiel wrote in his 2014 book *Zero to One*, you will fail. Smart capitalists know that competition is something they should exit from altogether rather than just try to win. Competition cuts profits, potentially down to zero. *Monopoly* creates them. "All happy companies," Thiel and his co-author Blake Masters wrote, "are different: each one earns a monopoly by solving a unique problem. All failed companies are the same: they failed to escape competition."[8] On the left, in contrast, Yanis Varoufakis has argued that Big Tech's monopoly behavior has overcome capitalism, meaning that we now live under "technofeudalism" instead.[9] Both overstate how successful capitalists are at achieving monopoly—but they are right that capitalists want to.

Amazon represents that impulse well. By the mid-2010s, Amazon was a multibillion-dollar business, selling everything you can imagine. Its "Prime" subscription, promising two-day delivery on most products, launched in 2005 and expanded with a video service in 2012. By the 2020s, Prime subscriptions topped 200 million.[10] Customers have bought hundreds of millions of devices with always-on microphones linked to the company's Alexa voice assistant, paying one of the world's richest men for the privilege of listening to their homes or—as the popular Ring doorbell does—watching everyone who enters them.[11]

Today Amazon is the world's second largest retailer, by revenue, and the world's largest provider of cloud computing, through Amazon Web Services (AWS). It is not quite a perfect monopoly in either field—it competes with Walmart in the former category and Microsoft in the latter. Yet Amazon exemplifies monopoly in the sense Thiel meant it, as well as the kind of rent-seeking fiefdoms Varoufakis referred to. Amazon wields its market power effectively. The company's marketplace is open to third-party sellers, and with Amazon's market share, it is increasingly mandatory for many businesses to sell there. Amazon collects not only fees from sellers but also data, which it uses to decide what product categories to develop in-house and sell on its own. Once it does so, Amazon then prioritizes its own products in search results.

A press release from the Federal Trade Commission, announcing a lawsuit with seventeen states against Amazon, put it this way: "By stifling competition on price, product selection, quality, and by preventing its current or future rivals from attracting a critical mass of shoppers and sellers, Amazon ensures that no current or future rival can threaten its dominance."[12] Because of the law and economics movement's role in shifting antitrust interpretation, it is unclear if what should be an obvious case against Amazon will actually go anywhere. Thanks to Robert Bork, the now-canonical antitrust legal standard in the US is consumer harm. While Amazon's behavior likely inflates prices in certain cases, the company's success comes from its low prices and fast shipping, which have won it enormous customer loyalty.

Those cheap goods and rapid shipments come courtesy of a precisely engineered system of surveillance and optimization. Behind the eyeless smile emblazoned on the side of an Amazon "fulfillment center" (FC) is a close analog to Samuel and Jeremy Bentham's Panopticon. Amazon's FCs do not use the Panopticon's literally centralized architecture because, thanks to modern technology, they do not have to. Centralized data architecture does the same thing. Through scanners and its logistics system, the company surveils workers' time down to the minute.[13] When everything works as intended, Amazon has a precise picture of how long and how hard each employee works, thanks to one of the most complete individualized productivity monitoring systems in the world. Workers who fail to meet productivity targets can be fired. Facing this individualized surveillance, Amazon workers have been afraid to take bathroom breaks, since doing so might lower their productivity rate. Amazon's panoptic architecture makes everyday workplace intimidation, like the harassment three Muslim women in Minnesota faced after protesting discrimination in their warehouse, that much more threatening.[14]

The company makes workers feel like lonely individuals as well. Individualized tasks and high turnover help produce the social isolation Jeremy Bentham called for, but so does explicit policy: Amazon workers at its Staten Island facility received warnings for talking to other employees.[15] When German writer Heike Geissler began suffering money troubles, she found work at Amazon as a "seasonal associate," a temporary worker, which became the title of a 2014 book she wrote about the experience. Written in the second person, to a "you" who starts work at Amazon, the book's narrator describes employment at Amazon as "work that leaves the employee no space to be human."[16] Just as Jeremy Bentham boasted in the Panopticon letters, Amazon warehouses render workers to their employer, "a *multitude*, though not a *crowd*; to themselves, they are *solitary* and *sequestered* individuals."[17]

Jeff Bezos's Panopticon took up one suggestion from the Benthams' proposals that prisons never did: you can visit fulfillment centers for a tour, physically or virtually. Jeremy Bentham had intended this as a transparency measure. In the hands of Jeff Bezos, it instead serves as a marketing tactic. My own virtual tour in summer 2024 began with an old-fashioned beeping film countdown, followed by chipper music, a video of Amazon's purchasing interface, and a warm voice asking, "*Have you ever wondered what happens after you click Buy?*" This set the tone for the rest of the tour: the entire affair assumes you are an interested customer.

Shortly after this, a smiling tour guide began with "exciting news about Prime Day," the company's annual astroturfed holiday, a sales event open only to subscribers. "[It was] our biggest ever! I hope you ordered some great stuff!" She appeared genuinely excited—exactly the kind of person you would want to hire to convince the world your facilities are not miserable Victorian workhouses.

When the tour moved to Minnesota facility MSP 1, the guide there greeted us with the same demeanor. He explained that facilities are named for airport codes. "Next time you get a package from us," he said smoothly over the harsh beep of a warehouse vehicle mostly out of frame, "why don't you take a look at that box and see where that package started?" This was an introduction to the first of seven steps in Amazon's logistics process, known as receive, stow, pick, pack, SLAM, shipping, and delivery. In the "receive" step, products come in and are unloaded into yellow boxes that Amazon calls "totes." Even before products arrive, they are categorized at a "crossdock" facility—in MSP 1's case, a crossdock in Chicago—where information like size is entered into Amazon's computer system. Minimizing human action as much as possible means maximizing computers' knowledge. After workers load items into totes, the boxes head off to "stow."

For the stow phase, a more relaxed guide with a horseshoe mustache introduced us to Amazon's robots. In years past, workers walked for miles through the labyrinthine warrens of the FC to stow and pick items. Now, in many warehouses, robots do the walking—they pick up large shelf units called "pods" and move them through the facility as needed. Stow workers in the facility I was shown stand at a station in a corner, with boxes and totes on their right and an opening in an otherwise fenced-off area to their left, where robot-mounted pods roll up. Workers take items out of boxes, scan them, and then place them into slots in the pod shelves. Automatically, thanks to "incredible innovation in technology" backed by AWS, the system tracks where items were placed, so Amazon knows exactly where they are. Once the pod is full, it zooms off into the warehouse.

The "pick" phase reverses this. Here, the older guide for this phase explained, the pod rolls up to another station, a corner arranged not unlike the stow station. On the right are a row of totes with light-up green buttons over each of them, and a computer monitor above all that. On the left is another opening where pods roll up. The monitor shows the worker the item and its location in the pod, so they can pick it; it also lights up the button above one of the totes, to indicate where to put it. If you do it right, the system emits an approving beep. Get it wrong, and an angry buzzer sounds.

What an Amazon FC employee does is keep the line rolling. Their every movement guided by machines, stow and pick workers are the ultimate version of the machine-tenders of Nathan Appleton's factories. To an extent, so are nonmanagement FC employees more generally. If there's a problem in the robot area, workers sent to fix it have to don a special belt that stops all robots in a certain radius in order to enter the fenced-off zone, which makes it clear whose space this is and whose it is not.

The stow guide explained to our tour that workers have the "autonomy" to place items wherever they want in the pods. While this is undoubtedly not the only *actual* place workers exert judgment, it is one of the few in which they are supposed to—generally speaking, Amazon treats the minds of its workers as something to avoid rather than make use of. As a manager named Norman puts it in Geissler's book, "you don't have to understand" Amazon's system, "you just have to know it." Her narrator tells the reader that "you," the Amazon worker, are "nothing but a placeholder for machines that have already been invented but aren't yet profitable enough to permanently replace you and your workmates."[18]

Amazon wants you to think that the company is a well-oiled machine that provides mutual benefits to its "associates." In theory, Amazon is not a particularly bad workplace compared to other warehouses or large retailers—Walmart, for example. Certainly, the work is monotonous, even dehumanizing, but most proletarianized work is. Amazon is often the best-paying employer in its area. Sometimes it is the only one, particularly for workers whose qualifications do not meet the shifting needs of employers. Amazon takes almost anyone—as the mustachioed guide told me, "you only need a high school diploma!" rather than an expensive college degree. The pick station's monitor switches language automatically for workers—our guide mentioned Tagalog—and for some "Amazonians," as they are called, Amazon might be one of only a few employers in their area without language barriers. Some Amazon associates can benefit from Amazon's "Career Choice" program, which pays for tuition and even books so students can take classes part time.

But the Amazon system looks different from the perspective of those who actually maintain it. Amazon's logistics system is an exploitative mess, held together by shortcuts and worker coercion. Geissler's book describes one shift of "pushy" and fast workers, which would seem to be exactly the optimized crew Amazon wants—but they achieve their speeds by gaming the system, concentrating easily loaded items into their workflow by getting on the "good list" of forklift operators, while shunting more troublesome cargo onto those in the next shift.[19] Turnover at Amazon warehouses has exceeded 100 percent annually, meaning that Amazon is hiring an entire new hourly workforce each year—and then some, by certain estimates. Documents leaked to the media outlet *Engadget* indicated that only one in three new hires during 2021 remained at the company for more than three months.[20]

Those who leave do so for good reason. A 2022 investigation found Amazon warehouse workers were twice as likely to suffer serious injuries as workers in other warehouses. Forty-two-year-old Rafael Reynaldo Mota Frias of New Jersey, an immigrant from the Dominican Republic, died on Prime Day in 2022 when his heart gave out in Amazon's EWR9 facility in Carteret, New Jersey. It was 92 degrees outside, and EWR9 was not air-conditioned. When sixty-one-year-old Rick Jacobs had a heart attack just before a shift change at Amazon's DEN4 warehouse in Colorado Springs, the company cordoned off his body with cardboard boxes and started the next shift running while waiting for the coroner.[21]

At one warehouse in Edwardsville, Illinois, DLI4, Amazon had done little to prepare workers for a tornado. Numerous personnel later questioned by Occupational Safety and Health Administration inspectors reported that they had never seen shelter-in-place drills, despite former employee LeeAnn Webster raising the issue repeatedly years earlier. Webster specifically tied Amazon's reticence to engage in safety drills to costs. Every minute spent on safety was a minute the Amazon machine could be fulfilling more orders. Even the megaphone meant to be used for emergency announcements was locked up and inaccessible.

Yet with tornado vortexes forming in the area in December 2021, Amazon refused to let workers leave the facility. One worker, Larry Virden, texted his girlfriend that "Amazon won't let us leave"; the Amazon machine could not stop for anything. Half an hour later she asked what he was doing, expressed hope that he was okay, and sent "I love you." He never saw it. Part of the warehouse had collapsed, killing Virden and five other workers.[22]

The final phase of an Amazon package's journey was not covered meaningfully in my virtual tour at all. Amazon delivers some of its packages through misclassified "independent contractor" drivers under its Amazon Flex program. Workers get to "be their own boss," as an Amazon spokesman put it when asked for comment on thousands of drivers trying to claim unpaid wages, overtime, and expense reimbursements they would be entitled to get if they were properly classified as employees.[23] Other packages are delivered through Amazon Delivery Service Partners, third parties whose workers drive Amazon-branded vans to deliver Amazon packages exclusively while monitored by Amazon AI cameras, but who are technically not employed by Bezos's empire. Like Flex, DSPs let Amazon avoid regulations and shift costs onto someone else. DSP owners, not Amazon, deal with costs like vehicle maintenance. If DSP workers dare unionize, Amazon simply cancels their contract.[24]

Instead of showing either Flex or DSP drivers, my virtual Amazon tour covered the "delivery" phase with a polished video on the experience of mule drivers who take packages down to a tourist lodge at the bottom of the Grand Canyon. This example works for them because it is everything an Amazon job is not: exciting, dynamic, difficult to replace. The mule packers in question are not, in fact, actually employed by Amazon at all—they are third-party carriers. Meanwhile, Amazon DSP drivers save time by urinating in bottles to keep up the company's demanding pace.[25]

The Career Choice program is about serving employers' needs, not those of workers. Amazon not only requires you to take classes in "qualified fields of study," it also must approve individual courses.[26] It is also only available to those with a "blue badge" marking them as nontemporary employees. A thread on the Amazon Fulfillment Center subreddit (an internet discussion board, useful because it is unfiltered, though not entirely reliable because it is anonymous) concerning the Career Choice program features multiple voices chiming in that "not many" workers take advantage of Career Choice, even among the subset who are allowed to.

While some individual workers manage to take advantage of it and find a career they like, Career Choice is a cruel political measure as much as anything else: it tells workers that their position is their fault. If they cannot fight through exhaustion, cobble together a degree out of one course a semester, and then manage to find a job with that degree, well, that's not Amazon's fault, is it? That same Reddit thread features workers sighing that they are too tired to use Career Choice anyway. One user reported they were "tired all the time" even after "12 hours of sleep," an experience Heike Geissler corroborates. Another responded, "You're going to live an unsuccessful life and you are the only reason for it."[27]

This victim-blaming analysis matches the underlying philosophy of Amazon. It manifests in Amazon's labor control strategies, corporate culture, and Jeff Bezos's personal philosophy. According to David Niekerk, a company vice president and one of the architects of its warehouse system, Bezos believes that "our nature as humans is to expend as little energy as possible to get what we want or need."[28] In other words, he believes in the pain-pleasure psychological egoism popular in labor control thought since John Locke. Jeff Bezos reinvented the Panopticon because centuries of economic history made it a profitable structure, and because centuries of political thought made it easy, obvious, and natural to see humans with the dim pessimism of control science. We have collectively accepted it for the same reasons.

Because his power comes from competition, eventually it will be replaced with something worse. Jeff Bezos might be able to escape Earth—though so far his Blue Origin company has had limited success—but he cannot escape competition. As a manager in *Seasonal Associate*'s orientation puts it, "nothing can grow forever."[29]

Bezos seems to be aware of this. One of his pet projects is a 10,000-year clock known as the Clock of the Long Now, built into a mountain and designed to survive virtually anything that could happen in the next ten millennia. Forced to think in terms of shareholder returns, pushed and pushing every day toward global ecological collapse, the billionaire class creates symbols of long-term thinking because of its inability to engage in it. Rather than avert civilizational collapse, Jeff Bezos is building a clock that can survive it.

From Bezos to . . . Jezos

Jeff Bezos was only one of many West Coast billionaires produced by the combination of internet innovation and neoliberal asset price inflation. He wasn't even the only one who dreamed of escaping to outer space: Paypal cofounder Peter Thiel did as well. Like Elon Musk, another PayPal billionaire, Thiel spent his childhood in Southern Africa, much of it specifically in occupied Namibia, where his father managed uranium mines. Thiel later defended apartheid with the same rhetoric the right had used in the 1970s, claiming that it "worked" economically.[30] He called himself a libertarian, and like others in that tradition since its nineteenth-century inception, he believed in a world of maximum property rights and a minimal state: a world free, as much as possible, of government "interference." Despite fabulous wealth and significant influence, he despaired that this vision was ever achievable. While neoliberalism had won, libertarianism had not.

In a 2009 essay for the Cato Institute, he wrote that he "no longer believe[d] freedom and democracy were compatible."[31]

This pessimism was nothing new for libertarians, who had long grappled with the unpopularity of their ideas. Thiel believed that "the 1920s were the last decade in American history during which one could be genuinely optimistic about politics." One reason was women's suffrage, which had "rendered the notion of 'capitalist democracy' into an oxymoron," because women vote for the wrong policies—a classic libertarian objection that went all the way back to Herbert Spencer.[32] Libertarians had long aimed to protect the competitive evolution of markets from the cooperative intention of democratic politics. Thiel proposed bold solutions for an "escape not via politics but beyond it."

The first was "cyberspace." Network technologies made it possible to bypass borders and regulations, creating a new world in parallel to the one that existed: a new world that could potentially supplant the old. PayPal, Thiel claimed, was originally based on a vision of a "new world currency, free from all government control and dilution—the end of monetary sovereignty, as it were." But while the internet was the easiest of his three new horizons to access, Thiel remarked that it might be a limited one: "any escape may be more imaginary than real." In contrast, outer space was distant and impractical but offered a "limitless possibility for escape from world politics." Thiel found it appealing but distant—at least decades away, if not more. So as a middle ground between the two, he proposed "seasteading"—settling the oceans, for example with floating cities.[33]

The internet, the first of these exit routes, offered enticing possibilities indeed for capitalists in the 2010s to escape government regulation. Flush with the easy cash of the zero-interest-rate era, venture capitalists pumped money into firms like Uber (an unregulated taxi service) and Airbnb (an unregulated hotel service). But no internet innovation better exemplified the libertarian dream of exit than cryptocurrency (an unregulated financial instrument). It seemed to promise many libertarians exactly the "end of monetary sovereignty" many of them desired.

Bitcoin, the first and most significant cryptocurrency, was an attempt to take money even further from democracy than central banks do. Alarmed by "money printing," but finding the real gold standard impossible to reinstate, libertarians hostile to fiat money invented an artificial currency with all of gold's drawbacks. Like gold, Bitcoin is limited in quantity and difficult to use for transactions—at the time I am writing this, one Bitcoin exchange takes more electricity to complete than one US household uses in an entire month.[34] This weakness was the very reason for Bitcoin's strength in the view of its proponents: like gold, it was deflationary. To this Bitcoin and cryptocurrency generally added another feature appealing to asset-holders: they were unregulated, making them useful for both crime and speculation.

Cryptocurrency soon played a role in the exit dreams of another group. The "effective altruism" (EA) movement began with efforts at optimizing charity efficiency. It had its roots in two organizations founded by Oxford philosophy students Toby Ord and Willam MacAskill: Giving What We Can, founded in 2009, and 80,000 Hours, founded in 2011. Giving What We Can urged individuals to pledge at least a tenth of their income to charities chosen for effectiveness. Applying utilitarian principles to charity, EA adherents argued both for giving away a greater share of income and for doing so effectively: giving to those charities with low overhead and serving important needs. They encouraged transparency in philanthropy and guiding giving with research, rather than intuition. This focus led effective altruists to make charitable decisions like prioritizing clean water and bypassing centuries of paternalist prohibitions by giving directly to those in need.[35]

Effective altruist and journalist Dylan Matthews described EA as an "escape from American politics"—its claustrophobic DC swamp, its blinkered short-term worldview, its bleak horse race politics. The movement's adherents talked about curing diseases that kill millions, or protecting against future disasters. After a weekend with them, Matthews wrote, it was "hard to go back to another DC panel where people rehearse the same arguments about whether taxes should be higher or lower."[36] While politicians squabbled, EA *dreamed*. Effective altruism was exciting, optimistic, forward-thinking. If the tech industry could "move fast and break things," as Facebook's motto went, perhaps a similar approach could move fast and fix things. Big ideas, big money, and big minds could take on the problems no one else seemed to solve. Neoliberalism had created the perfect conditions for such a movement by shrinking the horizons of politics and expanding the horizons of wealth.

All this optimism required was overlooking the profound distortions that come from working through private money, which they needed a lot of. 80,000 Hours, EA's other founding institution, urged adherents to seek high-paying employment in order to maximize the amount they could donate to charity. Specifically, this meant finance and banking. William MacAskill gave a talk in 2011 entitled, "Want an ethical career? Become a banker"; in a 2013 article on the topic, he explained that he had convinced a student to work at the proprietary trading firm Jane Street and donate half of his income, allowing him to "pay the wages of several people for the not-for-profit work he could have been doing."[37] "Earning to give" had obvious appeal to those few millennial professionals who had escaped the rising tide of the Great Recession—and in Britain especially, the austerity that followed—by fleeing to the high ground of tech and finance, or otherwise made it through finesse and fortune to their own islands of success. The combination of a tech boom and fantastically low interest rates pursued by central banks after the 2008 recession meant plenty of money was sloshing around for EA to suck up.

Benefiting from the broader pattern of philanthropy in the asset-price-inflation-forever economy and the tech world necessarily required EA to be a subculture that was comfortable with rather than critical of capitalism and its elites. While EA leans more centrist/center-left-liberal than libertarian, Peter Thiel gave the keynote at an EA Global conference in 2013. William

MacAskill's 2015 *Doing Good Better: How Effective Altruism Can Help You Make a Difference* was blurbed by *Freakonomics* author Steven Levitt and George Mason University's neo-Calhounite libertarian Tyler Cowen.[30] As of 2020, it appears that a majority of money donated by EA came from two people: Dustin Moskowitz (of Facebook) and Cari Tuna, a married couple who had given hundreds of millions of dollars to EA institutions and causes.[39] Flush with cash, effective altruism began to run out of obvious charitable causes altogether.[40]

So they found new ones, not in the present but in the future. Relatively early on, EAers were interested in more than philanthropy. Will MacAskill wrote that the founding of 80,000 Hours in 2011 moved "the focus in Oxford away from just charity and onto ethical life-optimisation more generally." Peter Thiel's 2013 EA Global keynote mentioned little about charity and concluded with an emphasis on the rapid growth and thus significance of attention to artificial intelligence (AI). The development and character of AI became one of the overriding concerns of a new tendency within EA called "longtermism."

Longtermists start with the laudable viewpoint that future lives matter, that we owe things to people in the future, including those who do not yet exist. But applied within a strict version of the utilitarian framework that defined EA more generally, attention to the long term produced strange consequences. Philosopher Nick Bostrom—an associate of and influence on Toby Ord and William MacAskill, and from 2005 to 2024 the head of an Oxford outlet called the Future of Humanity Institute—envisioned, in the far distant future, the conversion of all matter and energy in the universe itself into massive computers. These would run utopian simulations, producing the maximum possible number of happy people the universe could fit. He estimated that this could support some 10^{54} "human-brain-emulation subjective life-years"—though these individuals would be immortal, you can imagine this as 10^{52} full human lives of 100 years.[41]

This is an inconceivably large number, five times larger than the number of seconds since the Big Bang . . . multiplied by itself, then multiplied by itself again.[42] With such scale, "even the tiniest reduction of existential risk has an expected value greater than that of any 'ordinary' good, such as the direct benefit of saving 1 billion lives."[43] It's simple multiplication: increasing by one millionth of 1 percent (10^{-8}) the chances of a utopia in which 10^{54} human-life-years might be lived still gives an "expected value" of saving 10^{46} human-life-years. Therefore, long-term-minded EAs should focus their efforts on protecting this future rather than ameliorating suffering in the present. For some people, this kind of calculation demonstrates how dangerous mathematical ethics can be. But for these hard utilitarians, extending the Benthams' moral math onward to the stars was righteous, even necessary.

To be clear, Bostrom's view was only one version of longtermism, and longtermism was only one current—albeit an influential one attracting big money—within EA. Originally, EA had a complicated relationship to the kind of brutal utilitarianism Bostrom's arguments relied on. The movement was founded by utilitarian philosophers and drew significant inspiration from the work of Princeton University philosopher Peter Singer, a utilitarian infamous for arguing for the murder of disabled newborns.[44] But plenty of EAers were ethics-minded pragmatists rather than utilitarian ideologues; most early EA activity, intellectually and financially, was focused on matters like malaria nets and organ donation. Longtermists among the EA movement were right to identify nuclear war as an almost bafflingly overlooked cause (by the 2000s, compared to, say, the height of the disarmament movement in the mid-twentieth century).

A critique of utilitarian optimization was in fact at the heart of a growing concern by longtermists and other EAs: the risks posed by artificial intelligence. One impactful criticism of utilitarianism has been the "utility monster" thought experiment, which imagines a monster who gets more pleasure from the suffering of others than the sufferers themselves feel pain in the process; without certain modifications to utilitarianism, one would be obligated to serve this evil creature's whim. A utility monster is an agent who optimizes around something we would not want to optimize. This is what some longtermists feared an AI might do.

Nick Bostrom offered a thought experiment about AI that came to be known as the "paperclip maximizer": imagine a superintelligent AI in charge of a paperclip factory, with the objective "to make as many paper clips as possible." Pursuing this literally, the AI might take steps to ensure it was not shut off, convert the factory to produce death robots, take over the Earth, convert its mass into paperclips, and then head out into space to do the same to the rest of the universe. Bostrom's thought experiment was a distillation of decades of robot science fiction, like *Terminator*.[45] As neural network–based systems began rapidly achieving new capabilities, their proponents increasingly felt they were onto something transformative—perhaps even artificial intelligence, which turned out to be a handy marketing term for this array of new software techniques. Well-prepared for this moment, EA helped produce an "AI safety" movement focused on "alignment"—aligning the values of AI with human values in order to prevent catastrophe.

In 2015, a who's who of tech billionaires formed an AI research nonprofit called OpenAI. OpenAI's founding statement states that its "goal is to advance digital intelligence in the way that is most likely to benefit humanity as a whole." Because it would be "free from financial obligations," OpenAI would be able to make decisions based on values rather than money. EA's "AI safety" movement swooped in to try to steer progress; in time, effective altruists would make up half of OpenAI's board. Terror at the possibility of a utility monster AI could lead AI safety advocates to propose extreme measures: in a 2023 essay for *Time* magazine, Eliezer Yudkowsky—a notable figure in the EA-adjacent "rationalist" subculture—argued for bombing data centers if anyone gathered too many GPUs in one spot.[46]

Yet despite its fears of a utility monster, EA helped create one. Among those William MacAskill had encouraged to go into finance was a young man named Sam Bankman-Fried (later known as SBF). Over lunch, Sam, who had given up eating meat to minimize animal suffering, told MacAskill that he was interested in animal welfare issues.[47] MacAskill encouraged him to give his time instead of his money. After a short period at Jane Street, Sam began employing the same kind of arbitrage tricks he learned there to make a fortune on crypto, exploiting international price differences in Bitcoin. He started a crypto trading firm called Alameda Research and benefited from hiring EAs, his biographer Michael Lewis observed, because they provided much-needed trust in a risky business.[48] In 2019, he expanded his operations with the creation of a cryptocurrency exchange called FTX. It pitched itself to both venture capital funders and to customers as the responsible person's cryptocurrency exchange, a "safe and easy way to get into crypto"—more like a broker or bank than the seedy libertarian forums and dark web drug markets crypto was associated with.[49]

Money poured in. Soon worth some $10 billion, Sam became a relatively well-known public figure, the genius "SBF."[50] For its role in making Sam Bankman-Fried, and the manpower and important reputational benefits it provided to FTX, EA got billions of ill-gotten dollars to devote to doing good "effectively." Bankman-Fried even funded an EA campaign for Congress in Oregon.[51] SBF was at the top of the world, but *Sam* was troubled. "I don't feel happiness," he wrote one day in his diary—"I feel nothing but the aching hole in my brain where happiness should be." In a letter to his coworker and sometime-partner Caroline Ellison, he claimed, "I don't really have a soul."[52]

Sam's business was as hollow as his emotional state. The political economy of the 2020s simultaneously encouraged his worst tendencies and enabled his exploitative business. In a stagnating and staggeringly unequal global economy where nobody seemed able to go from "zero to one" anymore, cryptocurrency offered both struggling retail investors and hungry venture capitalists the false promise of profiting at zero, making money off of literally nothing. Someone would be left holding the bag, but the big players planned to make sure it was not them—maybe the libertarian true believers, or the duped ordinary investors pouring money into crypto, but not them. FTX and Alameda were already playing a shell game simply by trading in crypto. But in late 2022 it emerged that they were doing something worse: engaging in outright fraud, a scam on top of a scam, by stealing FTX deposits to make risky bets with Alameda, donate to politicians, and even for SBF's own use.[53]

FTX was a utility monster. It single-mindedly optimized its own ledgers, devouring venture capital money, private investments, and customer assets. Its collapse wiped out the savings of ordinary people who had dared to hope that the crypto money fountain might give them a win when the broader economy wouldn't.[54] The Ontario Teachers' Pension Plan lost $95 million.[55] EA had once focused on issues like the important but dry task of optimizing malaria mitigation. Now it was trying to buy a congressional seat with money stolen from Canadian teachers' pensions in order to speculate in bogus cryptocurrency. Effective altruism looked more like effective solipsism.

This had happened before. Jeremy and Samuel Bentham's utilitarian philosophy believed in optimizing society to quantitatively maximize good. While the Benthams believed that markets were a powerful tool for doing so, they did not trust the market to set goals—they apportioned that task to experts like themselves. In the mid- to late nineteenth century, Benthamite utilitarianism was succeeded by Herbert Spencer's laissez-faire competitive evolution, which wielded Bentham's own psychological egoism against him: if individuals were self-interested pleasure-optimizers, how could we trust them to make moral decisions at all? Instead, the markets Bentham favored should be, had to be, trusted for everything—the market was a judge rather than a tool. Spencer became wildly and internationally popular because he offered useful justifications for capitalism's ballooning profits.

In the early to mid-twentieth century, working-class and anticolonial movements defeated multiple manifestations of the

Spencerian ethos: fascism, European imperialism, and the most unregulated forms of capitalism. The failure to extend New Deal policies into social democracy or anything further left opened the way for a resurgent empirically minded economic technocracy, Keynesian Cold War liberalism, which was then toppled by market fundamentalism. Price theorists like Milton Friedman insisted that market evolution could do a better job of optimizing society than democratic intention could, assembled a coalition of capitalists with the help of business executives like Lemuel Boulware, and ultimately toppled the careful balance between labor and capital in favor of the latter. They ushered in a neoliberal era, explicitly meant as a return to the laissez-faire nineteenth century that Herbert Spencer had lived in and defended.

In the twenty-first century, a self-consciously neo-Benthamite movement has made the same political mistakes as Jeremy Bentham and has fallen victim to the resulting internal contradictions. EA's commitment to working within the status quo—to optimizing a calculable market economy rather than taking on its market structure—became its undoing. Its focus drew further and further from present reality, and its ethics became more and more compromised. This decay culminated in a new and decidedly farcical ideological formation: "effective accelerationism," or "e/acc" as its adherents know it. Among its "saints" was a man who went by the moniker "Beff Jezos."

"The Constrained Vision"

E/acc began because EA said no to the rich on something. Initially, EA-backed "AI safety" advocates were at the forefront of AI development, hoping to understand what was possible so that they could ensure its safety. OpenAI's nonprofit structure, and even its name, reflected the high-minded goals it was at least publicly devoted to. It took only four years for them to compromise this. In 2019, OpenAI became a for-profit business with the creation of a new subsidiary technically owned by the original nonprofit, whose board featured EAs. An influx of funding from Microsoft then enabled them to make further advances to their data-hungry models. AI safety advocates began to worry that things were moving too fast—a sentiment much of the public would soon come to share.[56]

"Beff Jezos" felt differently. A former quantum computing engineer at Google, he started a questionable hardware firm, Extropic, in 2022.[57] In August of that year, he began posting on Twitter as "BasedBeffJezos," just as Elon Musk was moving toward his October acquisition of the social network. On Twitter and its audio room "Twitter Spaces" function, "Beff Jezos" began telling both those who worked on AI and those who funded it what they wanted to hear: artificial intelligence was powerful, it was good, it was the future. This grew into an extreme online subculture—E/acc, which argues for a grand "acceleration" forward with technology. The most important conflict of our time, they believed, was between E/accs and "decels," "doomers" who sought to hold back progress so they could control it.[58] Through technology, "we are destined to be Gods. Don't let the decels take this future away from us."[59] And unlike the stuffy philosophers of EA, E/acc was *fun*, according to adherents.[60] Jezos legitimized his ludicrously grandiose claims with adolescent irony, tired memes, and language from the notoriously toxic forum 4chan.[61]

While the aesthetic was new, the message was not. Beff Jezos was selling control science, wrapped in self-important technobabble. In an interaction with venture capitalist Marc Andreessen, Beff quoted *Jurassic Park* author Michael Crichton on the unknowability of the future as evidence for "why you can't have centralized top-down control, and why decentralized adaptive feedback loops will always win (EA vs e/acc, communism vs capitalism)."[62] "Capitalism," according to Jezos, is "the real democracy."[63] It "reaches optima no centralized top-down control system ever could."[64] It is "thermodynamics," which everything is either "aligned with or dies."[65] These statements were, in tweet form, Ludwig von Mises "consumer's democracy,"

Milton Friedman's price theory, and Herbert Spencer's "there is no alternative" evolution, respectively.

As AI advanced rapidly, safety advocates tried to hit the brakes. On March 22, 2023, a week after OpenAI released its GPT-4 model to the public, numerous public figures and AI researchers signed an open letter calling for a six-month pause on further development.[66] The letter was published by the Future of Life Institute, an EA-linked institution connected specifically to longtermist "AI safety." It went nowhere. With governments unwilling or unable to act, mounting safety concerns, and increasing suspicion of OpenAI CEO Sam Altman, AI safety altruists tried another way to be effective: they leveraged the seats they held on the board of the nonprofit that legally controlled OpenAI. On November 16, 2023, the board fired Altman.[67]

A lesson in real power immediately followed. Microsoft hired Altman a day later, and OpenAI's employees threatened to go with him. So did all the money. Four days after the original decision, Altman was back, and the rebellious board members, including EA-linked AI safety researcher Helen Toner, were removed.[68] One of the new board members who replaced the forced-out safety advocates was Larry Summers, former Harvard president, National Economic Council director, and Treasury secretary. The safeguards OpenAI had placed on itself were even easier to bypass than those built into its models; like GPT, the profit-optimizing system of capitalism could not easily be controlled by the imposition of conscious rules.

E/acc was dedicated to making sure this kind of thing would happen whenever someone tried to wield cooperative intention against competitive evolution. The accelerationists believed in freeing markets and restricting humans, rather than the other way around. In October 2023, Marc Andreessen published a screed called "The Techno-Optimist Manifesto."[69] While Andreessen claimed that "techno-optimist" ideology would create "technological supermen" and a multiplanetary society of unparalleled prosperity, he insisted, "We are not Utopians" but rather "adherents to what right-wing economist Thomas Sowell calls the Constrained Vision." According to Sowell—another product of the postwar right-wing economic nexus, with a cushy job at the conservative Hoover Institution where he's paid to churn out books almost nobody reads—those who believe in the "constrained vision" know that humans are inherently selfish and cannot be changed.

Sowell's first example was Adam Smith and eighteenth-century psychological egoism. Constrained vision adherents rely on "moral traditions, the marketplace, or families," "social processes" which they understand as "evolved rather than designed." The "unconstrained vision," in contrast, foolishly holds that human beings can be improved, can do better, can change—that "wiser or more moral and humane social policies" can solve problems by designing a response intentionally instead of evolving one through competition. The constrained vision is also a vision *of* constraint: because human beings are selfish, we must not even try the idealistic schemes of the left.[70]

As long as the decels were constrained, "The Techno-Optimist Manifesto" promised, infinity would be ours. Written in a style similar to that of cryptocurrency boosters on Twitter and general hustle culture types on LinkedIn, with oppressively frequent line breaks, as well as Trumpian capitalization of Important Words, it did not so much fuse libertarianism and fascism as articulate the moral nihilism common to both. "We believe in ambition, aggression, persistence, relentlessness—*strength* [emphasis in original]," Andreessen wrote. "We believe in competition, because we believe in evolution." Quoting the 1909 Italian *Manifesto of Futurism*, a forerunner to actual Italian fascism, Andreessen explained, "Beauty exists only in struggle." He waxed poetic about "the eros of the train" (i.e., the locomotive) and the "Hero's Journey." As the movement's "saints" he cited Adam Smith, Ludwig von Mises, Friedrich Hayek, Ayn Rand's fictional hero John Galt, and . . . Beff

Jezos, who was in fact at the top of the list, named by his Twitter handle. Like the fascism it drew on, Andreessen's vision was as ridiculous as it was malevolent.

While Andreessen had the market structure of society on his side, he still faced a serious political problem: this vision was profoundly unappealing to most people. Tech was becoming increasingly unpopular—services from Google to Netflix were getting more expensive and worse, AI only exacerbated already-rampant misinformation on social media and spam clogging the internet more broadly, and platform-holders seemed more interested in making their services addictive rather than attractive. The last thing most people wanted was a *more* unregulated tech industry. Polling suggested that a majority of Americans were "more concerned than excited" about increasing use of artificial intelligence in daily life, and a supermajority of Americans—two out of three—were "more concerned about insufficient government regulation" of ChatGPT "than excessive regulation."[71]

So Silicon Valley billionaires plotted an exit. For some this looked like a very literal exit: Balaji Srinivasan—a former employee of Marc Andreessen, whose vision is popular with both him and with Beff Jezos—argued that a tech-aligned Grey Tribe (as opposed to the Republican Red Tribe and the Democratic Blue Tribe) should bribe the police, take over the San Francisco Bay area as a militarized corporate state, and ultimately secede from the US. Srinivasan's vision drew on 2010s exit schemes like the even more unhinged "neoreactionary" thought of Curtis Yarvin, an associate of Peter Thiel's.[72]

More practically, tech capital turned rightward politically. In 2016, Marc Andreessen had endorsed Hillary Clinton for president because Trump's stances on immigration, the Republican's signature issue, made him "sick to [his] stomach."[73] Eight years later he not only endorsed Trump but put money behind him. Within months of his inauguration, the president began kidnapping immigrants and flying them off to Salvadoran President Nayib Bukele's gulag CECOT, in defiance of both individual court orders and the general principle of law itself. This was easy enough for men like Andreessen to justify with accelerationism's bastardized longtermism—if pro-business Republicans were going to speed up techno-utopia, sacrificing migrants was a small price to pay. Trump's running mate, J. D. Vance, was a close associate of Peter Thiel's and part of a broader push by tech capital not only to support Republicans or even drive them rightward but to push them away from democratic politics and toward authoritarianism as a way to keep the masses, whom they could not seem to convince, in check.

Control science paved Donald Trump's road to the presidency. Textbooks and airport screeds, podcasts and increasingly common sense told the American electorate that everyone was out for themselves. Why not elect an utterly selfish man without virtue? He knew how the world really works. Art of the deal! As he memorably put it, "I could stand in the middle of Fifth Avenue and shoot somebody, and I wouldn't lose any voters, OK?" He was probably right; he was elected because he was a man who believed in nothing. More prosaically, the weakened state of American labor made for lower wages (and thus an angrier electorate) and less resistance to Republicans, exactly as the twentieth-century conservative movement intended. The Koch-backed victories of the "law and economics" movement had given the nation a ratchet screwdriver judiciary that only turned right.

Now capitalists no longer needed to carefully cultivate politicians over decades, as they had with Reagan, or even subtly pull on their strings with threats of market discipline. During the campaign for what became Trump's second term, Elon Musk realized that you could simply buy the president outright. He dumped hundreds of millions of dollars into the race and won himself several months effectively in charge of the executive branch, cutting whatever he wanted, illegally impounding congressionally appropriated funds, and firing federal workers through his "DOGE" group, named for a meme cryptocurrency. Musk never actually abandoned "AI safety" claims, partly (it seems) due to a feud with Sam Altman, but he otherwise spoke and acted like an effective accelerationist: breaking the federal government, ignoring the law, using AI to make decisions. The Tesla "Technoking" had long used longtermist rhetoric to justify whatever he wanted now. Robots and Mars were coming, so who cared about present earthly issues? USAID acting administrator for global health Nicholas Enrich estimated that Musk-driven cuts to his agency would kill millions of people.[74]

As the administration violated the law and then threatened the international free trade that neoliberalism had once treated as sacrosanct, America's most committed libertarians grew enraged: Wasn't the right about freedom? Small government? "Too many people and organizations are abandoning these principles," Charles Koch sniffed at a Cato Institute gala in the spring of 2025.[75] But his science of liberty had been the latest campaign in a long war against such principles altogether. The accelerationists and the fascists displaced the libertarians with even more ease than they had replaced the technocrats generations earlier.

"Love Doesn't Scale"

America's right-wing accelerationists sought to surpass material as well as legal and political limits. Andreessen believed that entrepreneurs "continually create new goods and services to satisfy those wants and needs, deploying unlimited numbers of people and machines in the process." This is, of course, false. The number of machines and people on Earth have been and will be finite. But Andreessen insisted that "technology lets you do more and more with less and less until eventually you can do everything with nothing."[76] And there was no need to limit humanity to Earth. With technological advances, he predicted, some 50 billion humans could live on the planet and expand to inhabit other worlds thereafter. This greater population would produce "scientists, technologists, artists, and visionaries beyond our wildest dreams." Despite having political differences with Andreessen, this was Jeff Bezos's vision as well: he claimed in 2023 that he wanted a trillion humans, because proportionally we would then "have, at any given time, 1,000 Mozarts and 1,000 Einsteins."[77] For Andreessen, the fact that "human wants and needs are infinite" means "economic demand is infinite, and job growth can continue forever."

It would be easy to criticize this vision for its rosy forecasts of endless growth on an increasingly hot and decidedly finite Earth—but there is a deeper problem with its infinity. Even if a future of infinite growth is possible—through unforeseen technology or space travel—Marc Andreessen and his ilk would ensure that it is a future of infinite coercion. Human needs do grow and change. In the United States today, most people *need* internet access, even though it did not exist until recently: it is necessary for their jobs, which in turn are how they get basic necessities such as food and shelter. The growth of human needs does not have to be an oppressive or coercive process. But capitalism is based on economic compulsion.[78] You must sell your labor to meet your needs. The capitalist competition that Andreessen and company took as an article of faith—"we believe in competition, because we believe in evolution"—relies on lack.

Practitioners of the science of control do not want to mitigate or regulate poverty, let alone abolish it. They hope instead to use it as fuel to accelerate new economic growth. The Trump administration made this almost explicit in April 2025, when, almost certainly pulling directly from Andreessen, the director of the White House Office of Science and Technology Policy called on individuals to "give themselves to scientific discoveries that will bend time and space," allowing us to "make more with less."[79] The accelerationists believe in preserving and magnifying rather than mitigating inequality and its economic coercion.

"The Techno-Optimist Manifesto" claimed that "scores of common causes of death . . . can be fixed with AI, from car crashes to pandemics to wartime friendly fire." AI's world-changing power would supposedly be enough to help send us to the stars, but it couldn't end war—only make it more efficient. As for the pandemic, billionaire action in the name of competition has already done enormous harm. In 2020, Oxford University scientists considered giving away the rights to their new COVID vaccine instead of patenting it. More broadly, a number of countries went to the World Trade Organization and asked for a suspension of intellectual property rights over the vaccines. For once—in this crisis—we could suspend competition and save lives.

Philanthropist Bill Gates and his Gates Foundation, a major player in public health, stepped in to warn them otherwise. He insisted that only Big Pharma and the existing intellectual property system could handle a major vaccination effort. Gates did not stand to gain from this intervention—he earnestly believed that this was the right choice. Oxford was convinced and partnered with the pharmaceutical company AstraZeneca. While Americans were beginning to breathe easy as the first vaccines released, people living in less wealthy countries died en masse, unable to afford the vaccines that wealthy countries were hoarding.[80]

Any paradise we make with technology, control science will simultaneously unmake with inequality. It already has. Today—right now—we can split atoms for energy, travel to the moon, and communicate anywhere on Earth in the blink of an eye. In short, we live with many of the material achievements portrayed in yesterday's science fiction, and some that exceed it. But we have not achieved the social vision that our forebears imagined for us. John Maynard Keynes predicted that by 2030, we might be working fifteen-hour weeks.[81] Most Americans are in fact lucky to work forty hours, toiling all the while for someone else's profit—someone like Musk or Andreessen.

Of course, we've made improvements since the early twentieth century. But most of the political and economic gains (for ordinary people) of the last century have come from limiting the effect of competition on our lives—with measures such as deposit insurance in banking, social safety nets, and labor law. These are results of the very political cooperation that effective accelerationism, like earlier incarnations of control science, seeks to destroy. People in the past like Andreessen have given us a future of material prosperity without liberation. Control science and the "constrained vision" would condemn us to that forever.

As economist Dan Davies put it regarding both the paperclip maximiser problem and economics, "every decision-making system set up as a maximiser needs to have a higher-level system watching over it," including a "red handle to pull" when something is unacceptable. Davies rightly concludes that this means we "can't have the economists in charge, not in the way they currently are."[82] Economics, the disciplinary home of the science of control, has preached against attempts to pull the red handle, or even such a handle existing at all. Accelerationism simply makes this ideology particularly explicit. Andreessen claimed: "Our enemy is the Precautionary Principle," an approach in international law and conventions that places the burden of proof regarding harm on proponents rather than detractors of new technology. Constraint is for humans, not for technology or corporations.

It seems unlikely that current generative AI methods will ever produce the humanlike "Artificial General Intelligence" their boosters are aiming for, but they do not have to in order to do harm. Contrary to Andreessen's promises about wartime friendly fire, AI has so far made warfare worse. The Israel Defense Forces' use of AI systems dramatically increased the speed at which it could convert data into targets, by dramatically reducing the role of human beings in making decisions about where to drop bombs on civilians.[83] This is a particularly violent example of AI and indeed control science's more general tendency to replace human intention with systemic imperatives. It is telling that the holy grail of AI development, an AI "agent" capable of independent action but entirely obedient to employers, is a mind without will, a person without a heart. Unwilling or unable to act against the market's profit imperative, control science's present-day adherents already act like this.

These exit schemes have failed, and they will continue to fail. The capitalist science of control works as an ideology for justifying exploitation but persistently falls short as a theory of how the world actually works—economically, politically, historically. Billionaires' dreams of space settlement are likely to meet a similar fate. Forget space—capitalists can't even manage to escape states or workers here on Earth. Thiel's aforementioned seasteading proposal has proven a total dead end. In one of the more promising efforts (in relative terms, which says something) libertarian crypto aficionados bought a cruise ship and tried to turn it into a libertarian paradise, the MS *Satoshi* (after Bitcoin's pseudonymous inventor, Satoshi Nakamoto). They soon ran into problems like fire safety and pet waste disposal. The company they formed banned microwaves from cabins and devised strict regulations on dog ownership—life aboard the proposed seastead was starting to sound more like life in a neighborhood with a particularly vicious HOA. Soon they abandoned the project altogether because they couldn't find . . . insurance.[84]

It is hard to imagine them faring any better with a space colony. In an environment completely hostile to human habitation, where every resource is scarce and precious, competition is dangerous and cost-cutting impossible. And should they succeed anyway, they won't achieve the paradise they claim they will. As long as control science reigns, Jeff Bezos's 1,000 future Mozarts won't do any better than the potential Mozarts who are already here on Earth now—and forced to make a living in places like Amazon warehouses because the market doesn't favor musicians.

Yet those who believe in market evolution insist to us that there is no alternative. Peter Thiel claimed in the summer of 2024 that Christianity was a "woke" obstacle to his agenda because it "always took the side of the victim."[85] If the meek inherit the Earth, they will waste it. The teachings of Jesus are holding us back. The gospel of Jezos will bring us forward. Cold as this might seem, they claim, any other worldview always fails. Paraphrasing Milton Friedman's less successful son David, Andreessen explains in his manifesto that people only act because of "love, money, or force." And "love," Andreessen writes, "doesn't scale."[86]

"I Have Nothing to Say to You"

This is wrong. Even after four centuries of hard work by the wealthiest people in the world, the science of control is still contested. Love *has* scaled, with an appropriate willingness to use money and force to achieve its ends. In the face of capitalists' well-funded efforts, workers ended slavery, expanded democracy, defeated fascism, and restrained markets. After capitalists achieved unprecedented global hegemony beginning in the 1980s and 1990s, it took them barely a generation or two to destabilize the world so severely that they now fear they need to flee Earth itself.

Many libertarians, the most extreme believers in control science, are also conspiracy theorists. One of the failed funders of the MS *Satoshi,* Chad Elwartowski, claimed that the "Great Reset" had "claimed another victim" when his plans collapsed—this was a reference to a conspiracy theory that COVID was a hoax perpetrated on the public by an elite seeking to remake the world.[87] Right-wingers are so terrified of intentional action, of "planning," that they see it in every shadow and around every corner. These people are a sad joke. Their ideas are cruel fictions.

To return to where we began: among the best-known science fiction novels of Iain Banks, whose work inspired Jeff Bezos and that Elon Musk names his SpaceX vehicles after, is 1990's *Use of Weapons*. The book deconstructs the traditional space opera hero through its protagonist, Zakalwe. In the past, he committed a terrible sin against his own family in a failed attempt to win a war. Banks's description of Zakalwe calls to mind both the men and more importantly the ideas this book has focused on: the protagonist is a man defined by "the adaptive, self-seeking urge to survive . . . [by the] taking and bending of materials and people to one purpose" and "the outlook that everything could be used in the fight; that nothing could be excluded, that everything was a weapon."[88] We learn in the novel's ending that Zakalwe is trapped in a cycle of failed redemption: the Culture asks him to carry out some unsavory task, he does it in exchange for a favor, he calls in that favor to have them bring him to his sister as he has before and will again, and she rejects him: "I have nothing to say to you. And there is nothing you can say to me."

The history of control science is not only a history of menace—it is also a history of failure. Certainly, these ideas are powerful, even hegemonic. They are not merely imposed from above—they are grounded in material reality (which they have helped make) and widely believed. Cynicism is self-reinforcing: the more the world is ruled by people who believe in nothing, the harder it becomes to believe in anything at all. But we *have* continued to believe. So far we have not overcome capitalists' market evolution, but we have made real progress in spite of it and forced capitalists to adapt again and again. Like Zakalwe's sister, humanity has repeatedly rejected control science, and like her, when we look upon men like Jeff Bezos, Charles Koch, Lemuel Boulware, Alfred Sloan, Herbert Spencer, Nathan Appleton, Samuel Bentham, Josiah Wedgwood, and William Petty, we should do so with pity, with hostility, and with disgust.

Conclusion

There Is an Alternative

The next time someone tells you we are all just out for ourselves, think of someone you love. Think of all the things they believe, all the ways their actions surprise you, all the things they have done for others. The people you have read about in this book would reduce all that complexity to simple selfishness. They have insisted that that is all we are and organized the world in an attempt to ensure it is all we ever can be. Psychological egoism is the final sneering defense of every oppressor: *in my position, you would do the same*. The science of control—and with it, much of orthodox economics, vernacular economic thought, and what passes now for common sense about human action—is based on that claim.

Now think of all you have done and would do for that person. Ask yourself: am I just an individual? Or can my actions only be understood through interactions with others? We are fundamentally social creatures. That includes the practitioners of control science themselves. John Locke's philosophy was shaped by decades of war and millennia of theology. Herbert Spencer's methodological individualism was an obvious product of his father's abuse. Thomas Cooper's turn from antislavery liberal to proslavery Calhounite came from his move into the social world of Southern slaveholders. Charles Koch's libertarianism developed through an entire postwar world of right-wing economic thought, and his influence came through funding and growing that community.

It took a particular society to make these men and their ideas actually matter as they did—under better economic and political conditions, Spencer would be a minor character in literary history, Koch a mere regional business figure, and "Beff Jezos" a nobody. Likewise, the defeats control science has suffered have come from collective dynamics, not individual impulses. It took millions of American laborers willing to risk everything to push FDR leftward. The Flint sit-down strikers acted not as autonomous selfish individuals motivated by material gain but as a valiant collective that believed in something better.

And so now ask yourself: what can we do better together? Since we are social creatures, since we are not purely selfish, since we can reason together, we can change the world for the better by cooperation, rather than mere competition. Control science's hostility to democratic planning and its preference for markets are two sides of the same coin. To rely on the market is to give up on deciding together. This might be acceptable, even necessary, in many areas of life—you should not need to call a town meeting in order to buy groceries. But right now markets are the rule, rather than the exception. The most important decisions in our lives—how much we will be paid, the conditions we work in, where we can find housing, how much carbon we can dump into our atmosphere—are not made as decisions at all but as competitions between bank accounts. This is not freedom. It is automated oppression. It can be painfully difficult for human beings to make any kind of plan together. It is even harder to do so democratically and thoughtfully. But we have done it before, and we can do it again.

Four hundred years of elite scheming have failed to produce either the technocratic control that utilitarians like the Benthams wanted or the pure competition advocated by market radicals like Ludwig von Mises. Every country in the world, even those with little or no political freedom, has major movements that demand better. Those movements do not always win. But every victory builds a foundation for the next. Today we have labor rights, voting power, and political freedoms—where we have them—because of the hard work of those who came before us. Building on their legacy, we can continue to make a better world now and to create conditions for yet more advances after we are gone.

Control science is not "human nature." It is not "how the world works." It is not *just* orthodox economics or economic common sense or advanced political discourse. Identifying the different intertwining strands that give control science its strength, and naming the total result, helps us take it on. Labeling control science—and labeling it accurately as a matter of control—is all the more important because of how it works.

The irony of control science is that it is ultimately not a theory of control by anyone at all. Control science respects no kings, no presidents, and no gods but what one of Herbert Spencer's followers called "that awful One to whom it is profanity to pray."[1] This is an ideology for control by no one, of everyone. Its advocates call this freedom. The science of control is an attempt at rule without rulers, an abstract authoritarianism, an art of excuses: centuries of elites finding themselves in positions of power and scrambling to justify that power to themselves and the world. What you have seen portrayed in this book is the accreted effort, over four centuries, of everyone who has ever looked at injustice and shrugged.

This vast program of institutionalized apathy has been developed through, and always relies on, the forceful control of workers themselves. Identifying this program does two things for us. First, it makes clear that cynical claims about "human nature" are social and political constructions, not an objective truth discovered by capitalists. Lemuel Boulware did not figure out how humans are, he aimed to determine how they could be. Second, then, this intellectual history of economic thought reveals how much it has always been about control of us, not by us. We can rally against it accordingly: control science is fake, and it is wrong.

Ideas alone will not be enough, of course. Control science has succeeded by embedding itself in the legal, political, and economic structures of the world around us. It does not describe actual human nature, but it does describe how many people do, and must, act, precisely because of the way capitalists have made the world. Selfishness is embedded in the real material relations we have with each other: the most responsible strategies for investing, for example, may include investments in oil companies. The cheapest products are produced under the worst labor conditions. Buying better or investing differently as an individual will accomplish little, and it is difficult to build collective movements around doing something that makes us, temporarily, worse off, in a world of economic scarcity and against constant competition by the preachers of selfishness. We cannot defeat control science as individual consumers—a social category Boulware helped create. But we can as workers, as voters, and as full human beings.

Over the last four centuries, many of the greatest victories for justice, equality, and freedom have relied on mass movements of working people, from the revolutions of the eighteenth century to the New Deal and decolonization in the twentieth century. The twenty-first century has been, in much of the world, a period of defeat and retreat for working-class left-wing politics. But it does not have to be that way. The science of control was made in the workplace. It can be unmade there as well. Labor organizing forces idealistic progressives to ground our projects in material incentives: better wages, improved working conditions, more free time. This is particularly necessary in the cynical world control science has made. We have been told that everyone is selfish and that an alternative world is impossible. This makes it all the more difficult to believe rousing appeals to empathy and ethics alone.

Organizing within workplaces must become part of a broader movement for democracy and equality at work—control *by* workers, not *of* them. Most of us recoil at the idea of an absolute monarch or a dictator. Yet we spend a good portion of our days, and our lives, doing the bidding of bosses over whom we have little power. We should abhor authoritarian company "presidents" and company boards the way we do dictatorship and monarchy. Working people should wield power through robust and assertive democratic unions to force our bosses to take our needs and desires and dreams into account.

A powerful labor movement alone will not end the science of control—we have already seen capitalists' ability to adapt to and weaken unions. And an economy of competing democratic cooperatives would still be one driven by markets and competition. Thus, we also need to aim for democratic control of the economy writ large. Human needs and collective desires, not the movement of markets, should determine what we make and do. A market is a forever skewed democracy: your voting power is proportional to your wealth, and the most exploitative actors are therefore the most powerful. We should find this an offense against democracy, and we should act accordingly. The people you have read about in this book would, not wrongly, warn that power corrupts. But so does the absence of it. Rule by market rules has only succeeded in leading us to a world that satisfies no one.

Mass working-class movements, wielding the power of democracy, can build an intentional and deliberate world that reflects our most meaningful and deeply held collective wants, democratically aggregated, rather than our individual purchasing choices, scaled by our wealth. We can undo the normative-positive collapse. We can build our moral principles and our material needs into the legal structure, social fabric, and collective ideals of our societies so that acting in the common good, instead of against it, becomes easier and more obvious every day.

We know collective effort can outcompete nihilist competition, because it has done so before: an imperfect fraction of this program of economic democracy saved the world from fascism. Imagine what a full-fledged collective program could do for living standards, economic growth, and climate change. Through public housing authorities, we can determine where housing is built and how much it costs based on our need for comfortable homes, instead of the political demand to keep housing prices up for those already locked into an expensive mortgage. With utility nationalization, we can replace hated telecommunications monopolies with less expensive, more functional infrastructure that we control.

By embracing the "planning" Hayek and company loathed, we can chart a course for the global economy instead of letting it determine the course of our lives. All of this requires no promises of or belief in a socialist utopia (though it will help us move toward one). Right now, it is right-wing economics that is in the way of lower rent, higher wages, shorter hours, full employment, and economic dignity, for all of us. If we take control of our work and our lives, we can secure a better life together.

Overturning control science and taking back control, not just of our work or our national economies but our global collective life, will require changes to all the areas of society this book has touched on and more. What is fair at work? What do we need for our families, our communities, our countries, our Earth? What should the world look like? No one has all the answers, and no one could or should. We have to insist on asking these questions, in the face of four centuries of economic thinkers telling us they don't matter. We should ask them not just every bargaining period or election cycle but each time the boss denies us a raise, each time an economist squawks at us from cable news, each time a politician tells us what we cannot do. And above all, we should ask them together, backing up labor actions with ongoing energy, and ballots with mass political action.

The sum total of this effort will be to give our ethics real political force—to place our best collective impulses, not our worst individual ones, in the driver's seat. Herbert Spencer's nihilistic and competitive description of the world is true when we operate only competitively. The more competitive the world is, the more everyone must treat each interaction as a competition to be won. But together we can suspend this game, refuse to fight, decide what is too much, pull the red handle. The economy is not a train on a linear track through history. It is a ship sailing through foggy seas at night. We can take the helm and find new futures together, beyond the limited horizons control science has charted for us. There are a near-infinite array of things we disagree on and places where our economic and political interests diverge. There probably always will be. But that is all the more reason not to hand power over to the dead hand of markets. We can have a workplace, an economy, and a world that are guided not by instrumental necessity but intentional hope.

As a starting point: the actual values behind a project of economic democracy are widespread. Most people believe in freedom, equality, and justice, even though we disagree about what they mean. Outside of economic thinking, control science's normative-positive collapse is hardly popular. Most of us believe deeply in altruism in a variety of circumstances. You don't act like a purely selfish individual, nor do the people around you. The religious traditions we have cultivated for millennia, the art we make and appreciate, and even the stories we read to our children, all valorize caring for others. Meanwhile, our most infamous movie villains sound like Herbert Spencer. We know that control science is wrong. And we do not have to always agree about what right and wrong are to believe that they matter. We still believe in care, in solidarity, in freedom, and in love. It is, as Carl Marzani put it once, as corny as that. Let's build something better together.

Notes

Introduction

1. Charles G. Koch, "Acceptance Remarks by Charles G. Koch, 2005 Herman W. Lay Memorial Award Recipient of the Association of Private Enterprise Education: Koch Industries, Market Process Analysis, and the Science of Liberty," *Journal of Private Enterprise* 22, no. 2 (2007): 1–6.
2. Various Glassdoor reviews, archived by author in summer 2024 in the likely event that they are not accessible for long.

1. Calculated Extraction, 1600–1700

1. Ted McCormick, *William Petty: And the Ambitions of Political Arithmetic* (Oxford University Press, 2009), 19.
2. John Aubrey quoted in McCormick, *William Petty*, 16.
3. Peter Linebaugh, *The London Hanged: Crime and Civil Society in the Eighteenth Century* (Verso, 2003), 382.
4. Lisa T. Sarasohn, "Motion and Morality: Pierre Gassendi, Thomas Hobbes and the Mechanical World-View," *Journal of the History of Ideas* 46, no. 3 (1985): 363–79.
5. Thomas Hobbes, *Leviathan: Or the Matter, Forme and Power of a Commonwealth, Ecclesiasticall and Civill*, ed. A. R. Waller (Cambridge University Press, 1904), xviii.
6. McCormick, *William Petty*, 36.
7. Gerrard Winstanley, "A Declaration from the Poor Oppressed People of England," in *Winstanley: "The Law of Freedom" and Other Writings*, ed. Christopher Hill (Cambridge University Press, 1983), 97–108.
8. Christopher Hill, *The World Turned Upside Down: Radical Ideas During the English Revolution* (Temple Smith, 1972), 90–1.
9. Hartlib quoted in McCormick, *William Petty*, 72.

10. Charles Webster, *The Great Instauration: Science, Medicine and Reform, 1626–1660* (Holmes & Meier Publishers, 1976), 29; McCormick, *William Petty*, 66–83.
11. McCormick, *William Petty*, 268–70 and 72 respectively.
12. Ibid., 47–8.
13. Alessandro Roncaglia, *The Wealth of Ideas: A History of Economic Thought* (Cambridge University Press, 2005), 57–65.
14. T. C. Barnard and Toby Christopher Barnard, *Cromwellian Ireland: English Government and Reform in Ireland 1649–1660* (Clarendon Press, 2000), 135; Paul Slack, *The Invention of Improvement: Information and Material Progress in Seventeenth-Century England* (Oxford University Press, 2015).
15. Ellen Meiksins Wood, *The Origin of Capitalism: A Longer View* (Verso, 2002), 106.
16. Hartlib quoted in Paul Slack, *The Invention of Improvement: Information and Material Progress in Seventeenth-Century England* (Oxford University Press, 2015), 138.
17. McCormick, *William Petty*, 88.
18. Sir William Petty, *Political Arithmetick* (R. Clavel, 1690), 108.
19. Ibid., 93.
20. Wood, *The Origin of Capitalism*, 163.
21. Petty quoted in, and the scheme discussed in, McCormick, *William Petty*, 194–6.
22. Ibid., 195.
23. Petty, *Political Arithmetick*, 98–9.
24. Ibid., 98.
25. See William Deringer, *Calculated Values: Finance, Politics, and the Quantitative Age* (Harvard University Press, 2018).
26. McCormick, *William Petty*, 13.
27. Petty, preface to *Political Arithmetick*.
28. William Petty, *A Treatise of Taxes and Contributions* (London, 1662), chapter 5.
29. See Wayne Modest, "WE HAVE ALWAYS BEEN MODERN: Museums, Collections, and Modernity in the Caribbean," *Museum Anthropology* 35, no. 1 (2012): 85–96.
30. Richard S. Dunn, *Sugar and Slaves: The Rise of the Planter Class in the English West Indies, 1624–1713* (University of North Carolina Press, 2012).
31. Peter Thompson, "Henry Drax's Instructions on the Management of a Seventeenth-Century Barbadian Sugar Plantation," *William and Mary Quarterly* 66, no. 3 (2009): 565–604, 571.

32. Ibid.; Edward Littleton, *The Groans of the Plantations* (M. Clark, 1689), 16–17.
33. Thompson, "Henry Drax's Instructions," 574.
34. Henry Drax's instructions in ibid., 585.
35. I discuss this briefly in Henry Snow, "Fugitive Harbour: Labour, Community, and Marronage at Antigua Naval Yard," *Slavery and Abolition* 42, no. 4 (April 2021): 1–24; and *Enemies of Order: Labor and Power at the Atlantic Dockside* (University of Georgia Press, forthcoming).
36. Thompson, "Henry Drax's Instructions," 587.
37. Stephanie E. Smallwood, *Saltwater Slavery: A Middle Passage from Africa to American Diaspora* (Harvard University Press, 2009), 35. See also Jennifer L. Morgan, *Reckoning with Slavery: Gender, Kinship, and Capitalism in the Early Black Atlantic* (Duke University Press, 2021).
38. See Randy M. Browne, *The Driver's Story: Labor and Power in the World of Atlantic Slavery* (University of Pennsylvania Press, 2024).
39. Marisa J. Fuentes, *Dispossessed Lives: Enslaved Women, Violence, and the Archive*, Early American Studies (University of Pennsylvania Press, 2016); Rashauna Johnson, *Slavery's Metropolis: Unfree Labor in New Orleans During the Age of Revolutions* (Cambridge University Press, 2016), 28.
40. See Stephanie M. H. Camp, *Closer to Freedom: Enslaved Women and Everyday Resistance in the Plantation South* (University of North Carolina Press, 2005); and Fuentes, *Dispossessed Lives*.
41. See Holly Brewer, "Slavery, Sovereignty, and 'Inheritable Blood': Reconsidering John Locke and the Origins of American Slavery," *American Historical Review* 122, no. 4 (October 1, 2017): 1038–78.
42. Fuentes, *Dispossessed Lives*, 38–9.
43. Boyrereau Brinch, *Memoirs of Boyrereau Brinch* (Prentiss, 1774), 91–4.
44. Richard Ligon, *A True and Exact History of the Island of Barbados*, (London, 1657), 44.
45. Ibid., 53.
46. Littleton, *The Groans of the Plantations*, 17.
47. John Locke, *An Essay Concerning Human Understanding* (T. Tegg and Son, 1836), 251.
48. Ibid., 147.
49. Ibid., 422.
50. Ibid., 251.

51. Ibid., 251.
52. Ibid., 162.
53. Ibid.
54. John Locke, "An Essay on the Poor Law (1697)," in *Locke: Political Essays* (Cambridge University Press, 1997), 182–200.
55. The London Lives project's website has a section on vagrancy that mentions this function of passes: *London Lives, 1690–1800*, londonlives.org.
56. Brewer, "Slavery, Sovereignty, and Inheritable Blood."
57. John Locke, *An Essay Concerning the True Original Extent and End of Civil Government* (Edes and Gill, 1773), 378.
58. Ibid., 211.

2. Labor Control and Psychological Egoism, 1700–1770

1. Eliza Meteyard, *The Life of Josiah Wedgwood* (Hurst and Blackett, 1865), 97–8; Simeon Shaw, *History of the Staffordshire Potteries* (Shaw, 1829).
2. Edwin A. Barber, "So-Called 'Red Porcelain,' or Boccaro Ware of the Chinese, and Its Imitations," *Bulletin of the Pennsylvania Museum* 9, no. 34 (1911): 17–23. See also Celia Fiennes, *The Illustrated Journeys of Celia Fiennes, c. 1685–c. 1712* (Webb & Bower, 1982), 156n2.
3. See R. L. Hobson, "Early Staffordshire Wares Illustrated by Pieces in the British Museum," *Burlington Magazine for Connoisseurs* 4, no. 10 (1904): 65–72.
4. Meteyard, *Life of Josiah Wedgwood*, 134–6 and 139; Shaw, *Staffordshire Potteries*, 150.
5. Ibid., 99.
6. Meteyard claims it was Samuel. Other accounts suggest that Samuel's brother John was behind the heist or did not necessarily steal the knowledge. See "Dictionary of National Biography, 1885–1900/Astbury, John," wikisource.org. See also "John Astbury, English Potter," britannica.com.
7. Meteyard, *Life of Josiah Wedgwood*, 158.
8. Bernard de Mandeville, *The Fable of the Bees: Or, Private Vices, Publick Benefits. With an Essay on Charity and Charity Schools. And a Search into the Nature of Society . . .* (J. Tonson, 1724), 4.
9. Ibid., 5.
10. Ibid., 8.
11. Ibid., 13.

12. Ibid., 18.
13. Ibid., 14–15.
14. Ibid., 20.
15. Mandeville, *Fable of the Bees*, 360–2.
16. Ibid., 357.
17. Ibid., 345–6.
18. Ibid., 330.
19. Ibid., 357.
20. Friedrich Engels, *The Condition of the Working-Class in England in 1844* (S. Sonnenschein, 1892), 257.
21. Sophie Audidière, "Helvétius, Claude Adrien (1715–71)," in *The Encyclopedia of Political Thought* (John Wiley & Sons, 2014), 1642–3.
22. Jean François de Saint-Lambert quoted in David Wootton, "Helvétius: From Radical Enlightenment to Revolution," *Political Theory* 28, no. 3 (2000): 307–36, 320.
23. "N'appercoivent qu'un joujou & qu'une occupation." The English translation renders this as "make their children their playthings and their pastimes." See Helvétius, *De l'esprit: Or, Essays on the Mind, and Its Several Faculties* (Vernor, Hood, and Sharpe, 1810), 432; Helvétius, *De l'esprit*, vol. 3 (Chez Durand, 1758), 127.
24. Helvétius, *De l'esprit: Or, Essays on the Mind*, 433; Helvétius, *De l'esprit* (French), vol. 3, 128–9.
25. Helvétius, *De l'esprit* (French), vol. 1, 62; *De l'esprit: Or, Essays on the Mind*, 29.
26. Helvétius, *De l'esprit* (French), vol. 1, 37; *De l'esprit: Or, Essays on the Mind*, 16.
27. Helvétius, *De l'esprit* (French), vol. 1, 49; *De l'esprit: Or, Essays on the Mind*, 23.
28. Helvétius, *De l'esprit* (French), vol. 1, 40; *De l'esprit: Or, Essays on the Mind*, 18. The English translation notably watered this down slightly to "all the privileges of humanity they have a right to demand."
29. Helvétius, *De l'esprit* (French), vol. 1, 36–55; *De l'esprit: Or, Essays on the Mind*, 15–26.
30. Helvétius, *De l'esprit* (French), vol. 1, 241; *De l'esprit: Or, Essays on the Mind*, 123.
31. See Pierre Foure, "Helvétius as an Epicurean Political Theorist," *Epicurus in the Enlightenment* 12 (2009): 105–18.
32. Helvétius, *De l'esprit* (French), vol. 1, 264; *De l'esprit: Or, Essays on the Mind*, 134.

33. Helvétius, *De l'esprit* (French), vol. 1, 234; *De l'esprit: Or, Essays on the Mind*, 120.
34. Originally published in 1754—the quotes here are from the 1765 fourth edition due to its availability: Samuel Martin, *An Essay upon Plantership*, 4th ed. (London, 1765).
35. Ibid., ix.
36. Ibid., xv.
37. Ibid., 36–7.
38. Ibid., 8–9.
39. Ibid., 3.
40. Ibid., 2.
41. David Barry, *Gaspar, Bondmen and Rebels: A Study of Master-Slave Relations in Antigua* (Johns Hopkins University Press, 1985).
42. Ibid., 3.
43. Ibid., 4, 3.
44. Ibid., 6.
45. Henry Laurens quoted in Joseph P. Kelly, "Henry Laurens: The Southern Man of Conscience in History," *South Carolina Historical Magazine* 107, no. 2 (2006): 82–123, 106.
46. Sean Kelley, "Scrambling for Slaves: Captive Sales in Colonial South Carolina," *Slavery and Abolition* 34, no. 1 (March 1, 2013): 1–21, 6.
47. Emma Hart, *Building Charleston: Town and Society in the Eighteenth-Century British Atlantic World* (University of Virginia Press, 2009), 62. For his advice on markets, see subsequent anecdotes.
48. *American Husbandry* (Bew, 1775), 358. For evidence of Oswald's authorship, see Robert Scott Davis, "Richard Oswald as 'An American': How a Frontier South Carolina Plantation Identifies the Anonymous Author of American Husbandry and a Forgotten Founder of the United States," *Journal of Backcountry Studies* 9, no. 1 (2014): 16.
49. *American Husbandry*, 407.
50. Kenneth Morgan, "Slave Sales in Colonial Charleston," *English Historical Review* 113, no. 453 (1998): 905–27, 920.
51. Michael Lawrence Dickinson, *Almost Dead: Slavery and Social Rebirth in the Black Urban Atlantic, 1680–1807* (University of Georgia Press, 2022), 19, 44.
52. Henry Laurens, *The Papers of Henry Laurens*, vol. 2, ed. Philip M. Hamer and George C. Rogers (University of South Carolina Press, 1968), 523–4.
53. Ibid., see footnote.
54. *American Husbandry*, 428–9.

55. Meteyard, *Life of Josiah Wedgwood*, 205.
56. Ibid., 299.
57. Ibid., 231.
58. Ibid., 308–10.
59. Margaret Canovan, "Paternalistic Liberalism: Joseph Priestley on Rank and Inequality," *Enlightenment and Dissent* 2 (1983): 23–37.
60. Priestley quoted in ibid., 32.
61. Isaac Kramnick, "Eighteenth-Century Science and Radical Social Theory: The Case of Joseph Priestley's Scientific Liberalism," *Journal of British Studies* 25, no. 1 (1986): 9.
62. Letter of June 20, 1768, in *Correspondence of Josiah Wedgwood*, vol. 1, *Letters of Josiah Wedgwood 1762 to 1772*, ed. Katherine Eufemia Farrer (Cambridge University Press, 2011), 218.
63. Josiah Wedgwood to Thomas Bentley, June 20, 1768, in ibid., 217–21.
64. Wedgwood, quoted in Neil McKendrick, "Josiah Wedgwood and Factory Discipline," *Historical Journal* 4, no. 1 (1961): 34.
65. Ibid., 40.
66. Ibid., 33.
67. Ibid., 39.
68. E. P. Thompson, "Time, Work-Discipline, and Industrial Capitalism," *Past and Present*, no. 38 (1967): 56–97, 83n87.
69. McKendrick, "Josiah Wedgwood and Factory Discipline," 41.
70. Wedgwood, quoted in ibid., 39.
71. Ibid., 33.
72. Ibid., 47.
73. Ibid., 47–50.
74. Ibid., 54, 51.
75. Josiah Wedgwood to Thomas Bentley, September 27, 1769, in *Correspondence*, 284–93.
76. See Josiah Wedgwood to Thomas Bentley, September 30, 1769, in *Correspondence*, 294–7.
77. Kelly, "Henry Laurens."
78. Laurens, *The Papers of Henry Laurens*, vol. 1, 242.
79. Jenny Uglow, *The Lunar Men: The Friends Who Made the Future, 1730–1810* (Faber & Faber, 2002).

3. Mechanized Labor and the Original Panopticon, 1760–1810

1. Mary Bentham, *The Life of Brigadier-General Sir Samuel Bentham* (Longman, Green, Longman, and Roberts, 1862), 2.

2. Ibid., 3–4.
3. James M. Haas, "The Introduction of Task Work into the Royal Dockyards, 1775," *Journal of British Studies* 8, no. 2 (1969): 44–68. I have forthcoming work on this as well.
4. See *The Correspondence of Jeremy Bentham*, as well as his correspondence as Inspector General of Naval Works, in the National Archives, Kew under ADM 1/3527.
5. Jeremy to Samuel, 10 April 1775, in *The Correspondence of Jeremy Bentham*, vol. 1, *1752–1756*, ed. Timothy L. S. Sprigge (UCL Press, 2017), 228–30.
6. Jeremy Bentham quoted in Roger Bartlett, *The Bentham Brothers and Russia: The Imperial Russian Constitution and the St Petersburg Panopticon* (UCL Press, 2022).
7. Ibid., 58.
8. Jeremy Bentham to Samuel Bentham, 17 June 1775, in *The Correspondence of Jeremy Bentham*, vol. 1, 238–9, addressed to Samuel at Chatham Dockyard; Jeremy Bentham to Samuel Bentham, 25–26 September 1775, in *The Correspondence of Jeremy Bentham*, vol. 1, 260–6, which mentions "le divin Helvetius" and forwards a letter from Priestley.
9. James Henderson Burns and Herbert Lionel Adolphus Hart, eds., *Bentham: A Fragment on Government* (Cambridge University Press, 1988).
10. Akihito Matsumoto, "Happiness and Religion: Joseph Priestley's 'Theological Utilitarianism,'" *Kyoto Economic Review* 79, no. 2 (2010): 55–66; J. H. Burns, "Happiness and Utility: Jeremy Bentham's Equation," *Utilitas* 17, no. 1 (March 2005).
11. Joseph Priestley, *Institutes of Natural and Revealed Religion* (Pearson and Rollason, 1782), 17–18, 65–6.
12. See Mary Bentham, *Life of Brigadier-General Sir Samuel Bentham*, 60.
13. Bentham quoted in Jeremy Bentham, *The Works of Jeremy Bentham*, vol. 10, ed. J. Bowring (Tait, 1843), 66.
14. See Ian R. Christie, *The Benthams in Russia, 1780–1791* (Berg, 1993); Bartlett, *Bentham Brothers and Russia*.
15. Mary Bentham, *Life of Brigadier-General Sir Samuel Bentham*, 70.
16. Christie, *The Benthams in Russia*, 97–100.
17. Alessandro Stanziani, "The Traveling Panopticon: Labor Institutions and Labor Practices in Russia and Britain in the Eighteenth and Nineteenth Centuries," *Comparative Studies in Society and History* 51, no. 4 (October 2009): 715–41, 719; Bartlett, *Bentham Brothers and Russia*, 18. Regarding serfs, see

Simon Werrett, "Potemkin and the Panopticon: Samuel Bentham and the Architecture of Absolutism in Eighteenth Century Russia," *Journal of Bentham Studies*, June 1, 1999, 4, which indicates Samuel was given "a large serf labour force" by Potemkin.
18. Mary Bentham, *Life of Brigadier-General Sir Samuel Bentham*, 83.
19. Mary uses the phrase, and Samuel did frequently in his correspondence and published work.
20. See Matsumoto, "Happiness and Religion," 57, 63–4.
21. See Jeremy Bentham, "Nonsense upon Stilts, Or, Pandora's Box Opened," in Philip Schofield, Catherine Pease-Watkin, and Cyprian Blamires, eds., *The Collected Works of Jeremy Bentham: Rights, Representation, and Reform; Nonsense upon Stilts and Other Writings on the French Revolution* (Clarendon, 2002), 317–75.
22. Jeremy Bentham, *An Introduction to the Principles of Morals and Legislation* (Clarendon Press, 1907 [1789]), 187–8, 1.
23. Bartlett, *Bentham Brothers and Russia*, 22.
24. Jeremy Bentham, *The Panopticon Writings*, with an introduction by Miran Božovič (Verso, 1995), 51.
25. Ibid., 66.
26. Ibid., 52.
27. Ibid., 54.
28. Ibid., 66.
29. Michel Foucault, *Discipline and Punish: The Birth of the Prison* (Vintage, 1995), 28–30.
30. Mary Bentham, *Life of Brigadier-General Sir Samuel Bentham*, 96.
31. See Roger Morriss, "Dockyard Operations and Logistics," in *Science, Utility and British Naval Technology, 1793–1815: Samuel Bentham and the Royal Dockyards* (Routledge, 2020).
32. For the mini Panopticon and visitors, see later in this chapter. For speaking tubes, see Jeremy Bentham, *Correspondence of Jeremy Bentham*, vol. 4, ed. Alexander Taylor Milne (UCL Press, 2017), xxxiii.
33. Jeremy Bentham to Archbishop Markham, August 15, 1793, in ibid., 451–2.
34. Samuel Bentham to Evan Nepean, 21 December 1797, ADM 1/3525.
35. Peter Linebaugh, *The London Hanged: Crime and Civil Society in the Eighteenth Century* (Verso, 2003), 399. See also William J. Ashworth, System of Terror': Samuel Bentham, Accountability and Dockyard Reform During the Napoleonic Wars," *Social History* 23, no. 1 (January 1, 1998): 63–79.
36. Mary Bentham, *Life of Brigadier-General Sir Samuel Bentham*, 186–8.

37. Jedediah Stephens Tucker, *Memoirs of Admiral the Right Honorable the Earl of St. Vincent*, vol. 1 (Richard Bentley, 1844), 303–8.
38. R. A. Morriss, "Labour Relations in the Royal Dockyards, 1801–1805," *Mariner's Mirror* 62, no. 4 (January 1, 1976): 337–46.
39. Morriss, *Science, Utility, and British Naval Technology*, 245.
40. See J. M. Haas, *A Management Odyssey: The Royal Dockyards, 1714–1914* (University Press of America, 1994), 192.
41. William Wilberforce to Jeremy Bentham, November 21, 1796, in Jeremy Bentham, *The Correspondence of Jeremy Bentham*, vol. 5, *1794–1797*, ed. Alexander Taylor Milne (UCL Press, 2017), 309–10.
42. Jeremy Bentham, *The Panopticon Writings*, 50.
43. Jeremy Bentham, *The Correspondence of Jeremy Bentham*, vol. 7, *January 1802 to December 1808*, ed. J. R. Dinwiddy (Clarendon, 1988), 120.
44. William Wilberforce, *A Practical View of the Prevailing Religious System of Professed Christians: In the Higher and Middle Classes in This Country, Contrasted with Real Christianity* (W. Collins, 1829), 388–9.
45. Jeremy Bentham, *The Correspondence of Jeremy Bentham*, vol. 6, *January 1798 to December 1801*, ed. J. R. Dinwiddy (Clarendon, 1984), 166.
46. By men associated with the disbanded Association for the Protection of Liberty and Property Against Republicans and Levellers, see ibid., 359.
47. Wilberforce, *A Practical View*, 393.
48. Joseph Townsend, *Dissertation on the Poor Laws*, 2nd ed. (C. Dilly, 1787), 34–5; Raymond G. Cowherd, "The Humanitarian Reform of the English Poor Laws from 1782 to 1815," *Proceedings of the American Philosophical Society* 104, no. 3 (1960): 328–42; Norman E. Himes, "Jeremy Bentham and the Genesis of English Neo-Malthusianism," *Economic History* 3, no. 11 (1936): 267–76, 269, citing Townsend as a "friend of Jeremy Bentham."
49. Cowherd, "Humanitarian Reform," 339. For "nasty" bread, see also E. P. Thompson, "The Moral Economy of the English Crowd in the Eighteenth Century," *Past and Present* 50, no. 1 (1971): 76–136, 81.
50. Cowherd, "Humanitarian Reform," 335–6.
51. Gertrude Himmelfarb, "Bentham's Utopia: The National Charity Company," *Journal of British Studies* 10, no. 1 (November 1970): 80–125, 83.
52. Lea Campos Boralevi, *Bentham and the Oppressed* (Walter de Gruyter, 2012), 146–7.

53. Roger Anstey, *The Atlantic Slave Trade and British Abolition, 1760–1810* (Humanities Press, 1975), 346–63.
54. See Henry Snow, *Enemies of Order: Labor and Power at the Atlantic Dockside* (University of Georgia Press, forthcoming); Padraic X. Scanlan, "The Great Distress: Wage Labor and British Antislavery After 1815," *Journal of Modern History*, September 1, 2024.

4. Political Economy in Antebellum America, 1800–1865

1. Nathan Appleton, 1844 notes on political economy, in Appleton Family Papers, Massachusetts Historical Society holdings, Ms. N-1778, Box 12.
2. Nathan Appleton, "Memoir at New Ipswich," in Appleton Family Papers, Box 13.
3. Ibid.
4. See Isaac Appleton Jewett, *Memorial of Samuel Appleton of Ipswich, Massachusetts: With Genealogical Notices of Some of His Descendants* (Boston: 1801); "Nathan Appleton—Lowell National Historical Park (U.S. National Park Service)," nps.gov.
5. See Thomas Dublin, *Women at Work: The Transformation of Work and Community in Lowell, Massachusetts, 1826–1860* (Columbia University Press, 1979); Frances W. Gregory, *Nathan Appleton, Merchant and Entrepreneur, 1779–1861* (University Press of Virginia, 1975); and Hannah Josephson, *The Golden Threads: New England's Mill Girls and Magnates* (Russell & Russell, 1967).
6. Gregory, *Nathan Appleton*, 147; Carroll D. Wright, *Comparative Wages, Prices, and Cost of Living: From the Sixteenth Annual Report of the Massachusetts Bureau of Statistics of Labor, for 1885* (Wright & Potter Printing, 1889).
7. Gregory, *Nathan Appleton*, 143.
8. Joseph Priestley, *An Account of a Society, for Encouraging the Industrious Poor, with a Table for Their Use . . .* (Pearson and Rollason, 1787), 4.
9. Harriet Jane Hanson Robinson, *Loom and Spindle: Or, Life Among the Early Mill Girls, with a Sketch of "The Lowell Offering" and Some of Its Contributors* (T. Y. Crowell, 1898), 215.
10. Ibid., 68.
11. Mary Beth Sievens, *Stray Wives: Marital Conflict in Early National New England* (New York University Press, 2005).
12. Robinson, *Loom and Spindle*, 31, discusses Robinson's wages at Lowell as a child, while page 4 covers the other professions.

13. Ibid., 72–3.
14. Ibid., 61.
15. Ibid., 73.
16. Dublin, *Women at Work*, 79.
17. Robinson, *Loom and Spindle*, 43.
18. Ibid., 19.
19. Ibid., 42.
20. Dublin, *Women at Work*, 60.
21. Ibid., 59–60.
22. Robinson, *Loom and Spindle*, 30.
23. Ibid., 31.
24. Ibid., 34.
25. Dublin, *Women at Work*, 59.
26. Ibid., 59–65.
27. Thomas Cooper, *Lectures on the Elements of Political Economy* (Doyle E. Sweeny, 1826), 97.
28. Dublin, *Women at Work*, 61.
29. Robinson, *Loom and Spindle*, 13.
30. Ibid., 14.
31. Dublin, *Women at Work*, 78–80.
32. Nathan Appleton, *Introduction of the Power Loom; And, Origin of Lowell* (B. H. Penhallow, 1858), 13.
33. Ibid., 32.
34. Nathan Appleton, 1804–5 journal, in Appleton Family Papers, Box 23.
35. Thomas Brown, *Lectures on the Philosophy of the Mind* (Adam & Charles Black, 1851), vol. 4, 34–105, discusses the "selfish system" and then Smith's modification of it.
36. At least at the time of his death: Smith's work appears among the volumes listed in his will. See Will of Nathan Appleton, in Appleton Family Papers, Box 13.
37. This and subsequent relevant quotes come from Nathan Appleton, document labeled "selfishness," dated possibly 1828, in Appleton Family Papers, Box 13.
38. Thomas Cooper, *Lectures on the Elements*, 16.
39. Ibid., 9.
40. See Daniel Kilbride, "Slavery and Utilitarianism: Thomas Cooper and the Mind of the Old South," *Journal of Southern History* 59, no. 3 (1993): 469–86. See also H. M. Ellis, "Thomas Cooper—A Survey of His Life: Part I—England, 1759–1794," *South Atlantic Quarterly* 19, no. 1 (January 1, 1920): 24–42.

41. Thomas Cooper, *Letters on the Slave Trade: First Published in Wheeler's Manchester Chronicle* ... (C. Wheeler, 1787).
42. Ibid., 5, for the quote.
43. Ibid., 30.
44. Ibid., 31.
45. Ibid., 33, 35, 36. For Ramsay's role in abolitionist control projects, see Sasha Turner, *Contested Bodies: Pregnancy, Childrearing, and Slavery in Jamaica* (University of Pennsylvania Press, 2017), in particular 100–1.
46. Thomas Cooper, *Letters on the Slave Trade*, 32.
47. R. B. Rose, "The Priestley Riots of 1791," *Past and Present* 18 (1960): 68–88. The precise makeup and motivations of the rioters are unknown, but the presence of both reasonably well-off men and a common "mob" is reasonably well-established.
48. Ellis, "Thomas Cooper—A Survey of His Life: Part I," 33–5.
49. Details here come from a friend of Cooper's, recording Cooper's later recollections of his time in France, reported in Evert Augustus Duyckinck and George Long Duyckinck, *Cyclopædia of American Literature: Embracing Personal and Critical Notices of Authors, and Selections from Their Writings* ... vol. 2 (W. Rutter, 1875), 141–4.
50. Caroline Robbins, "Honest Heretic: Joseph Priestley in America, 1794–1804," *Proceedings of the American Philosophical Society* 106, no. 1 (1962): 60–76; 62 mentions him traveling with "two of the younger Priestleys."
51. Thomas Cooper, *Some Information Respecting America* (J. Johnson, 1795), 57.
52. Ibid., 78–80.
53. Ibid., 235–8, criticizes European-style manufacturing subsidies.
54. Ibid., 69.
55. Thomas Cooper, *Lectures on the Elements*, 207–9, argues against a hypothetical national emancipation law; 95–6 argues for its economic necessity in the South.
56. Thomas Cooper, *Some Information*, 78.
57. Thomas Cooper, *Lectures on the Elements*, 98.
58. Ibid., 184.
59. Francis Wayland, *The Elements of Political Economy* (Leavitt, Lord, 1837), 43–4.
60. Josephson, *Golden Threads*, 89. Political economy influences *Moral Science*'s discussion of subjects like property and interest and appears more directly in Wayland's discussion of slavery. See

Francis Wayland, *The Elements of Moral Science* (Cooke and Company, 1835), 222.
61. Cooper, *Lectures on the Elements*, 185.
62. Ibid., 77–8.
63. Ibid., 16–18, for negative advice, 212 for the quote.
64. Gregory, *Nathan Appleton*, 72.
65. Salim Rashid, "Dugald Stewart, 'Baconian' Methodology, and Political Economy," *Journal of the History of Ideas* 46, no. 2 (1985): 245–57, 251.
66. Thomas Cooper, *Lectures on the Elements*, 95–6.
67. Dublin, *Women at Work*, 111.
68. Quoted in ibid., 112.
69. Ibid.
70. Ibid.
71. Dublin, *Women at Work*, 115; Massachusetts Legislature Committee on Manufactures, Committee Report and Female Labor Reform Association Response, 1845 in Massachusetts General Court, House of Representatives, House Documents, No. 50, 1845, 1–6, 15–17. Originally accessed in excerpt form on the "Voice of Industry" website at industrialrevolution.org.
72. Ibid.
73. "Copy from Proprietors' Records of the Merrimack Manufacturing Company," Appleton Family Papers, Box 13.
74. Dublin, *Women at Work*, 10.
75. Ibid.
76. "Copy from Proprietors' Records of the Merrimack Manufacturing Company."
77. John C. Calhoun, "Address to the People of South Carolina, Prepared for the Members of the Legislature, at the Close of the Session of 1831," in John Caldwell Calhoun, *The Works of John C. Calhoun: Reports and Public Letters* (D. Appleton, 1855), 124–44, 130.
78. Joel Poinsett to President Andrew Jackson, October 23, 1830, reproduced in Charles J. Stillé, *The Life and Services of Joel R. Poinsett, the Confidential Agent in South Carolina of President Jackson During the Nullification Troubles of 1832* (Philadelphia, 1888), 56–8. Benjamin E. Park, "The Angel of Nullification: Imagining Disunion in an Era Before Secession," *Journal of the Early Republic* 37, no. 3 (2017): 507–36, 512, also characterizes Cooper as an important nullifier in this period.

79. Nathan Appleton, *Speech of Mr. Appleton of Massachusetts on the Bill to Reduce and Otherwise Alter the Duties on Imports: Delivered in the House of Representatives in Committee of the Whole, Jan. 23, 1833* (Gales and Seaton, 1833), 16.
80. Ibid., 11, 16.
81. Ibid., 16.
82. Ibid., 14.
83. Nathan Appleton and William C. Rives, *Letter to the Hon. Wm. C. Rives of Virgina, on Slavery and the Union* (J. H. Eastburn's Press, 1860), 4.
84. Susan Hale, ed., *Life and Letters of Thomas Gold Appleton* (D. Appleton, 1885), 17.
85. Appleton, *Letter*, 4.
86. Ibid., 5.
87. The phrase appears in what seems to be an earlier draft of the letter, labeled "Scrap Book p 66," in Appleton Family Papers, Box 13. The quotation itself is removed in the printed version of the letter, which condemns abolitionists' opposition to the Constitution without quoting them. Appleton angrily brought up the same abolitionist slogan in correspondence found in John Gorham Palfrey and Nathan Appleton, *Correspondence Between Nathan Appleton and John G. Palfrey Intended as a Supplement to Mr. Palfrey's Pamphlet on Slave Power* (J. H. Eastburn's Press, 1846), 20, quoting Wendell Phillips.
88. Gregory, *Nathan Appleton*, 211–12, covers Appleton's absence in management and his tariff advocacy; for the latter, see also Josephson, *Golden Threads*, 143.
89. Lynn Gordon Hughes, "Biography of Nathan Appleton," in Dictionary of Unitarian and Universalist Biography, an online resource of the Unitarian Universalist History and Heritage Society. Accessible via the Internet Archive.
90. Donald Yacovone, *Teaching White Supremacy: America's Democratic Ordeal and the Forging of Our National Identity* (Pantheon Books, 2022), 169.
91. Kenneth E. Shewmaker, "Forging the 'Great Chain': Daniel Webster and the Origins of American Foreign Policy Toward East Asia and the Pacific, 1841–1852," *Proceedings of the American Philosophical Society* 129, no. 3 (1985): 225–59, 225, 247 (the latter indicates that Webster "completed and countersigned" the letter and thus had a hand in its writing as well).

5. Competitive Evolution and Japanese Industrialization, 1850–1905

1. Tetsuo Najita, *Visions of Virtue in Tokugawa Japan: The Kaitokudō Merchant Academy of Osaka* (University of Hawaii Press, 1997), 8.
2. For Egypt, see Taylor M. Moore, "'Living Fossils': Anatomies of Race and Reproduction in Modern Egypt," *American Historical Review* 130, no. 1 (March 1, 2025): 19–52, 36.
3. Beatrice Webb, *The Diaries of Beatrice Webb* (Virago, 2000), 32.
4. Marian Evans quoted in Mark Francis, *Herbert Spencer and the Invention of Modern Life* (Routledge, 2014), 62.
5. Francis, *Herbert Spencer*, 56, 60–3.
6. Herbert Spencer, *An Autobiography*, vol. 1 (D. Appleton, 1904), 321.
7. See Francis, *Herbert Spencer*, particularly the introduction.
8. Francis, *Herbert Spencer*, 312.
9. Spencer, *Social Statics (D. Appleton, 1888)*, 42.
10. Ibid., 50.
11. Francis, *Herbert Spencer*, 177.
12. Ibid., 510.
13. For the phrase, see ibid., 69.
14. Spencer, *Social Statics*, 83, for this phrase: 91–3 for the argument.
15. Ibid., 92.
16. Ibid., 92.
17. Ibid., 164–6.
18. Ibid., 131–44. For his later abandonment of land socialization, see Albert Jay Nock's introduction in Herbert Spencer, *The Man Versus the State: With Six Essays on Government, Society, and Freedom* (Liberty Classics, 1981), xx.
19. Spencer, *Social Statics*, 229.
20. Ibid., 29.
21. Ibid., 238.
22. All of this comes from Spencer's summary in ibid., 498–502.
23. Ibid., 149–54, for his critique of socialism.
24. Ibid., 72.
25. Ibid., 26.
26. Ibid., 71–2.
27. Ibid., 92.
28. Ibid., 101–7.
29. Ibid., 353.
30. Ibid., 354.

31. See, for instance, the title of Herbert Spencer, *Illustrations of Universal Progress: A Series of Discussions* (D. Appleton, 1864).
32. Ibid., 404.
33. Ibid., 386.
34. Spencer, *Social Statics*, 151, 152.
35. Francis, *Herbert Spencer*, 294.
36. Herbert Spencer, *The Principles of Sociology*, vol. 2 (D. Appleton, 1898), 608–11. *Principles of Sociology* was originally published in 1873.
37. Herbert Spencer, *The Principles of Biology*, vol. 2 (D. Appleton, 1901), 523–5. Francis, *Herbert Spencer*, 223–4, summarizes this strand of thought in Spencer's work more broadly.
38. Francis, *Herbert Spencer*, 173–4, discusses his blurring of psychological distinctions, such as between reason and instinct, in *Principles of Psychology*.
39. Beatrice Webb, *My Apprenticeship* (Longmans, Green, 1926), 7.
40. Sorai, quoted in Kim Young-Chin, "On Political Thought in Tokugawa Japan," *Journal of Politics* 23, no. 1 (1961): 127–45. See also W. J. Boots and Takayama Daiki, eds., *Tetsugaku Companion to Ogyū Sorai* (Springer Nature, 2019). I have called him "Sorai" following the style of the latter book.
41. Sorai, quoted in Takashi Shogimen, "Treating the Body Politic: The Medical Metaphor of Political Rule in Late Medieval Europe and Tokugawa Japan," *Review of Politics* 70, no. 1 (2008): 77–104, 100.
42. J. R. McEwan, introduction to Ogyū Sorai, *The Political Writings of Ogyū Sorai*, ed. J. R. McEwan (Cambridge University Press, 1962), 8.
43. Webb, *My Apprenticeship*, 329–30.
44. McEwan, *The Political Writings of Ogyū Sorai*, 77–8.
45. Ibid., 77–83.
46. Najita, *Visions of Virtue*, 161–2.
47. Ibid., 33, 135.
48. Sorai quoted in Eiko Ikegami, *Taming of the Samurai: Honorific Individualism and the Making of Modern Japan* (Harvard University Press, 1997), 313.
49. Keiichi Sawai, "An 'Intellectual-Historical' Biography of Ogyū Sorai," in W. J. Boot and Daiki Takayama, eds., *Tetsugaku Companion to Ogyu Sorai* (Springer Verlag, 2019), 45–69, 53.
50. Olivier Ansart, "Gods, Spirits, and Heaven in Ogyū Sorai's Political Theory," in Boot and Takayama, *Tetsugaku Companion to Ogyu Sorai*, 97.

51. Ikegami, *Taming of the Samurai*, 313.
52. McEwan, *Political Writings of Ogyū Sorai*, 100–9.
53. Ansart, "Gods, Spirits, and Heaven," 97.
54. Najita, *Visions of Virtue*, 161–4.
55. John Sagers, *Origins of Japanese Wealth and Power: Reconciling Confucianism and Capitalism, 1830–1885* (Palgrave Macmillan, 2006), 21–2; Thomas R. H. Havens, "Origins of Japanese Wealth and Power: Reconciling Confucianism and Capitalism, 1830–1885 (Review)," *Journal of Japanese Studies* 34, no. 1 (December 2008): 166–7.
56. E. Patricia Tsurumi, *Factory Girls: Women in the Thread Mills of Meiji Japan* (Princeton University Press, 2020), 20.
57. Ibid., 21; and Thomas C. Smith, *Political Change and Industrial Development in Japan: Government Enterprise, 1868–1880* (Stanford University Press, 1955), 29–30.
58. Smith, *Political Change*, 25.
59. Albert M. Craig, *Chōshū in the Meiji Restoration* (Lexington Books, 2000), 92–3.
60. Ibid., and Junji Banno, *Japan's Modern History, 1857–1937: A New Political Narrative* (Routledge, 2014), 1.
61. Aurora Hunt, "The Civil War on the Western Seaboard," *Civil War History* 9, no. 2 (1963): 178–86, 183.
62. See Tosh Minohara and Kaoru Iokibe, "America Encounters Japan" in Makoto Iokibe and Tosh Minohara, eds., *The History of US-Japan Relations: From Perry to the Present* (Springer, 2017), 3–22, 13; and Craig, *Choshu in the Meiji Restoration*, 232–3.
63. Ian Nish, *The Iwakura Mission to America and Europe: A New Assessment* (Routledge, 2008).
64. Kume quoted in ibid., 29.
65. Kume quoted in ibid.
66. Webb, *My Apprenticeship*, 335.
67. Ōkubo, quoted in Nish, *Iwakura Mission*, 33.
68. Ibid., 16–19.
69. Ibid., 21.
70. Iwakura, quoted in Smith, *Political Change*, 26.
71. Tsurumi, *Factory Girls*, 26–9.
72. Ibid., 84.
73. Spencer, *Social Statics*, 100.
74. Akiko Sashinami, "New Perspectives on Wages, Production Technologies, and the Peasantry in Japan's Capitalist Development," *Social Science Japan Journal* 4, no. 1 (April 2001): 103–9, 106.

75. Tsurumi, *Factory Girls*, 34.
76. Ibid., 37–9.
77. Ibid., 34, 33.
78. Ibid., 39–46.
79. Akitoshi Monden and company records quoted in Matao Miyamoto, "The Products and Market Strategies of the Osaka Cotton Spinning Company: 1883–1914," *Japanese Yearbook on Business History* 5 (1989): 117–59, 120–1.
80. Tsurumi, *Factory Girls*, 41.
81. E. Patricia Tsurumi, "Yet to Be Heard: The Voices of Meiji Factory Women," *Bulletin of Concerned Asian Scholars* 26, no. 4 (December 1, 1994): 18–27, 22.
82. Toshiaki Chokki, "Labor Management in the Cotton Spinning Industry," in Michael Smitka, ed., *The Textile Industry and the Rise of the Japanese Economy* (Taylor & Francis, 1998), 1–26, 11.
83. Ibid., 9–12
84. Quoted in ibid., 19.
85. Tsurumi, *Factory Girls*, 99–100.
86. Ibid., 101–2.
87. Michio Nagai, "Herbert Spencer in Early Meiji Japan," *Far Eastern Quarterly* 14, no. 1 (November 1954): 55–64, 59.
88. Craig, *Choshu in the Meiji Restoration*, 268, references the "Meiji oligarch"; more broadly, the political and economic situation outlined here should make it obvious why oligarchy was a problem.
89. Marius Jansen, foreword to Nakae Chōmin, *A Discourse by Three Drunkards on Government*, trans. Nobuko Tsukui, ed. Nobuko Tsukui and Jeffrey Hammond (Weatherhill: 1984).
90. Chōmin, *Discourse*, 95–7.
91. Ibid., 92.
92. Nagai, "Herbert Spencer in Early Meiji Japan," 57.
93. Chōmin, *Discourse*, 125–6.
94. Nagai, "Herbert Spencer in Early Meiji Japan," 61.
95. Chōmin, *Discourse*, 93–4.
96. Ibid.
97. Ibid., 62.
98. Spencer, *Social Statics*, 85.
99. Spencer, *Illustrations of Universal Progress*, 385.
100. Nagai, "Herbert Spencer in Early Meiji Japan," 62–3, discusses Nagao's conservative views.
101. Spencer, *Social Statics*, 441–2.
102. Smith, *Political Change*, 41.

103. Ibid., 36–66.
104. See Alistair Swale, *The Political Thought of Mori Arinori: A Study of Meiji Conservatism* (Routledge, 2013).
105. Spencer, quoted in David Duncan, ed., *Life and Letters of Herbert Spencer* (Methuen, 1908), 161.
106. See Banno, *Japan's Modern History*, 117.
107. Spencer to Kaneko Kentarō, August 21, 1892, in Duncan, *Life and Letters*, 319–21.
108. Tsurumi, *Factory Girls*, 98–9.
109. Ibid., 98, 160.
110. Tsurumi, "Yet to Be Heard," 27.
111. Tsurumi, *Factory Girls*, 112–14.
112. Andrew Gordon, "Workers Movements in Late Meiji Tokyo," *Bulletin de l'École Française d'Extrême-Orient* 84 (1997): 285–308, 291.
113. Tsurumi, *Factory Girls*, 114.
114. Gordon, "Workers Movements in Late Meiji Tokyo," 290–2.
115. For "closest friend and teacher," see Royden J. Harrison, *The Life and Times of Sidney and Beatrice Webb: 1858–1905, the Formative Years* (Palgrave Macmillan, 2000), 95. "The Employers' Gospel" comes from Webb, quoted in Harrison, *Life and Times*, 136.
116. Webb, diary entry, October 4, 1886, quoted in Webb, *My Apprenticeship*, 284.

6. Scientific Management and "Free Enterprise," 1880–1945

1. Frederick Winslow Taylor, *Principles of Scientific Management* (Harper and Brothers, 1911), 48–50.
2. Ibid., 51, 50.
3. Roger W. Ohnsorg, *Robert Lindley Murray: The Reluctant U.S. Tennis Champion: Includes "The First Forty Years of American Tennis"* (Trafford, 2011), 25; "Clarence Clark, Financier, Was 77; Partner in Philadelphia Firm of Private Bankers Dies—Executive in Utilities," *New York Times*, June 30, 1937.
4. Taylor, *Principles*, 52–3.
5. Daniel Nelson, "Scientific Management, Systematic Management, and Labor, 1880–1915," *Business History Review* 48, no. 4 (1974): 479–500, 483; see also Daniel Nelson, "Taylorism and the Workers at Bethlehem Steel, 1898–1901," *Pennsylvania Magazine of History and Biography* 101, no. 4 (1977): 487–505.

6. Taylor narrates this in Taylor, *Principles*, 41–73. For the story behind this story, see Charles D. Wrege and Amedeo G. Perroni, "Taylor's Pig-Tale: A Historical Analysis of Frederick W. Taylor's Pig-Iron Experiments," *Academy of Management Journal* 17, no. 1 (1974): 6–27.
7. Wrege and Perroni, "Taylor's Pig-Tale," 14.
8. Taylor describes such a law in *Principles*; Wrege and Perroni explain the misleading logic involved in it in "Taylor's Pig-Tale," 19–25.
9. Taylor, *Principles*, 39.
10. Nelson, "Scientific Management, Systematic Management, and Labor," 484–5, 491.
11. Wrege and Perroni, "Taylor's Pig-Tale," 14, indicates that Gillespie and Wolle shifted 45 tons per day; Taylor's later recollection in *Principles* was 47.5.
12. F. W. Taylor, "A Piece Rate System," *Economic Studies* 1, no. 2 (June 1, 1896): 89–129.
13. Ibid., 114.
14. Both Taylor's piece-rate article and *Principles* indicate as much.
15. Wrege and Perroni, "Taylor's Pig-Tale," 13–17. The quote is from Gillespie and Wolle.
16. Taylor, *Principles*, 142–3.
17. Nelson, "Scientific Management, Systematic Management, and Labor," 479.
18. Taylor, *Principles*, 28.
19. Ibid., 62.
20. Wrege and Perroni, "Taylor's Pig-Tale," 15n8.
21. Taylor quoted in Daniel Nelson, "Taylorism and the Workers at Bethlehem Steel," 493.
22. Ibid., 500n45.
23. Raymond E. Callahan, *Education and the Cult of Efficiency: A Study of the Social Forces That Have Shaped the Adminstration of the Public Schools* (University of Chicago Press, 2010), 23; Shailer Mathews, *Scientific Management in the Churches* (University of Chicago Press, 1912).
24. Irene S. Rubin, "Early Budget Reformers: Democracy, Efficiency, and Budget Reforms," *American Review of Public Administration* 24, no. 3 (September 1, 1994): 229–52.
25. Speech by Woodrow Wilson regarding labor, 1912, audio recording from the Michigan State University Vincent Voice Library.
26. Testimony of Mr. Frederick W. Taylor, in United States Commission on Industrial Relations, *Industrial Relations: Final Report and*

Testimony, vol. 1 (US Government Printing Office, 1916), 765–810, 766.
27. "Report of Basil M. Manly, Director of Research and Investigation, Signed by Commissioners Walsh, Lennon, O'Connell, and Garretson," in Commission on Industrial Relations, *Industrial Relations*, vol. 1, 11–152, 142.
28. Taylor testimony, in Commission on Industrial Relations, *Industrial Relations*, vol. 1, 788.
29. Ibid., 788–90.
30. Ibid., 793–5.
31. Ibid., 795–806.
32. Testimony of Mr. John F. Tobin, in Commission on Industrial Relations, *Industrial Relations*, vol. 1, 810–22.
33. Manly report, in Commission on Industrial Relations, *Industrial Relations*, vol. 1, 133.
34. Tobin testimony, in Commission on Industrial Relations, *Industrial Relations*, vol. 1, 819.
35. Manly report, in Commission on Industrial Relations, *Industrial Relations*, vol. 1, 70–1, 73–9, 72, 119, respectively.
36. In addition to Commons's report, see Adams Graham Jr., *Age of Industrial Violence, 1910–15: The Activities and Findings of the United States Commission on Industrial Relations* (Columbia University Press, 1966), 215.
37. Testimony of Mr. Carl G. Barth, in Commission on Industrial Relations, *Industrial Relations*, vol. 1, 886–99, 888.
38. Alfred P. Sloan, *Adventures of a White-Collar Man* (Doubleday, Doran, 1941), 3–21.
39. Ernest Dale, "Contributions to Administration by Alfred P. Sloan, Jr., and GM," *Administrative Science Quarterly* 1, no. 1 (June 1956): 30–61.
40. David Farber, *Sloan Rules: Alfred P. Sloan and the Triumph of General Motors* (University of Chicago Press, 2002), 62–6. See also Stefan Link, "The Charismatic Corporation: Finance, Administration, and Shop Floor Management Under Henry Ford," *Business History Review* 92, no. 1 (April 2018): 85–115.
41. Farber, *Sloan Rules*, 58–9.
42. Sloan quoted in Link, "The Charismatic Corporation," 94.
43. Farber, *Sloan Rules*, 167–9.
44. See Dale, "Contributions to Administration by Alfred P. Sloan, Jr. and GM"; Dale L. Flesher and Gary John Previts, "Donaldson Brown (1885–1965): The Power of an Individual and His Ideas over

Time," *Accounting Historians Journal* 40, no. 1 (June 1, 2013): 79–101; Jeffery D. Houghton, "What Is Good for General Motors: The Contributions and Influence of Alfred P. Sloan, Jr.," *Journal of Management History* 19, no. 3 (June 21, 2013): 328–44.
45. Farber, *Sloan Rules*, 166–8.
46. Ibid., 179–87.
47. Farber, *Sloan Rules*, 183; Kim Phillips-Fein, *Invisible Hands: The Businessmen's Crusade Against the New Deal* (W. W. Norton, 2010), 10–25.
48. Phillips-Fein, *Invisible Hands*, 11.
49. Farber, *Sloan Rules*, 188–9.
50. Alonzo L. Hamby, "Sixty Million Jobs and the People's Revolution: The Liberals, the New Deal, and World War II," *Historian* 30, no. 4 (August 1, 1968): 578–98.
51. Alfred P. Sloan, *My Years with General Motors* (eNet Press, 2015), 472.
52. See Frances Perkins interview transcript, from oral history by Dean Albertson, Columbia University Oral History Research Office, part 6, 208, library.columbia.edu.
53. The song is quoted in Sidney Fine, *Sit-Down: The General Motors Strike of 1936–1937* (University of Michigan Press, 1969), 163. I have changed the punctuation in order to better match the rhythm of Gallagher and Shean.
54. Perkins interview transcript, part 6, 199–212. Farber, *Sloan Rules*, 198–208, also relays this story.
55. Farber, *Sloan Rules*, 205; Perkins interview transcript, Part VI, 205–6. The exclamation marks are not in Perkins's original, or at least in her transcript, but seem obvious from context.
56. Perkins interview transcript, part 6, 209–12.
57. Ibid., for her analysis of Sloan; for the Sloan Foundation, see later in this chapter.
58. F. Taylor Ostrander, "Notes and Other Materials from John Ulrich Nef's Course on French Industrial History Since the Reformation, Economics 322, University of Chicago, Spring 1934," in W. J. Samuels, ed., *Further University of Wisconsin Materials: Further Documents of F. Taylor Ostrander*, Research in the History of Economic Thought and Methodology, vol. 23 (Emerald Group, 2005), 155–239, 171.
59. F. Taylor Ostrander, "Materials from Chester Whitney Wright's Courses," in Samuels, *Further University of Wisconsin Materials*, 279–367, 314.

60. Ibid., 334.
61. Ostrander's father, Frank T. Ostrander, is described as "Vice President in charge of the New York City office of National Supply Export Corp.," where he worked from 1905 until his retirement in 1948. See George M. Merten to F. Taylor Ostrander, November 9, 1948, in F. Taylor Ostrander Papers, Box 3, Folder Personal Correspondence, Germany. The Ostrander family's presence in Westchester County is discussed in F. Taylor Ostrander, "F. Taylor Ostrander: His Long and Wide-Ranging Career," in Jeff E. Biddle and Ross B. Emmett, eds., *Research in the History of Economic Thought and Methodology*, vol. 23B (Emerald Group, 2005), 89–110, 89. For Marzani's childhood, see Carl Marzani, *The Education of a Reluctant Radical*, book 1, *Roman Childhood* (Topical Books, 1992).
62. Carl Marzani, *The Education of a Reluctant Radical*, book 4: *From Pentagon to Penitentiary* (Topical Books, 1992), 8.
63. "Statement by F. Taylor Ostrander Concerning the Activities and Associations of Carl A. Marzani," February 22, 1947, in F. Taylor Ostrander Papers, Box 3, Folder Personal Correspondence, Germany; see also F. Taylor Ostrander to J. D. Beam, Office of Political Affairs, OMGUS (Office of the Military Government of the United States), March 25, 1947, in the same folder.
64. Friedman worked for the National Resources Committee, while Ostrander's job was for the Works Progress Administration. See Jennifer Burns, *Milton Friedman: The Last Conservative* (Picador, 2024), 84; Ostrander, "F. Taylor Ostrander: His Long and Wide-Ranging Career," 90–1.
65. "Statement by F. Taylor Ostrander Concerning the Activities and Associations of Carl A. Marzani."
66. Marzani, *Education of a Reluctant Radical*, book 4, 54–5.
67. Ibid., 68.
68. Ibid.; Ostrander, "F. Taylor Ostrander: His Long and Wide-Ranging Career," 91.
69. Quinn Slobodian, *Globalists: The End of Empire and the Birth of Neoliberalism* (Harvard University Press, 2018), 86.
70. Brian Doherty, *Radicals for Capitalism: A Freewheeling History of the Modern American Libertarian Movement* (PublicAffairs, 2009), 68–70.
71. See Jörg Guido Hülsmann, "Introduction to the Third Edition: From Value Theory to Praxeology," in Ludwig von Mises, *Epistemological Problems of Economics* (Ludwig von Mises Institute, 2003), ix–lv; originally published in 1960 in English and 1933 in German. See

also Ludwig von Mises, *Human Action: A Treatise on Economics* (Ludwig von Mises Institute, 1998 [1949]), 215.
72. Mises, *Epistemological Problems of Economics*, 13.
73. Mises, *Human Action*, 215.
74. "Materials from Charles O. Hardy's Course on Money and Banking, Economics 330, University of Chicago, 1933–1934," in Samuels, *Further University of Wisconsin Materials*, 241–69, 243. This is a quote from Robert Dimand about Hardy's position.
75. Burns, *Milton Friedman*, 38.
76. Ibid., 46.
77. James M. Buchanan, *Better Than Plowing, and Other Personal Essays* (University of Chicago Press, 1992), 68.
78. Henry Hazlitt, *Economics in One Lesson* (Mises, 2008), 92–3. This is a reprint of the original.
79. Ibid., 95.
80. Milton Friedman, *Free to Choose*, Episode 1, freetochoosenetwork.org.
81. Burns, *Milton Friedman*, 44–6.
82. Milton Friedman and Anna Jacobson Schwartz, *A Monetary History of the United States, 1867–1960* (Princeton University Press, 2008).
83. Burns, *Milton Friedman*, 91.
84. Ludwig von Mises, *Epistemological Problems in Economics* (Liberty Fund, 2013 [1933]), 184.
85. Friedrich A. Hayek, *The Road to Serfdom, with the Intellectuals and Socialism* (IEA, 2005), 40. This is a reprint of the Reader's Digest version which most readers actually encountered—see Burns, *Milton Friedman*, 165–7.
86. Andrew Farrant and Edward McPhail, "Supporters Are Wrong: Hayek Did Not Favor a Welfare State," *Challenge* 55, no. 5 (2012): 94–105, 100.
87. Sloan Foundation 1938 report, 9, 16, Alfred P. Sloan Foundation Annual Reports, 1938–1946, sloan.org. The "after the sit-down strike" timing assessment is based on this report, which says they shifted direction in December 1937 (which would appear to have been the next annual meeting year to do so after the strike's end) and began some projects toward their new economic education direction already earlier that year.
88. Ibid., 15.
89. Farber, *Sloan Rules*, 210.
90. Sloan Foundation 1944 report, 20, Alfred P. Sloan Foundation Annual Reports, 1938–1946, sloan.org.

91. Ibid., 10.
92. Sloan Foundation 1940 report, 24, Alfred P. Sloan Foundation Annual Reports, 1938–1946, sloan.org.
93. Dan Streible, "The Failure of the NYU Educational Film Institute," in Devin Orgeron, Marsha Orgeron, and Dan Streible, eds., *Learning with the Lights Off: Educational Film in the United States* (Oxford University Press, 2011), 271–94. The film itself is available via the Internet Archive.
94. Sloan Foundation 1945 report (entitled "1945–1946" report), 20, Alfred P. Sloan Foundation Annual Reports, 1938–1946, sloan.org.
95. Harold Glenn Moulton et al., *Capital Expansion, Employment, and Economic Stability* (Brookings Institution, 1940).
96. Burns, *Milton Friedman*, 187–9; Phillips-Fein, *Invisible Hands*, 42–51.
97. Sloan Foundation 1944 report, 28–9.
98. This is clear from the Sloan Foundation reports, which name members of the committee and list publications. The PAC's treasurer in 1938, for example, Luther Gulick, was a Roosevelt ally and taught at Columbia. Another member was Columbia PhD economist William T. Foster. For the differences between Columbia and Chicago's paradigms, see Burns, *Milton Friedman*.
99. Paul Charles Milazzo, "Henry Hazlitt Unbound: Pamphlets, Markets, and Economic Education After World War II," *History of Political Economy* 55, no. S1 (December 1, 2023): 75–101.
100. University of Chicago Round Table, no. 370, April 22, 1945, available via the Internet Archive. This is the print version of the radio discussion.
101. Hugh Richard Slotten, "Commercial Radio, Public Affairs Discourse and the Manipulation of Sound Scholarship Isolationism, Wartime Civil Rights and the Collapse of the Attractiveness of Communism in America, 1933–1945," *Historical Journal of Film, Radio and Television* 25, no. 3 (August 1, 2005): 371–98, 379–81.
102. Phillips-Fein, *Invisible Hands*, 16–17.
103. Milazzo, "Henry Hazlitt Unbound," 84–6.
104. For Keynes's epistemology and methodology, see Anna Carabelli and Nicolò De Vecchi, "Hayek and Keynes: From a Common Critique of Economic Method to Different Theories of Expectations," *Review of Political Economy* 13, no. 3 (July 1, 2001): 269–85.
105. John Maynard Keynes, 1942 radio broadcast, in *The Collected Writings of John Maynard Keynes* (Cambridge University Press, 2013), vol. 27, 264–71, 270.

106. F. Taylor Ostrander, "Recollections of a Dinner for John Maynard Keynes, Washington, D.C., 1941," in Warren Samuels and J. E. Biddle eds., *Research in the History of Economic Thought and Methodology*, vol. 20, part 1 (Emerald Group, 2002), 43–50.
107. See R. M. Hartwell, *A History of the Mont Pelerin Society* (Liberty Fund, 1995).

7. Factory Discipline and the Postwar Right, 1946–67

1. F. Taylor Ostrander, "F. Taylor Ostrander: His Long and Wide-Ranging Career," in Jeff E. Biddle and Ross B. Emmett, eds., *Research in the History of Economic Thought and Methodology*, vol. 23B (Emerald Group, 2005), 89–110, 90.
2. *Deadline for Action*, Union Films, 1946. Available (split into two parts) via the Internet Archive.
3. M. Kalecki, "Political Aspects of Full Employment," *Political Quarterly* 14, no. 4 (1943): 322–30.
4. Nelson Lichtenstein, *Walter Reuther: The Most Dangerous Man in Detroit* (University of Illinois Press, 1997), 221–46.
5. Ibid., 246.
6. Truman quoted in William E. Leuchtenburg, "New Faces of 1946," *Smithsonian Magazine*, November 2006. See also Meg Jacobs, *Pocketbook Politics: Economic Citizenship in Twentieth-Century America* (Princeton University Press, 2007).
7. Jonathan Kissam, "Seventy Five Years Later, Toll of Taft-Hartley Weighs Heavily on Labor," UE, June 23, 2022, ueunion.org.
8. See Charles Musser, "Carl Marzani and Union Films: Making Left-Wing Documentaries During the Cold War, 1946–53," *Moving Image* 9, no. 1 (2009): 104–60; Carl Marzani, *The Education of a Reluctant Radical*, Book 4, *From Pentagon to Penitentiary* (Topical Books, 1992).
9. Lemuel R. Boulware, *The Truth About Boulwarism: Trying to Do Right Voluntarily* (Bureau of National Affairs, 1969), 3.
10. Lemuel Boulware/GE Employee Relations, *Supervisor's Guide to General Electric Job Information* (General Electric, 1947).
11. Ibid., 33–4.
12. Ibid., 35.
13. Thomas W. Evans, *The Education of Ronald Reagan: The General Electric Years and the Untold Story of His Conversion to Conservatism* (Columbia University Press, 2008), 53.
14. Boulware/GE, *Supervisor's Guide*, 29.

15. Lichtenstein, *Walter Reuther*, 301.
16. "Rise and Fall of General Electric in Somersworth," *Foster's Daily Democrat*, June 12, 2016. I have also relied here on conversations with my father, Peter Warburton, who grew up in 1950s–1960s Somersworth and whose father worked in the shoe factory.
17. Boulware/GE, *Supervisor's Guide*, 78.
18. Ibid., 83.
19. Ibid., 34.
20. Court decision cited in Irving Abramson, "The Anatomy of Boulwarism with a Discussion of Forkosch," *Catholic University Law Review* 19, no. 4 (January 1, 1970): 459–88, 463.
21. Kim Phillips-Fein, *Invisible Hands: The Businessmen's Crusade Against the New Deal* (W. W. Norton, 2010), 100.
22. For phone calls, see Kim Phillips-Fein, "'If Business and the Country Will Be Run Right': The Business Challenge to the Liberal Consensus, 1945–1964," *International Labor and Working-Class History* 72, no. 1 (October 2007): 192–215, 202. For local leaders, see Evans, *Education of Ronald Reagan*, 52.
23. Boulware/GE, *Supervisor's Guide*, 47.
24. Boulware, "Salvation Is Not Free," reproduced in Evans, *Education of Ronald Reagan*, 229–37, 233.
25. Ibid.
26. Evans, *Education of Ronald Reagan*, 50.
27. Friedman said this frequently, including in a 1963 lecture entitled "Inflation: Causes and Consequences" and a 1970 lecture, "The Counter-Revolution in Monetary Theory."
28. Jennifer Burns, *Milton Friedman: The Last Conservative* (Picador, 2024), 48–50.
29. Boulware, "Salvation Is Not Free," in Evans, *Education of Ronald Reagan*, 236.
30. Boulware/GE, "Supervisor's Guide," 57.
31. Ibid.
32. Ludwig von Mises, *Socialism: An Economic and Sociological Analysis* (Yale University Press, 1962), 443.
33. Leonard Read, "'I, Pencil: My Family Tree' as Told to Leonard E. Read," Liberty Fund, December 1958, libertyfund.org.
34. Wilhelm Röpke, *Economics of the Free Society* (Regnery, 1963).
35. Phillips-Fein, "If Business and the Country Will Be Run Right," 202.
36. Evans, *Education of Ronald Reagan*, 52.

37. Phillips-Fein, "If Business and the Country Will Be Run Right," 202.
38. Röpke, *Economics of the Free Society*, 254, 237.
39. Earl B. Dunckel oral history, April 27, 1982, accessed via the Internet Archive.
40. Evans, *Education of Ronald Reagan*, 6.
41. Ibid., 65; and Ronald Reagan and Richard G. Hubler, *Where's the Rest of Me? The Ronald Reagan Story* (Arcadia, 1965), 267.
42. Ronald Reagan, *An American Life: The Autobiography* (Simon and Schuster, 1990), 129–30.
43. See Earl Dunckel oral history.
44. Reagan, *An American Life*, 132–4.
45. Reagan, *Where's the Rest of Me?*, 265.
46. Evans, *Education of Ronald Reagan*, 55, 57.
47. Röpke, quoted in Quinn Slobodian, *Globalists: The End of Empire and the Birth of Neoliberalism* (Harvard University Press, 2018), 129.
48. William Henry Chamberlin, "The GAP Between Earning and Receiving," *Freeman*, April 1967, 235–42.

8. Multinationals, Macroeconomics, and the Road to Reagan, 1967–80

1. "Some Aspects on the Copperbelt," May 31, 1962, in the papers of F. Taylor Ostrander, Box 3, Folder "Ostrander Genealogy and Other Materials," at the American Heritage Center, Laramie, Wyoming.
2. See F. Taylor Ostrander, "F. Taylor Ostrander: His Long and Wide-Ranging Career," in Glenn Johnson and Warren Samuels, eds., *Research in the History of Economic Thought and Methodology*, vol. 27C (Emerald Group, 2009), 89–107; this is also clear from his papers.
3. Ostrander, "Some Aspects on the Copperbelt."
4. Prain quoted in Ian Phimister, "Workers in Wonderland? White Miners and the Northern Rhodesian Copperbelt, 1946–1962," *South African Historical Journal* 63, no. 2 (June 1, 2011): 183–233, 217.
5. R. Sklar, *Corporate Power in an African State: The Political Impact of Multinational Mining Companies in Zambia* (University of California Press, 1975), 105–6, quoted in Phimister, "Workers in Wonderland," 193.

6. Jane L. Parpart, *Labor and Capital on the African Copperbelt* (Temple University Press, 1983), 140–1.
7. Ibid., 140–9. For a period in 1955 the union reluctantly recognized MASA but only under serious pressure; this was part of the reason for the 1956 strikes.
8. Ibid.,154.
9. FTO memo, June 1, 1962, in the papers of F. Taylor Ostrander, Box 3, Folder "Ostrander Genealogy and Other Materials," at the American Heritage Center.
10. Parpart, *Labor and Capital on the African Copperbelt*, 155–7.
11. Press Release No. 1422/67, July 19, 1967, in FTO Papers, Box 12, Folder "Rhodesian Selection Trust- Labor."
12. Lewis Changufu to Mining Companies, May 24, 1968, in FTO Papers, Box 12, Folder "Rhodesian Selection Trust—Labor."
13. Andrew Sardanis, *Zambia: The First 50 Years* (I. B. Tauris, 2014), 66.
14. Kaunda memorandum reproduced in ibid., 330–7.
15. Kenneth Kaunda, April 20, 1968, speech, newspaper copy in F. Taylor Ostrander (hereafter FTO) Papers, Box 12, Folder "Roan Selection Trust—"Takeover," Basic Zambian Documents. For "Zambian Humanism" and this language, see Henry S. Meebelo, "The Concept of Man-Centredness in Zambian Humanism," *African Review* 3, no. 4 (1973): 559–75.
16. Ronald T. Libby and Michael E. Woakes, "Nationalization and the Displacement of Development Policy in Zambia," *African Studies Review* 23, no. 1 (1980): 33–50, 35.
17. J. M. Mwanakatwe, "A Message to the Mineworkers of Zambia from the Hon. J. M. Mwanakatwe, Minister of Lands and Mines," in FTO Papers, Box 12, Folder "Rhodesian Selection Trust—Labor." My date estimate is based on its placement in FTO's papers and the timing of Mwanakatwe's tenure in the Ministry of Land and Mines. See J. M. Mwanakatwe, *John M. Mwanakatwe: Teacher, Politician, Lawyer: My Autobiography* (Bookworld Publishers, 2003).
18. Libby and Woakes, "Nationalization and the Displacement of Development."
19. Mwangi S. Kimenyi and Nelipher Moyo, "The Late Zambian President Fredrick Chiluba: A Legacy of Failed Democratic Transition," *Brookings* (blog), June 24, 2011, brookings.edu.
20. See Irving Abramson, "The Anatomy of Boulwarism with a Discussion of Forkosch," *Catholic University Law Review* 19, no.

4 (1970), 459–88; Kim Phillips-Fein, If Business and the Country Will Be Run Right': The Business Challenge to the Liberal Consensus, 1945–1964," *International Labor and Working-Class History* 72, no. 1 (October 2007): 192–215.
21. Peter M. Garber, "The Collapse of the Bretton Woods Fixed Exchange Rate System"; Michael D. Bordo, "The Bretton Woods International Monetary System: A Historical Overview," in Michael D. Bordo and Barry Eichengreen, eds., *A Retrospective on the Bretton Woods System: Lessons for International Monetary Reform* (NBER, 1993), 461–94 and 3–108, respectively.
22. Melinda Cooper, *Counterrevolution: Extravagance and Austerity in Public Finance* (Princeton University Press, 2024), 14.
23. Conference program in FTO Papers, Box 53, US-EEC Businessmen's Conference—1972 February–March.
24. William Blackie, Remarks at Opening Session, in FTO Papers, Box 53, US-EEC Businessmen's Conference—1972 February–March.
25. Joint Working Group on Multinational Investment Problems Paper, in FTO Papers, Box 53, US-EEC Businessmen's Conference—1972 February–March; Blackie, Remarks at Opening Session.
26. Edwin L. Dale Jr., "Shultz Names Monetary Reform Panel," *New York Times*, August 23, 1973; Youn Ki and Yongwoo Jeung, "Ideas, Interests, and the Transition to a Floating Exchange System," *Journal of Policy History* 32, no. 2 (April 2020): 151–82.
27. Jennifer Burns, *Milton Friedman* (Picador, 2024), 342–5.
28. Ibid., 342.
29. See "F. Taylor Ostrander: His Long and Wide-Ranging Career," 96; US Congressional Budget Office, *The Effects of the Tokyo Round of Multilateral Trade Negotiations on the U.S. Economy: An Updated View* (US Government Printing Office, 1979), 23–39.
30. Program and Hans-Günther Sohl, "E.C. Economic Overview," both in Report of the Second Annual Meeting—E.C.—U.S. Businessmen's Council, 5–8 and 26–34, in FTO Papers, Box 53, Folder EEC Businessmen's Council, 1974–1975. Sohl's resentment at being treated as a criminal following the war is discussed in Armin Grünbacher, "'Honourable Men': West German Industrialists and the Role of Honour and Honour Courts in the Adenauer Era," *Contemporary European History* 22, no. 2 (May 2013): 233–52. Nuremberg trial records indicate that in 1940 Sohl was chief of ore mining at Krupp, a firm that "had manifested not only its willingness but its ardent desire to employ forced labor." He was directly involved in the expansion of mining operations in occupied

Yugoslavia, including via the seizure of shares in a local company using laws targeting Jews. See "KRUPP et al.," US Military Tribunal Nuremberg, Judgment of July 31, 1948.

31. Summary of Third Plenary Session, October 10, 1975, in Second Annual Meeting Report, 16–24, 24, 18, respectively.
32. Joint Working Group on Multinational Investment Problems Paper, in FTO Papers, Box 53, US-EEC Businessmen's Conference—1972 February–March.
33. Melinda Cooper, *Counterrevolution*, 117–19.
34. Ibid., 40.
35. Josh Levin, *The Queen: The Forgotten Life Behind an American Myth* (Little, Brown, 2019).
36. Melinda Cooper, *Counterrevolution*, 136.
37. Eric Helleiner, *States and the Reemergence of Global Finance: From Bretton Woods to the 1990s* (Cornell University Press, 2015), 131–5; W. Carl Biven, *Jimmy Carter's Economy: Policy in an Age of Limits* (University of North Carolina Press, 2003), 101–20.
38. Melinda Cooper, *Counterrevolution*, 53.
39. Ibid., 141.
40. Letter by Pierre Gousseland to the President, December 11, 1978, in FTO Papers, Box 7, Folder "AMAX Inc. Speeches 1972–1979."
41. Melinda Cooper, *Counterrevolution*, 54; William L. Silber, *Volcker: The Triumph of Persistence* (Bloomsbury, 2012); Tim Sablik, "Recession of 1981–82," *Federal Reserve History*, November 22, 2013, federalreservehistory.org.
42. A rough estimate based on Diane N. Westcott and Robert W. Bednarzik, "Employment and Unemployment: A Report on 1980," *Monthly Labor Review*, February 1981, 4–14.
43. Milton Friedman, *Free to Choose*, Episode 1.
44. Gary Penner, "Fifth Graders Hear Candidates, Then Give Political Views," *Fort Wayne News-Sentinel*, October 11, 1980; Jerry Graff, "Moses Scored for Trying to Nix Auto Union," *Fort Wayne News-Sentinel*, October 25, 1980; Raymond A. Friedman, "Interaction Norms as Carriers of Organizational Culture: A Study of Labor Negotiations at International Harvester," *Journal of Contemporary Ethnography* 18, no. 1 (April 1, 1989): 3–29.
45. Ronald Reagan, "Televised Campaign Address 'A Vital Economy: Jobs, Growth, and Progress for Americans,'" October 24, 1980, Ronald Reagan Presidential Library and Museum, reaganlibrary.gov.
46. "It Gave Me a Happy Feeling Inside," *Fort Wayne News-Sentinel*, October 25, 1980, lists one "Ronald Baden" as her father. There is

a "Ron Baden" of appropriate age who worked as an accountant; see Mark Brohan, Forced Savings' Spark Good Habits," *Fort Wayne News-Sentinel*, April 6, 1867.
47. See Dave Leip's Atlas of US Presidential Elections, uselectionatlas.org.
48. See Melinda Cooper, *Counterrevolution*, this is one of the entire book's arguments.
49. Elizabeth Anderson, *Hijacked: How Neoliberalism Turned the Work Ethic Against Workers and How Workers Can Take It Back* (Cambridge University Press, 2023); Brohan, Forced Savings' Spark Good Habits."

9. Popular Economics, 1981–2008

1. David Owen, "Vaclav Smil and the Value of Doubt," *New Yorker*, February 20, 2024.
2. Alan Greenspan, *The Age of Turbulence: Adventures in a New World* (Penguin, 2007), 492.
3. Daniel Schulman, *Sons of Wichita: How the Koch Brothers Became America's Most Powerful and Private Dynasty* (Grand Central Publishing, 2014), 11.
4. Ibid., 11–26.
5. Bill Koch quoted in Bryan Burrough, "Wild Bill Koch," *Vanity Fair*, June 1994.
6. Fred C. Koch, *A Business Man Looks at Communism* (self-published, 1960), 9. Accessed via HathiTrust.
7. Schulman, *Sons of Wichita*, 55.
8. F. A. Harper, *Why Wages Rise* (Foundation for Economic Education, 1957).
9. Charles G. Koch, "Acceptance Remarks by Charles G. Koch, 2005 Herman W. Lay Memorial Award Recipient of the Association of Private Enterprise Education: Koch Industries, Market Process Analysis, and the Science of Liberty," *Journal of Private Enterprise* 22, no. 2 (2007): 1–6, 2; Abraham Maslow, *Religions, Values, and Peak-Experiences* (Ohio State University Press, 1964), xii–xv.
10. Charles Koch, "Eulogy of Baldy Harper," Foundation for Economic Education, 1973; F. A. Harper, "Morals and Liberty," Foundation for Economic Education, July 1, 1971. All subsequent Harper quotes come from the latter.
11. Charles G. Koch, *The Science of Success: How Market-Based Management Built the World's Largest Private Company* (John Wiley & Sons, 2007), 31–7.

12. Ibid., 38–40.
13. William M. Tsutsui, "W. Edwards Deming and the Origins of Quality Control in Japan," *Journal of Japanese Studies* 22, no. 2 (1996): 295–325, 319.
14. Christopher Leonard, *Kochland: The Secret History of Koch Industries and Corporate Power in America* (Simon and Schuster, 2019), 53–79.
15. For Director's career trajectory and role in law and economics, see Jennifer Burns, *Milton Friedman: The Last Conservative* (Picador, 2024).
16. Gary S. Becker, "Crime and Punishment: An Economic Approach," *Journal of Political Economy* 76, no. 2 (1968): 169–217.
17. Henry G. Manne, "How Law and Economics Was Marketed in a Hostile World: A Very Personal History," in *The Collected Works of Henry G. Manne*, vol. 3 (Liberty Fund, 2009), 291–313, 295, 291.
18. Ibid., 297–9.
19. Ibid., 302–4.
20. Elliott Ash, Daniel L Chen, and Suresh Naidu, "Ideas Have Consequences: The Impact of Law and Economics on American Justice," National Bureau of Economic Research Working Paper, February 2022.
21. See Nancy MacLean, *Democracy in Chains: The Deep History of the Radical Right's Stealth Plan for America* (Penguin, 2017).
22. Charles Koch, *Science of Success*, 39–40.
23. Ibid., 161.
24. Ibid., 162.
25. Katelynn Harris, "Forty Years of Falling Manufacturing Employment," *Beyond the Numbers* 9, no. 16 (November 2020), bls.gov.
26. Thomas Gryta and Ted Mann, *Lights Out: Pride, Delusion, and the Fall of General Electric* (HarperCollins, 2020), 18. Initially GE Capital was known as GE Credit Corporation.
27. Jack Welch and John A. Byrne, *Jack: Straight from the Gut* (Grand Central Publishing, 2003), 231–3.
28. Gryta and Mann, *Lights Out*, 18–19.
29. Welch and Byrne, *Jack*, 158–62.
30. Ibid., 158–9.
31. Ibid., 162–6.
32. Gryta and Mann, *Lights Out*, 27.
33. Welch and Byrne, *Jack*, 163–4.

34. Gryta and Mann, *Lights Out*, 14–20, quote on 21.
35. Charles Koch, *Science of Success*, 31.
36. Charles Koch's personal website has a page listing his top four books. The others are journalist Tom Wolfe's *Bonfire of the Vanities*, eugenicist Charles Murray's *In Pursuit of Happiness and Good Government*, and philosopher of science Michael Polanyi's *Personal Knowledge*.
37. Charles Koch, *Science of Success*, 31.
38. Ibid., viii, 67, 84–7. For critique of Gardner's model, see Perry D. Klein, "Multiplying the Problems of Intelligence by Eight: A Critique of Gardner's Theory," *Canadian Journal of Education / Revue Canadienne de l'éducation* 22, no. 4 (1997): 377–94.
39. Charles Koch, *Science of Success*, 124–34.
40. Ibid., 26.
41. Ibid., 110.
42. Ibid., 44.
43. Ibid., 19.
44. Tim Dickinson, "Inside the Koch Brothers' Toxic Empire," *Rolling Stone*, September 24, 2014; Leonard, *Kochland*, 11–33, 132–46.
45. Marcus Baram, "Koch Brothers Accused of Hiring Former NYPD Chief to Dig Up Dirt on Journalist," *Fast Company*, January 22, 2016.
46. Charles Koch, *Science of Success*, 44.
47. Leonard, *Kochland*, 138–9.
48. Browner quoted in Dickinson, "Inside the Koch Brothers' Toxic Empire."
49. Bill Clinton, speech to Business Roundtable, June 9, 1993, c-span.org.
50. See Nelson Lichtenstein and Judith Stein, *A Fabulous Failure: The Clinton Presidency and the Transformation of American Capitalism* (Princeton University Press, 2023).
51. Greenspan, *Age of Turbulence*, 179.
52. Franklin R. Edward, "Hedge Funds and the Collapse of Long-Term Capital Management," *Journal of Economic Perspectives* 13, no. 2 (June 1999): 189–210.
53. John Mullin, "The Fed, the Stock Market, and the 'Greenspan Put,'" *Econ Focus*, First Quarter 2023, richmondfed.org.
54. Melinda Cooper, *Counterrevolution: Extravagance and Austerity in Public Finance* (Princeton University Press, 2024), 83.
55. Marcus Miller, Paul Weller, and Lei Zhang, "Moral Hazard and the US Stock Market: Analysing the 'Greenspan Put,'" *Economic Journal* 112, no. 478 (2002): C171–86, C172.

56. Melinda Cooper, *Counterrevolution*.
57. Relevant laws include the Airline Deregulation Act of 1978, the Telecommunications Act of 1996, the Motor Carrier Act of 1980. See Bert J. Kellerman, "The Impact of 1994's Further Deregulation of the Trucking Industry: The Rural Shippers' View," *Journal of Marketing Theory and Practice* 6, no. 4 (October 1, 1998): 92–103; Philip Weinberg, "Masquerade for Privilege: Deregulation Undermining Environmental Protection," *Washington and Lee Law Review* 45 (Fall 1988): 1321–43.
58. Greenspan, *The Age of Turbulence*, 174; Bush quoted in Jo Becker, Sheryl Gay Stolberg, and Stephen Labaton, "Bush Drive for Home Ownership Fueled Housing Bubble," *New York Times*, December 21, 2008.
59. Greenspan, *Age of Turbulence*, 492.
60. N. Gregory Mankiw, *Principles of Economics*, 6th ed. (South-Western, 2012), 4.
61. Peter Bofinger, "Best of Mankiw: Errors and Tangles in the World's Best-Selling Economics Textbooks," Institute for New Economic Thinking blog, January 3, 2021.
62. Leon S. Robertson, "A Critical Analysis of Peltzman's 'The Effects of Automobile Safety Regulation,'" *Journal of Economic Issues* 11, no. 3 (September 1, 1977): 587–600.
63. Mankiw, *Principles*, 10–17.
64. Ibid., 120–1.
65. Elinor Ostrom, *Governing the Commons: The Evolution of Institutions for Collective Action* (Cambridge University Press, 1990), 3–4.
66. Ibid.
67. Derek Wall, *The Sustainable Economics of Elinor Ostrom: Commons, Contestation and Craft* (Routledge, 2014), xv, 28–30.
68. Adam Miller, "The Pioneer Fund: Bankrolling the Professors of Hate," *Journal of Blacks in Higher Education*, no. 6 (1994): 58.
69. Mankiw, *Principles*, 224–8.
70. Ibid., 223–4.
71. Steven D. Levitt and Stephen J. Dubner, *Freakonomics: A Rogue Economist Explains the Hidden Side of Everything* (HarperCollins, 2005).
72. Stephen J. Dubner, "The Probability That a Real-Estate Agent Is Cheating You (and Other Riddles of Modern Life)," *New York Times Magazine*, August 3, 2003.

73. Steven D. Levitt, "Juvenile Crime and Punishment," *Journal of Political Economy* 106, no. 6 (December 1998): 1156–85.
74. Dubner, "The Probability That a Real Estate Agent Is Cheating You."
75. Levitt and Dubner, *Freakonomics*, 206, 14.
76. Ibid., 1–5, viii.
77. Levitt and Dubner, *Freakonomics*, 206. For a thorough review of this particular argument, see Theodore Joyce, "Abortion and Crime: A Review," NBER Working Paper no. 15098, June 2009. The Romania case study in question is Cristian Pop-Eleches, "The Impact of an Abortion Ban on Socio-Economic Outcomes of Children: Evidence from Romania," Job Market Paper, November 2002. See also Andrew Gelman and Kaiser Fung, "Freakonomics: What Went Wrong?," *American Scientist* 100, no. 1 (January–February 2012); Michael Hobbes and Peter Shamshiri, "Freakonomics," *If Books Could Kill* (podcast), November 2022.
78. Levitt and Dubner, *Freakonomics*, 206.
79. Ibid., 20, 70.
80. US Department of the Treasury, "Homeowner Affordability and Stability Fact Sheet," press release, February 18, 2009; archived on home.treasury.gov.
81. Rick Santelli's "rant" is widely available on the internet with a quick search; it was delivered on CNBC news on February 19, 2009.
82. Numbers based on estimates in Ronald P. Formisano, *The Tea Party: A Brief History* (Johns Hopkins University Press, 2012), 8.
83. See Gary B. Nash, *The Urban Crucible: Social Change, Political Consciousness, and the Origins of the American Revolution* (Harvard University Press, 1979); David S. Lovejoy, *Rhode Island Politics and the American Revolution, 1760–1776* (Brown University Press, 1958). For Black maritime workers attacking the customs house, see Henry Snow, *Enemies of Order: Labor and Power at the Atlantic Dockside* (University of Georgia Press, forthcoming).
84. Formisano, *The Tea Party*, 63–80.
85. Jane Mayer, "The Koch Brothers' Covert Ops," *New Yorker*, August 23, 2010.
86. Yakov Feygin, "The Deflationary Bloc," *Phenomenal World*, January 9, 2021.

10. Dreams of Exit, 2009–2024

1. Franklin Foer, "Jeff Bezos's Master Plan," *Atlantic*, October 10, 2019.
2. Kurt Schiller, "The Culture War: Iain M. Banks's Billionaire Fans," *Blood Knife* (blog), January 22, 2021.
3. Isaac Asimov, *Robots and Empire* (Doubleday, 1985); Travis M. Andrews and Roxanne Roberts, "The Love Affair Between Jeff Bezos and 'Star Trek,'" *Washington Post*, October 13, 2021.
4. *Mobile Suit Gundam: Char's Counterattack*, released in 1988.
5. Dana Mattioli, "The Tactics Elon Musk Uses to Manage His 'Legion' of Babies—and Their Mothers," *Wall Street Journal*, April 15, 2025.
6. Tad Friend, "Sam Altman's Manifest Destiny," *New Yorker*, October 3, 2016; Mark O'Connell, "Why Silicon Valley Billionaires Are Prepping for the Apocalypse in New Zealand," *Guardian*, February 15, 2018.
7. Douglas Rushkoff, "The Super-Rich 'Preppers' Planning to Save Themselves from the Apocalypse," *Observer*, September 4, 2022.
8. Peter Thiel with Blake Masters, *Zero to One: Notes on Startups: Or, How to Build the Future* (Crown Business, 2014), 29, 34.
9. Yanis Varoufakis, *Technofeudalism: What Killed Capitalism* (Melville House, 2024).
10. Alex Weprin, "Amazon Prime Passes 200 Million Subscribers," *Hollywood Reporter*, April 15, 2021.
11. "Amazon Introduces Four All-New Echo Devices: Sales of Alexa-Enabled Devices Surpass Half a Billion," press release, May 17, 2023.
12. Federal Trade Commission, "FTC Sues Amazon for Illegally Maintaining Monopoly Power," press release, September 26, 2023. See also FTC complaint filed with United States District Court, Western District of Washington, Federal Trade Commission et al. v. Amazon.com Inc., No. 2:2023cv01495, Document 188 (W.D. Wash. 2024).
13. In some facilities and jobs, this means handheld scanners; the facility I toured instead relied on scanning systems built into workers' stations. This seems to be the direction Amazon is heading in, and it is certainly more reminiscent of the Panopticon than the handheld scanner systems already were.
14. Abha Bhattarai, "Lawsuits Accuse Amazon of Discriminating Against Muslim Women," *Washington Post*, May 13, 2019.

15. Lauren Kaori Gurley, "Internal Documents Show Amazon's Dystopian System for Tracking Workers Every Minute of Their Shifts," *Vice*, June 2, 2022; "Amazon Fined for 'Excessive' Surveillance of Workers," BBC, January 23, 2024.
16. Heike Geissler, *Seasonal Associate* (MIT Press, 2018), 169.
17. For this quote and all subsequent Bentham references, see chapter 3.
18. Geissler, *Seasonal Associate*, 70, 137.
19. Ibid., 174–5.
20. Avery Ellis, "Exclusive: Amazon's Attrition Costs $8 Billion Annually According to Leaked Documents. And It Gets Worse," *Engadget*, October 17, 2022. See also "Amazon's Disposable Workers: High Injury and Turnover Rates at Fulfillment Centers in California," National Employment Law Project, March 2020.
21. Kate Briquelet and Josh Fiallo, "Amazon Employee Who Died on Prime Day Was Hardworking Dad," *Daily Beast*, July 27, 2022; Michael Sainato, "'Lack of Respect': Outcry over Amazon Employee's Death on Warehouse Floor," *Guardian*, January 9, 2023.
22. Ken Klippenstein, "After Deadly Warehouse Collapse, Amazon Workers Say They Receive Virtually No Emergency Training," *Intercept*, December 13, 2021; Celina Tebor, "Feds Have 'Concerns,' but No Punishment, for Amazon After Deadly Warehouse Collapse in Tornado," *USA Today*, April 26, 2022; More Perfect Union (@MorePerfectUS), Twitter, December 13, 2021, 4:56 p.m. ET, of a screenshot of texts from Larry Virden; letter by Aaron Priddy, Occupational Safety and Health Administration Area Director, to Amazon.com Services LLC, April 26, 2022, dol.gov.
23. Nilutpal Timsina, "Thousands of Amazon Flex Drivers File for Arbitration over Contractor Status," Reuters, June 12, 2024.
24. Caitlin Harrington, "His Drivers Unionized—Then Amazon Tried to Terminate His Contract," *Wired*, June 13, 2023.
25. Katherine Hamilton, "Delivery Drivers Sue Amazon for Being Forced to Pee in Bottles," *Forbes*, May 24, 2023.
26. This is clear from the requirements Amazon lists for schools for its Career Choice program on its website.
27. -talktoghosts-, reply to "How many people actually use Career Choice?," AmazonFC subreddit, May 10, 2024.
28. David Niekerk, quoted in David Leonhardt, "The Amazon Customers Don't See," *New York Times*, June 15, 2021.
29. Geissler, *Seasonal Associate*, 35.
30. Max Chafkin, *The Contrarian: Peter Thiel and Silicon Valley's Pursuit of Power* (Penguin, 2021), 19.

31. Peter Thiel, "The Education of a Libertarian," *Cato Unbound*, April 3, 2009.
32. Mark Francis, *Herbert Spencer and the Invention of Modern Life* (Routledge, 2014), 73.
33. Thiel, "The Education of a Libertarian."
34. Estimates from Bitcoin Energy Consumption Index, *Digiconomist*, December 30, 2024.
35. Giving What We Can's website suggests both of these as examples.
36. Dylan Matthews, "How Effective Altruism Went from a Niche Movement to a Billion-Dollar Force," *Vox*, August 8, 2022. I find it necessary to disclose that I have met Matthews and went to graduate school with his wife. This has not impacted my approach to EA here.
37. William MacAskill, "To Save the World, Don't Get a Job at Charity; Go Work on Wall Street," *Quartz*, February 27, 2013.
38. For Cowen's Calhoun sympathies, see Alexander Tabarrok and Tyler Cowen, "The Public Choice Theory of John C. Calhoun," *Journal of Institutional and Theoretical Economics (JITE) / Zeitschrift Für Die Gesamte Staatswissenschaft* 148, no. 4 (1992): 655–74.
39. sapphire, "How Dependent Is the Effective Altruism Movement on Dustin Moskovitz and Cari Tuna?," September 21, 2020, on the Effective Altruism Forum.
40. See Matthews, "How Effective Altruism Went from a Niche Movement."
41. Nick Bostrom, "Existential Risk Prevention as Global Priority," *Global Policy* 4, no. 1 (February 2013): 15–31, 18.
42. Rounding to $4.3*10^{17}$ seconds; cubed, this comes out to about $2*10^{32}$.
43. Bostrom, "Existential Risk Prevention," 19.
44. Jeff Sparrow, "Giving, Good, and the Fallout of FTX: Peter Singer on Effective Altruism Now," *Guardian*, December 23, 2022, describes him as "generally regarded as EA's philosophical originator." For Singer and infanticide, see (among many others) Peter Singer, *Practical Ethics* (Cambridge University Press, 1993 [1979]).
45. Nick Bostrom, "Ethical Issues in Advanced Artificial Intelligence," nickbostrom.com; this is an edited version of an earlier paper published in Iva Smit, Wendell Wallach, and G. E. Lasker, eds., *Cognitive, Emotive and Ethical Aspects of Decision Making in Humans and in Artificial Intelligence*, vol. 2 (International Institute

of Advanced Studies in Systems Research and Cybernetics, 2003), 12–17.
46. Eliezer Yudkowsky, "Pausing AI Developments Isn't Enough. We Need to Shut It All Down," *Time*, March 29, 2023.
47. Nicholas Kulish, "How a Scottish Moral Philosopher Got Elon Musk's Number," *New York Times*, October 8, 2022; Michael Lewis, *Going Infinite: The Rise and Fall of a New Tycoon* (W. W. Norton, 2023), 46–51.
48. Lewis, *Going Infinite*, 86–8.
49. Advertisement for FTX quoted in Ayesha Rascoe, "FTX Is Now Defunct. Does Crypto Have a Future?," NPR, November 5, 2023.
50. Michael Lewis, *Going Infinite*, 114–66.
51. Miranda Dixon-Luinenburg and Dylan Matthews, "Carrick Flynn May Be 2022's Unlikeliest Candidate. Here's Why He's Running," *Vox*, May 14, 2022; Lewis, *Going Infinite*, 181–3.
52. Bankman-Fried quoted in Lewis, *Going Infinite*, 72–3; Ellison quoted in Lewis, *Going Infinite*, 132.
53. Lewis, *Going Infinite*, 193–210.
54. Chris Arnold, "FTX Investors Fear They Lost Everything, and Wonder if There's Anything They Can Do," NPR, November 18, 2022; Emily Stewart, "How Crypto Failed Black Investors," *Vox*, February 16, 2023.
55. Divya Rajagopal, "Ontario Pension Says Any Loss from FTX Investment to Have Limited Impact," Reuters, November 10, 2022.
56. Benjamin Hilton and 80,000 Hours, "Preventing an AI-Related Catastrophe," 80,000 Hours, August 2022, 80000hours.org; updated March 24, 2025.
57. Emily Baker-White, "Who Is @BasedBeffJezos, the Leader of the Tech Elite's 'E/Acc' Movement," *Forbes*, December 4, 2023.
58. This and other broad claims about language and style come from reading far too many of Beff Jezos's tweets.
59. Beff Jezos (@BasedBeffJezos), Twitter, December 29, 2022, 6:20 a.m. ET.
60. Kevin Roose, "This A.I. Subculture's Motto: Go, Go, Go," *New York Times*, December 10, 2023.
61. Beff Jezos frequently directs tweets to "anon," a formulation that originated on 4chan.
62. Beff Jezos (@BasedBeffJezos), responding to Marc Andreessen, Twitter, December 26, 2022, 2:30 a.m. ET.
63. Beff Jezos (@BasedBeffJezos), Twitter, June 13, 2024, 6:07 p.m. ET.
64. Beff Jezos (@BasedBeffJezos), Twitter, June 10, 2024, 4:32 a.m. ET.

65. Beff Jezos (@BasedBeffJezos), Twitter, June 16, 2024, 7:28 p.m. ET.
66. "Pause Giant AI Experiments: An Open Letter," Future of Life Institute, March 22, 2023.
67. Keach Hagey, "The Secrets and Misdirection Behind Sam Altman's Firing from OpenAI," *Wall Street Journal*, March 28, 2025.
68. Jeffrey Dastin et al., "OpenAI Appoints New Boss as Sam Altman Joins Microsoft," Reuters, November 21, 2023; Jeffrey Dastin and Aditya Soni, "Sam Altman to Return as OpenAI CEO After His Tumultuous Ouster," Reuters, November 22, 2023; Luciana Lopez, "Economist Larry Summers Joins the Board of OpenAI as Ousted CEO Sam Altman Returns," cnn.com, November 22, 2023.
69. Marc Andreessen, "The Techno-Optimist Manifesto," Andreessen Horowitz, October 16, 2023, a16z.com.
70. Thomas Sowell, *A Conflict of Visions* (William Morrow, 1987).
71. Michelle Faverio and Alec Tyson, "What the Data Says About Americans' Views of Artificial Intelligence," Pew Research Center, November 21, 2023, pewresearch.org.
72. See Quinn Slobodian, *Crack-Up Capitalism: Market Radicals and the Dream of a World Without Democracy* (Metropolitan Books, 2023).
73. Andreessen quoted in Dawn Chmielewski, "Asked Why He Supports Clinton over Trump, Marc Andreessen Responds, 'Is That a Serious Question?,'" cnbc.com, June 15, 2016.
74. Apoorva Mandavilli, "U.S.A.I.D. Memos Detail Human Costs of Cuts to Foreign Aid," *New York Times*, March 2, 2025.
75. Phillip Elliott, "In DC Speech, Charles Koch Speaks of 'the Mess' He Sees the Country In," time.com, May 1, 2025.
76. This is supposedly a quote from Buckminster Fuller, but as far as I can tell he never actually said this. It seems more likely Andreessen got it from a misquotation at the beginning of the Wikipedia article on Fuller's concept of "ephemeralization," which does have this quote. It cites a section from Fuller's *Nine Chains to the Moon*, originally published in 1938. While it is unclear from this citation which edition is intended, those I found did not include this quote.
77. Lex Fridman, "Jeff Bezos: Amazon and Blue Origin," *Lex Fridman Podcast* #405, YouTube, December 14, 2023.
78. See Søren Mau, *Mute Compulsion: A Marxist Theory of the Economic Power of Capital* (Verso, 2023) in particular the discussion of human needs, 89–103.
79. Michael Kratsios, "Remarks by Director Kratsios at the Endless Frontiers Retreat," White House, April 15, 2025, whitehouse.gov.

80. Erin Banco, Ashleigh Furlong, and Lennart Pfahler, "How Bill Gates and Partners Used Their Clout to Control the Global Covid Response—with Little Oversight," *Politico*, September 14, 2022.
81. John Maynard Keynes, "Economic Possibilities for Our Grandchildren" (1930), in *Essays in Persuasion* (W. W. Norton, 2011 [1932]), 258–374.
82. Dan Davies, *The Unaccountability Machine: Why Big Systems Make Terrible Decisions—and How the World Lost Its Mind* (Profile Books, 2024), 270.
83. Bethan McKernan and Harry Davies, "'The Machine Did It Coldly': Israel Used AI to Identify 37,000 Hamas Targets," *Guardian*, April 3, 2024.
84. Sophie Elmhirst, "The Disastrous Voyage of *Satoshi*, the World's First Cryptocurrency Cruise Ship," *Guardian*, September 7, 2021.
85. "The Real Risk Is Totalitarian Government—Peter Thiel," *TRIGGERnometry* (podcast), YouTube, July 28, 2024.
86. Andreessen, "Techno-Optimist Manifesto."
87. Elmhirst, "The Disastrous Voyage of *Satoshi*."
88. Iain M. Banks, *Use of Weapons* (Orbit, 1992 [1990]).

Conclusion

1. William Winwood Reade, *The Martyrdom of Man* (J. Lane, 1910 [1872]), 543.

Index

AMAX, Inc., 189–90, 193–4, 196, 200, 206, 210
Amazon, 246–53, 273
amorality, 32, 105, 239
Appleton, Nathan, 76–9, 82, 84–6, 91–2, 94–101, 122, 250, 275
Astbury, Samuel, 44
Austrian School, 157–61, 165, 168, 170, 210, 220, 223, 235

Bankman-Fried, Samuel, 261
Bentham, Jeremy, 45, 54, 57–8, 61–3, 65–7, 69–72, 74, 76–7, 87, 106, 109, 111, 114, 129, 247–8, 262–3, 277
Bentham, Samuel, 70, 72, 77, 111, 136–7, 225, 275, 277
    and John Stuart Mill, 76
    and machines, 83
    and the Panopticon, 53, 66, 247
    and pile-driving machine, 59–60
    and Royal Dockyards, 54
    and shipbuilding, 3, 55, 58
    and strikes, 56
    and utilitarianism, 262
    and worker efficiency, 60–2, 67–9
Benthamism, 37, 86, 92, 107–8, 113, 192, 259, 263
Boulware, Lemuel Ricketts, 174–83, 185–7, 192, 196, 205, 207–9, 211–12, 214, 243, 263, 275, 278–9
Boulwarism, 178, 181, 186, 188, 197–8

capitalism, 3, 14, 37, 69, 91, 95, 97, 113, 149, 161, 169, 181–4, 211, 245–6, 257, 261–5, 279–80
    and Charles Koch, 225
    and class interests, 171
    and competition, 96, 112, 129, 270
    and conservatism, 185, 268
    and constraints, 123
    and control, 94
    and democracy, 255
    and economic coercion, 101

capitalism (*continued*)
   and economic compulsion, 270
   and empire, 53, 60
   European, 13
   and exploitation, 18, 125, 203
   global, 103, 195, 197
   and government intervention, 158
   and greed, 128
   and hegemony, 274
   and Herbert Spencer, 114
   and hierarchy, 145, 186
   and human nature, 278
   industrial, 104, 120
   and Japan, 121, 131
   and labor, 27, 48
   and management, 66
   and manufacturing, 90
   market, 112
   and market dependence, 51
   and market evolution, 275
   and market order, 131
   modern, 17
   and monetary policy, 200
   and pottery, 44
   and poverty, 90
   and profit imperative, 50, 52
   and profits, 81
   and proto-monetarism, 183
   and rationalism, 43
   and resource allocation, 72
   and right-wing economists, 217
   and science of control, 12, 135, 210, 273
   and self-interest, 35, 96
   and terms, 9
   and United States, 154, 163–65, 167, 173–74, 188
   and workers, 120, 146, 172
Capitalism and Slavery (Williams), 75
capitalist labor system, 48, 69
Chicago Mercantile Exchange, 240
Chicago school of economics, 154, 156, 158–60, 163–6, 168, 170, 181, 190, 207, 217–18, 232, 235
   and price theory, 187, 230
Chicago Tea Party, 240
Chōmin, Nakae, 126, 128, 133
class, 125–6, 151, 175–6, 180, 245, 254
   and capitalists, 97, 171
   conflict, 142
   consciousness, 97, 192
   hierarchy, 34, 155
   and Japan, 128
   justice, 58
   and lower-class political movements, 7, 91
   merchant, 119
   middle, 207, 209, 232
   and race, 101
   renter, 25
   repression, 17–18
   ruling, 181, 237
   socioeconomic, 114
   solidarity, 152
   struggle, 174, 194

upper, 115
and wage labor, 25
warfare, 109
working, 119, 136–8, 147, 182, 186, 192, 209–10, 262, 279–80
Clay, Henry, 99
competition, 2, 79, 84, 96, 112–13, 123, 131, 147, 162, 218, 222, 254, 266, 271, 273
and capitalists, 112, 129, 245–7, 270
and cooperation, 122, 173
economic, 229
free market, 142
and General Motors, 177
global, 209
and Herbert Spencer, 160, 203
horizontal, 125
interdivision, 150
and laissez-faire, 130
market, 69, 76, 277, 279–80
Western, 120
Cooper, Thomas, 46, 77, 83, 86–94, 98, 101, 276
cryptocurrency, 255–6, 261–2, 266, 268, 273

dehumanization, 11, 19, 41, 146, 250
dockyards, 48, 54–6, 58, 67–9
Drax, Henry, 15–16, 18–20

economic activity, 121, 233

economic analysis, 1
economic coercion, 48, 88, 101, 270
economic compulsion, 101
economic consensus, 228
economic consulting, 142
economic convenience, 11
economic democracy, 135, 280, 282
economic development, 131, 196
economic equality, 204
economic exploitation, 20, 75
economic force, 3
economic freedom, 207
economic growth, 164, 183, 199, 208, 232, 270, 280
economic hegemony, 188
economic hierarchy, 34, 88, 188
economic history, 253
economic inequality, 6, 36, 45
economic interest, 9, 97
economic liberty, 186
economic life, 2, 163
economic necessity, 21
economic opportunity, 33
economic planning, 165
economic policy, 117, 208, 229
economic power, 5, 28, 94–5, 118, 123, 130, 160, 188, 216
economic reform, 27
economic rights, 170, 174
economic royalism, 151, 223
economics, 2, 116, 154, 163, 167, 172, 179, 188, 190, 231, 237, 272

economics (*continued*)
   Austrian, 220
   and Board of Economic
      Warfare, 157
   classical, 235
   conservative, 186
   and David Ricardo, 135
   free enterprise, 166, 201
   free market, 159
   imperial, 75
   industrial, 202
   and institutionalist school,
      147, 155
   and Keynesianism, 167
   law and, 217–19, 226, 247, 268
   military-industrial, 157
   and Nobel Prize, 234
   orthodox, 276, 278
   positive, 238
   right-wing, 161–2, 164, 181,
      187, 206, 210, 218–19,
      224, 226, 232, 236,
      239–40, 276
   and University of Chicago,
      156, 158, 217–18, 235
economic scarcity, 279
economic self-interest, 233
Economic Stabilization Act
   (170), 198
economic stagflation, 205
economic stimulus, 183
economic structures, 112, 278
economic technocracy, 263
economic thought, 3, 104–5,
   130, 162, 165, 175, 183,
   217, 242, 278, 281–2

economic utility, 222
economic value, 9, 48
effective altruism, 256–8, 262
Ely, Richard T., 147, 155
European Economic Community
   (EEC), 200

Federal Trade Commission, 247
Ford, Henry, 148–50
   Fordist economy, 230
Foundation for Economic Education, 167–8, 184, 186, 214
Friedman Institute (Chicago),
   236
Friedman, Milton, 156, 159–60,
   181, 184, 202, 206–7,
   211, 263, 274
   and price theory, 203, 265
Future of Humanity Institute,
   258

General Agreement on Tariffs
   and Trade (GATT), 202–3
General Electric, 174–9, 182,
   185–8, 205, 220–2
General Motors, 148–53, 171–2,
   177, 243
Greenspan, Alan, 212–13,
   227–30

Hartlib, Samuel, 8–9
Harwood, Richard, 15
Hazlitt, Henry, 159, 161, 165–6,
   176, 185–6, 211
Helvétius, Claude Adrien, 35–8,
   56, 72

Homo economicus, 92, 111
human behavior, 2, 110, 216
human deprivation, 16
human dignity, 180
human invention, 28
humanism, 196
humanity, 6, 21–2, 24, 36–7, 40, 46, 71, 74, 92, 104, 106–7, 109–11, 113–14, 129–30, 244, 260, 269, 275
human labor, 76, 87
human law, 23, 129
human nature, 58, 107, 110–11, 115, 278
human relations, 6, 28
human self-interest, 36–7
human selfishness, 24
human society, 38, 114, 126
human value, 66
human values, 260
human virtue, 85

Japan, 123, 127, 205–6, 234
   and Britain, 132
   and class structure, 128
   and conservatives, 129–30
   and diplomats, 120
   and elites, 104, 117–19, 121
   Emperor of, 102
   and factory owners, 121
   and factory workers, 133
   and global capitalism, 103
   government of, 125–6
   and industrial capitalism, 120
   and industrialization, 104, 130–1
   and industry, 216
   and intellectuals, 114
   and liberal movement, 125–6
   and mill executives, 124
   and Pearl Harbor, 157
   and political economy, 117
   and politics, 116
   Tokugawa, 103
   and trade imbalance, 120
   and troops, 172
   and United States, 117
   and workers, 131–4

Kaunda, Kenneth, 193–5
Keynes, John Maynard, 167–8, 174, 181, 183, 207, 235, 239, 243, 263, 271
Kissinger, Henry, 203
Koch, Charles, 213, 220, 226, 234, 237, 275, 277
   and Americans for Prosperity, 242
   and Cato Institute, 219, 269
   and F. A. Harper, 214
   family of, 213
   and FreedomWorks, 242
   and labor management, 223
   and law and economics movement, 268
   and legal establishment, 217
   and libertarianism, 276
   and management philosophy, 216, 223, 237

Koch, Charles (*continued*)
   and Market-Based Management (MBM), 223–5, 227, 237
   philosophy of, 1–2
   and property rights, 224
   and science of liberty, 1, 219, 224
   and *Why Wages Rise* (Harper), 214
Koch, Fred, 213
Koch Industries, 219, 224–6

labor control, 17, 33, 63, 245, 253
   advancements, 101
   and Amazon, 253
   and democratic efforts, 131
   and factories, 3
   failures of, 103
   and industrial relations, 202
   methods of, 9, 76, 220
   and moral law, 109
   and plantations, 3
   and profits, 65
   problem of, 175
   and rationalist market philosophy, 190
   and scientific management, 140
   and slavery, 75
   threat to, 135
laborers, 151, 207, 268, 270
   and autonomy, 5
   artisan, 5, 31
   Black, 93
   and capital, 194, 263
   child, 28
   and conflicts, 194
   convict, 60–1
   and discipline, 46, 81, 124, 174
   and disruptions, 73
   and division of labor, 83, 111
   domestic, 80
   enslaved, 39, 43
   and exploitation, 66, 87, 104
   and extraction of labor, 86
   factory, 52, 80, 109, 125
   forced, 204
   free, 4, 15, 20, 93
   and hard labor, 26
   heavy, 39
   and indentured servants, 14
   and management, 141, 143, 146, 171, 223, 225
   organized, 13, 205, 279
   and patriarchy, 128
   penal, 13
   price of, 12, 37, 78, 89, 170
   and prolabor policies, 150
   and protections, 54
   and radicalism, 141
   and relations, 178
   resistance, 140
   and rights, 277
   and surveillance, 30
   tenant, 117
   and value, 65
   wage, 7, 25, 37, 117, 121
labor unions, 156, 165
laissez-faire economics, 35, 94, 105–6, 108, 112, 126, 130–1, 158, 186, 262–3

Laurens, Henry, 41–3, 51, 77
Law and Economics Center, 219
Ligon, Richard, 19–20, 34
Locke, John, 22–9, 34–7, 40–1, 45–6, 49, 57, 62, 66, 72, 76, 87, 107–8, 110, 253, 276

Mandeville, Bernard, 32–7
Manne, Henry, 218–19
Market-Based Management (MBM), 1–2, 223–5, 227, 237
Martin, Samuel, 38–41, 43, 46, 87, 110
Marzani, Carl, 155–7, 173, 282
Massachusetts, 78, 94–5, 98, 172
moral economy, 61
morality, 103, 107–8, 113, 130, 212, 214–15, 237–9
  of commerce, 44
  conservative, 35, 70, 72
  and John Locke, 24–5, 29
  mathematical, 62
  and neutrality, 52
  science of, 38, 57
  sexual, 84
moral law, 108–9, 215, 217
moral nihilism, 266
moral perfection, 45
moral pessimism, 116
moral philosophy, 45, 57, 85, 91
moral restraint, 74
Musk, Elon, 244, 254, 264, 268–9, 271, 274

National Economic Council, 265
National Labor Relations Board, 197–8
New World, 13
Noll, Henry, 140–2

Ostrander, F. Taylor, 154–8, 168, 170, 173, 181, 189–91, 193–4, 200–1, 203, 210
Oswald, Richard, 41, 43
overwork, 4, 64

Panopticon, 53, 61, 63–7, 69–71, 74, 114, 247–8, 253
Petty, William, 4–6, 8–13, 22–3, 29, 35, 77, 275
Phillips, Wendell, 99, 101
pot-works, 31, 44

Reagan, Ronald, 186–8, 205, 208–11, 220, 233, 243–4, 268

slavery, 13–14, 18, 21, 33, 58, 97, 143, 183, 215–16, 274
  and abolition, 51–2, 69, 74–5, 99, 276
  and brutality, 20
  and capitalism, 17
  Caribbean, 38
  and Claude Adrien Helvétius, 35
  and colonialism, 44
  and fugitives, 15, 42
  and Nathan Appleton, 100–1
  opposition to, 28

slavery (*continued*)
   and resistance to, 16
   and Samuel Martin, 40–1
   and Thomas Cooper, 87–8, 91–3
   and West Indies, 78
Sloan, Alfred Pritchard, 148–54, 161–7, 172, 176, 211, 243, 275
Sloan Foundation, 162, 165–6
socioeconomic class, 114
Spencer, Herbert, 2, 103–8, 117, 207, 275, 277–8, 282
   and Ariga Nagao, 129–30
   and Austrian school, 210–11
   and Beatrice Webb, 114, 119, 134–5
   and behavioral quietism, 113
   and capitalism, 121
   and competition, 147
   and competitive evolution, 110, 113
   and competitive process, 111
   and Friedrich Hayek, 161, 184, 203
   and heredity, 112
   ideology of, 111, 128
   and individualism, 210, 276
   and industrial society, 111
   and laissez-faire, 126, 262–3
   and libertarianism, 255
   and Japan, 125–30, 133
   and Milton Friedman, 265
   and moral law, 109
   and nihilism, 281
   and social statics, 158

Spencerism, 107, 111, 114, 125–6, 129–30, 132–3, 147, 160, 184, 203, 263
surveillance, 13, 16–17, 30, 37, 47, 49, 66, 91, 173, 241, 247

Taylorism, 138, 142, 147
Taylor, Frederick Winslow, 3, 136–8, 176
   and Carl Barth, 147
   and Commission on Industrial Relations, 143
   and John F. Tobin, 145–6
   and principles, 146
   and scientific management, 140
   and worker efficiency, 145, 148
   and worker management, 139, 141, 143–4
Thiel, Peter, 245–6, 254–5, 257–8, 267–8, 273

United Electrical and Radio and Machine Workers of America (UE), 170–4, 198
United States, 1, 49, 58, 78, 102, 120, 163–4, 192, 205–6, 240–1, 267–8, 271
   and abolitionism, 100–1
   and Alfred Pritchard Sloan, 148–9
   and American Liberty League, 151
   and Austrian School, 210

and Black Americans, 101
and capital accumulation, 80
and capitalism, 174, 188
and Charles Koch, 225
and conservatism, 214
corporate, 220, 223
and democracy, 148
and economic education, 162
and economic growth, 208, 230–1
and economic policy, 229
and economics, 147, 154, 165, 207, 217, 235–6, 242
and enslaved people, 11, 15, 42
and Franklin D. Roosevelt, 155
and Frederick Winslow Taylor, 136
and Great Recession, 243
and Harvard Business, School, 180
and industry, 76, 177
and Japan, 118, 124, 216
and John Maynard Keynes, 168
and Joseph Priestley, 89
and legal establishment, 217–18
and libertarianism, 214–15, 269
and manufacturing, 79, 84
and McCarthyism, 173
and military budget, 228
and mills, 79
and monetary policy, 199–200
and Native Americans, 28
and Office of Strategic Services, 157
and plantations, 11, 13
and postwar economy, 170
and revolution, 22, 28, 56
and Ronald Reagan, 209
and slave trading, 41
and South, 77
and standard of living, 176
and tariffs, 98
and Thomas Cooper, 89
and unions, 171
and voters, 172
and women, 80, 94
and workers, 94, 174, 212, 277
and working class, 209
and Zambia, 197
University of Chicago Graduate School of Business, 202

Wallace, Henry, 173
Walsh Commission, 142–7
Wedgwood, Josiah, 44–52, 54, 57, 61, 66–7, 77, 80, 96, 275
Welch, Jack, 220–3, 240
Welch, Richard, 149
workers, 46, 50, 57–8, 65–6, 68–9, 81, 86, 90–1, 100, 109, 135–9, 150, 168, 180, 189, 200, 204, 207, 225, 229–30, 239, 245, 279
African, 191–92
alienation of, 47–8

workers (*continued*)
   Amazon, 247–8
   American, 170–1, 174, 209, 212, 249–52
   auto, 152–3
   and Boulwarism, 181, 196–8, 205, 214
   British, 133
   Career Choice, 253
   and children, 26
   coercion of, 114
   construction, 32
   cooperative, 224
   controlling, 3, 53, 60, 82, 192, 220
   displacement of, 117
   efficiency of, 9, 59
   enslaved, 17, 43
   expatriate, 195–6
   exploitation of, 51–2, 112
   federal, 268
   General Electric, 175–9, 221
   General Motors, 152
   health, 146
   and hierarchy of, 29
   interests, 146, 194
   iron, 141
   Japanese, 120–5, 131, 133–2
   management of, 1, 61, 83, 95, 140, 143–4, 185, 217
   manufacturing, 49, 220
   maritime, 241
   mill, 76, 80, 84, 94, 101
   mine, 191, 196
   and NAFTA, 227
   overseers of, 14
   pay, 233
   and productivity, 93
   rail, 155
   rights, 198
   sawmill, 184
   self-interest of, 56
   and solidarity, 222
   and strikes, 154, 192
   and Taylorism, 147–8
   urban, 25
work ethic, 55
work exploitation, 5
workhouses, 46, 74, 248
working conditions, 20, 54, 93, 112, 121, 124, 279
working schools, 26–7
workshops, 31, 37
World Trade Organization, 245, 271
World War I, 164, 173
World War II, 169–70, 173–4, 199

Zambia, 189, 192–7